THE ROLE OF FINANCE IN INDUSTRIAL INNOVATION

- Aspects of financial systems

Jesper Lindgaard Christensen

Ph.d. dissertation
Serie om Industriel Udvikling
Institute of Production
Aalborg University

THE ROLE OF FINANCE IN INDUSTRIAL INNOVATION

- Aspects of financial systems

ISBN 87-7307-457-8

© 1992   Jesper Lindgaard Christensen

Publisher   Institute of Production

Distribution   Aalborg University Press
                Postbox 159
                9100 Aalborg
                Denmark
                Telephone (45) 9815 5031

Tryk   Thy Bogtryk & Offset A/S

This publication is no. 39 in a Series on Industrial Development.

THE ROLE OF FINANCE IN INDUSTRIAL INNOVATION
- Aspects of financal systems

LIST OF TABLES AND FIGURES

PREFACE AND ACKNOWLEDGEMENTS

This book is the main part of my Ph.d. thesis which is a part of my programme for obtaining a Ph.d. in economics at the University of Aalborg.

The process of writing this book has had many similarities with the situation noticed in small, innovative firms. To develop and implement ideas external capital needed to be raised. A "business" plan was consequently conducted and a number of potential sources of funds were contacted. I am grateful to The Danish Social Science Research Council for being a (risk) willing investor who carried the project through financially during its start-up and growth stages. In later stages expansion external financing from The Danish Ministry of Industry is gratefully acknowledged.

Small firms often need additional competence and advice both when business plans are conducted and when faced with unforeseen or new problems during their development. This role in my work has been fulfilled by a number of people of whom I am particularly indebted to my supervisors Esben Sloth Andersen and Bengt-Åke Lundvall.

A stimulating environment is an important prerequisite for innovations. In the IKE-group I found such an intellectual and social stimulating environment. In particular I am grateful for many comments on earlier drafts by the "writing group". I am also grateful to Institute of Production for providing me with facilities. Finally, an important part of the stimulating environment has been my family Hanne and Malene.

A network of suppliers is another factor in innovative ability. I would like to thank the bankers who supplied me with material for the empirical survey. Jan Christensen and Keld Laursen helped with the computing of data for this survey.

For most small, innovative firms it is a hard process to reach break-even and there are many failures among such firms. I shall leave the judgement of whether the present attempt is successful or a failure to the reader.

Jesper Lindgaard Christensen
University of Aalborg, September 4th 1992

Chapter 1. Introduction

"Risk, nevertheless, enters into the pattern in which entrepreneurs work. But it does so indirectly and at one remove: riskiness - and every new thing is risky in a sense in which no routine action is - makes it more difficult to obtain the necessary capital and thus forms one of the obstacles entrepreneurs have to overcome and one of the instances of resistance of the environment which explain why innovations are not carried out smoothly and as a matter of course." (Schumpeter, 1939, p.79)

1.1. The core of the problem

Doing something new usually implies some degree of uncertainty. Innovation is by definition characterized by some novelty and therefore uncertainty. It thus should not be surprising that financiers are reluctant to join innovation projects. On the other hand, people do not always dislike taking risks. In a background report OECD (1982, p.119) compares innovation financing with expenses on gambling:

"In many countries about 5% of the GNP is spent on traditional gambling - casinos, lotteries, football pools, horse-racing - and one must ask why is so little spent on innovation financing?"

As in gambling the chances of a successful innovation are relatively small but the potential gains are large. A consequence of uncertainty is that innovators, be it firms, individuals or governments, must carefully consider the technical practicability and market prospects before putting the innovation process into effect. An important pre-condition for the process is initial financing. But a problem may arise when financing that process. In essence the problem is that there is a time lag between investments in the process and proceeds from sales. The process cannot finance itself before the outcome of the process is sold or used.

Whether the innovation is successful or not, can be evaluated from both a technical and a commercial point of view. In a market economy the commercial evaluation is the important one in the long run, but it is very difficult to predict the success and failure in innovation projects before execution and finalizing of the project. The decision to undertake such projects is thus dependent on an uncertain ex ante anticipation of technical and commercial success.

If the process is financed internally the only relevant anticipation is the innovator's. But if external funding is necessary, the situation is different. Then the ex ante perception of the project must also be positive with the financier. Risky investments in innovations are often initially financed internally. This applies especially to large companies, whereas small and medium sized firms may have less possibilities for self-financing. However, large companies also increasingly tend to use external finance.[1] Higher R & D costs and shorter life cycles for most high technology products, make technology based firms more dependent on external finance. Underlying this very general statement there are important differences, not only between the financial strength of firms, but also between countries. In some countries firms are less dependent on external finance.

It is my primary purpose in this book to show implications for innovation financing of how and why the form, availability and amount of external capital varies according to the project in question and to the specific financial institution and - system.

Uncertainty can be an obstacle to innovation projects if financial institutions are risk avers and if they are not sufficiently competent to screen or monitor innovation projects. However an acceptable level of knowledge can reduce the problems of uncertainty about a project and the persons undertaking it, and often this will ease access to finance. One way to provide information and confidence is by repeated contracts between a borrower and a lender[2], accumulating knowledge through the learning processes. Another way is to create financial institutions suited to accumulate and diffuse knowledge already generated, and to support the creation of new knowledge. Different

---

1 This observation is not new. Even Gurley & Shaw (1955, p.518) points to increased use of external finance: "Over the very long term, the trend has been away from self-finance. Government, business, and consumers alike have come to lean more heavily on external finance."

2 In some contexts the theoretical problems treated will present themselves differently if the financing is by equity rather than debt, but for the sake of clarity the terminology will be kept as "lender-borrower" if nothing else is stated.

institutional set-ups of financial systems can support or limit the development of these relationships between the lender and the borrower, and this is more precisely the topic of the present analysis.

It is not straightforward to determine if or not there is a lack of finance for innovations. A priori it is impossible to select exactly those projects which will succeed, and it is not possible to determine if too many or too few projects are being selected. Thus, some rejected projects may have been a success had they been financed, and a large number of failures within the first years of a firms' development could perhaps indicate that too much finance is available. However, to discuss this issue it is necessary to have criteria for the quantity that is too much or too little. Is it socially desireable that some kinds of projects are financed at the expense of others and are there differences in what projects would be selected by criteria of social benefits or by private business criteria?

On this basis it might be possible to reject that there is a lack of finance for innovation projects but even if some - perhaps most - of the start-ups fail[3] they are beneficial both for employment and for the evolutionary viability of industry. The latter refers to the fact that a large number of different industrial firms may be an advantage when rapid, exogenous changes demand shifts in the structure of production. A final point is that even though there might be enough resources for the aggregate, there seems to be problems at the interface between firms and financial institutions which makes the *allocation* of the resources non-optimal.

One could argue, provisionally, that, in principle, there are three ways of financing:-through markets, hierarchies (internal allocation), or the in between, through an intermediary[4]. The three ways of allocating funds have their respective advantages concerning transaction costs and capabilities. Moreover, there are considerable differences, both between nations and between national firms, in how frequently one is used rather than another and in how they complement each other. I shall show that

---

3 OECD (1982, p.119) estimate based on a number of country studies, that "the ratio of successful projects out of initial ideas is very small - about 1 per 1000 was suggested".

4 Prakke (1988, p.97) uses this Williamsonian (1988) terminology although only with the two extreme dimensions, whereas Neave (1991) uses the present three dimensional distinction.

financial and industrial development are closely knit, in that the specific mix of financing mechanisms in an economy depends on the kinds of transactions necessary, and vice versa the financing of industrial and technological development depends on the available allocation mechanisms. As there are a number of different kinds of transactions going on simultaneously in a financial system the above mentioned financing mechanisms will co-exist.

In summation, I intend to demonstrate the validity of the following working hypotheses:

i)   financing innovations are different from financing ordinary investments. In particular the technical and market uncertainty is more fundamental when financing innovations. This has implications for the possibilities of financing such investments.

ii)   firm size and stages in a project matter to financing. External financiers are, for several reasons, biased towards financing larger firms and later stages of the process.

iii) financial barriers to innovation are to a large extent due to information and competence gaps between the firm and the financier. The learning process and close relationship between borrower and lender can ease these obstacles to get innovations financed.

iv)   the institutional set-up of different financial systems support, maintain and generate these learning processes differently.

1.2. The perspective: individual, firm, nation

The working hypotheses above necessitates an analysis on several levels of aggregation.

Personal relations between the borrower and the lender is essential to the analysis. Uncertainty affects the behaviour of both the innovator and the financier, and a microeconomic discussion is also valuable for subsequent analysis at a higher level of aggregation.

"Analyzing how agents deal with uncertainty is thus profoundly important to studying financial system evolution. For, financiers' strategic choices determine how financial firms, and consequently the financial system, will change through time. Equally, clients' strategic choices influence the kinds of demands that financiers will face." (Neave, 1991, p.19)

An innovator may be an individual, but more often it is a firm. If it is an individual innovator he/she will eventually establish a firm. In addition to the individual level I shall deal with financing innovations at the firm level, as the characteristics, strategies and financial position of firms affect financing decisions.

At the level of the national system I shall consider national, institutional factors in financial systems important to firms, when they need to finance investments in new technology. One could argue that the concept of a *national* financial system has become more irrelevant due to internationalization, deregulation and globalization of financial markets in recent years. I shall discuss if, and how, these trends affect the possibilities for innovation financing. The systemic perspective is likewise relevant in relation to understanding the context in which the innovation process takes place.

Thus, the discussion has both a micro- and a macro aspect, but as it will be made evident, the systemic factors have feed-backs on micro behaviour and vice versa. For example, the well-documented question of capital structure in a firm cannot be seen in isolation. The firms' choice between debt and equity is conditioned by the availability, forms and prices of funds, which in turn is closely related to how the financial system as a whole is working.

1.3. The relevance of the subject in relation to economic policy

Why consider this subject? Contemporary financial systems are, broadly speaking, characterized by internationalization, turbulence, potential or actual instability - reflected in an increasing number of bank failures-, financial scandals, and bank crises. Technological development is extremely

17

fast and unpredictable, and in addition, there is an increasing need for finance - in particular external finance. With regards to this background it is important to assess processes of change of financial systems, because the institutional set-ups of the systems affects corporate behaviour and viability. Changes may come from within the system, but for a large part external factors induce the changes. These external factors are for example, the results of the political process of moving towards the European single market. It is an important political assignment to ensure that these changes are adequately adapted to the needs of national industry. However, the basis for effective policy measures is an understanding of the interplay between the corporate sector and the financial system.

It is, of course, also a prerequisite for such measures that policy makers recognizes the needs for supporting innovation financing. In Denmark there has recently been intense debates on how to support innovations financially, and major institutional changes in government agencies for innovation support have resulted.

The evolutionary viability of a national industry depends heavily on a pool of potentially innovative firms and persons. However, there is also a need for a financial, institutional set-up for selecting good projects and supporting their successful realization. At first sight only a part of the financial system seems relevant to innovation financing. However it is difficult to keep the parts of the financial system separate as changes in performance, financial innovations etc. in one part of the system are bound to have an influence on other parts. One issue intensely debated and under political supervision is the large losses incurred in corporate lending in 1991 in Danish banks. It may be that risky, innovative projects are affected by resulting changes in credit policies in banks. Other examples could be mentioned. The point is that politically it is crucial to take into account how the interplay between the financial system and industry takes place. This interplay must be better understood than it is to date. The present investigation can, hopefully, contribute to a clarification of the basis for such policies.

1.4. The relevance of the subject for economic theory

In general, economic theory has tended to make a sharp distinction between monetary and real phenomena. Even disregarding this fact there are, to my knowledge, only few attempts to analyze the role of finance in innovations. One remarkable exception is the work by Schumpeter (1912/1934), who made the first thorough treatment of the financing aspect of innovations. Since then the subject has been close to non-existent in economic theory - at least in the sense that most of the contributions are either limited in depth or scope - or both.

One line of research focuses on the financing of R&D, sometimes on how the sources are distributed between private and public financing. Even if R&D is an important part of innovation - and increasingly so - it is far from being the only one. Another branch of literature is occupied with the analysis of the venture capital industry. Again, although this is a highly relevant subject, venture capital is only a small fraction of the total risk capital pool. Other studies are concerned with differences in banking systems or financial systems as a whole. These studies are valuable but rarely focused upon the special features of financing innovation. On the other hand innovation theories are preoccupied with the real side of the process and, with few exceptions, barely mention the financial aspects.

Financial theory similarly suffers from even more fundamental deficiencies. Most often agents are assumed to take decisions under conditions of risk rather than uncertainty and their computational abilities are assumed to be unlimited. Innovations are, however, by definition characterized by novelty and uncertainty. Therefore, standard, financial theory is inadequate in relation to innovations. In relation to analysis of financial systems it is also insufficient for the present purpose. Rather than developing a systemic perspective financial theory has been preoccupied with price relations and arbitrage. As Neave (1991, p.5) puts it:

> "Neoclassical financial theory is similarly limited in its ability to explain financial system change. Indeed, it may fairly be said that the theory is better at explaining well established practices rather than it is at illuminating the creative or exploratory aspects of finance, the

dynamics of technological change, or the evolution of sophisticated financial systems from primitive ones."

In conclusion there is a gap in the literature in this area. This is not to say that it is necessary to start from scratch to construct a new theory. Elements from existing theories and applications to financing innovation, may help bridge the gap. In other words, an important part of a theory of financing innovations is in some respect analogue to how Schumpeter defines an innovation. In his definition an innovation is a combination of existing knowledge, which can be straightforward or difficult to identify.

> "Sometimes, an innovation might be almost inevitable - the new combination might be easy to find and realise. In other cases, it might take an enormous intellectual effort or an extremely creative mind, to identify a potential new combination." (Lundvall, 1992, p.8)

In this present approach I shall combine elements from innovation theory with selected aspects of financial theory, institutional economics and microeconomic considerations. Obviously there is only room and reason for selecting and merging a few elements of these theories and they are not necessarily equally represented in the resultant synthesis. Thus, the weight of inspiration from innovation theory is likely to be easily traceable in the following chapters. The other main body of theory considered is financial theory, but the merging process has left this theoretical inspiration less recognizable if one looks for a standard paradigm of financial theory. An application of standard financial theory to innovation financing is difficult for reasons explained in chapter three, but financial considerations are nevertheless highly integrated throughout the discussions.

Institutional economics and microeconomic theory are also deemed necessary to an understanding of decisions to finance or innovate and the circumstances under which these decisions are taken. I shall apply these element to the special case of financing innovations in order to highlight the basic mechanisms of how financial systems work with respect to financing innovations. In addition, I hope to provide an understanding of the interaction between the major actors in this play - that is the borrower and the lender. The methods used to fulfill this, admitted, immodest ambition, are explained in the following sections.

1.5. Design of the investigation and methodological considerations

When Sir John Hicks wrote his "Causality in Economics" (1979), his intentions were, among other things, to point out that uncertainty, time and the perceptions of the socio-economic environment affect how economic theories are made, which causalities are seen as relevant, and what (limited) degree of generality is appropriate.

It is important to recognize that economic theories are not universally valid. They are created in a specific period in a certain institutional setting and are thus more or less related to the specific context in which they are created. Moreover, the very choice of what is considered relevant subjects to study is determined by the socio-economic setting and development. Similarly, the considerations below relate to the specific technological and financial development in contemporary Western economies. However, the present enquiry is mainly oriented towards studying changes, and a static analysis of the situation today would be inadequate. Consequently, I supplement the analysis of the present situation with prospective and past experiences. In order to understand the character, strength and future development of the present bank-industry relationship it is useful to go back in history to trace how and why these relationships were established. In order to make adequte policies it is useful to consider how these relationships are affected by present and future changes in financial systems.

The weight one places on theory and empirical material respectively varies in economic studies. The task which I have set myself in this study is primarily theoretical and therefore the major part of the subsequent chapters are theoretical. The empirical investigations are concentrated in the latter part of the book. More specifically, by using secondary data, I shall in chapter seven illustrate the theoretical analysis by comparing financial systems in some of the major Western economies. The purpose of which is to demonstrate that the institutional set-up of financial systems affects

21

possibilities for innovation financing. At a more specific level I shall focus upon the Danish system of innovation financing.

Descriptions of the working of financial systems are difficult to take seriously if based purely on whim or duplication of common beliefs. Pure theory, on the other hand, may not be sufficient. To avoid problems of a biased approach I shall conduct an empirical analysis of the Danish banking sector focusing on the interplay between banks and firms and on the criteria used for screening innovation projects in the 1980s and 1990s. The purpose is to clarify if what are normally considered common established facts are actually tenable and to confront this limited empirical evidence with theory. The theoretical results in this book are compared to innovation through combinations of existing knowledge. The empirical study of the Danish banking sector is, on the other hand, novel in its own right, and provides surprisingly, important conclusions with regards to the central aspects of the subject with great implications for potential policy implications.

1.6. Limitations and reservations to the analysis

Financing is an extremely important precondition for the innovation process. I do not claim, though, that the availability of external capital totally determins the speed and direction of technical change. I recognize that there are other important inputs to the innovation process, and even though the focus in this study is primarily on external finance, a large part of innovations are financed internally. Internal finance will also be dealt with here, but to a lesser extent than external capital.

A fundamental problem of analysising this subject is that it may often be difficult to separate expenses in a firm from what is used for innovations and what is used for the ordinary operating of the business. Therefore, it may be difficult to give a precise classification of financing sources related to types of investments.

There are topics which I do not intend to give equal priority, or even touch upon in the following pages even though it may be argued that they are, in some way or another, related to financing innovations. This applies to for example, the financing of the education system[5]. The education system is, directly and indirectly, an underlying base for a large part of innovative activity. Scientists need a formal education and high level of skills which are a prerequisite for much activity in innovation. Indirectly, even primary schools, and indeed also higher level education institutions like universities, are part of the innovation system in a nation. University research is often directly used in the private sector[6], and the private sector often has its own education for scientists.

Another topic that I shall not be treating thoroughly is the role of various government programmes and specific instruments aimed at promoting innovations. This topic is wide scoping in itself and I shall not discuss the particular instruments in detail.

For a number of purposes it would be interesting to see if there are differences between industries in their needs and opportunities for financing. However, in the following I shall deal with industry as a whole.

Merging two large, apparently very distinct, bodies of literature into a consistent framework of analysis for this special problem, is an immense task. I do not claim to fulfil this task to perfection. Instead I hope to take the first steps towards the development of a comprehensive theory on financing innovations.

1.7. A road map of the book

A normal procedure in economic research is to refer to major theories and classical articles related to, or dealing with, the topic in question. Often this is a useful exercise because it helps to clarify possible deficiencies in the prevailing theories and may be used to emphasize the purpose of the work. When investigating a relatively new area of research, like the present one, this avenue is closed, or at best limited. With the possible exception of the contribution by Schumpeter, the treatment of financing innovations has been

---

5 Included in the education system in this connection is an increasing amount of institutions and courses aimed at educating people to become skillful entrepreneurs.

6 The use of university research is particularly profound in the U.S. as dealt with in further detail by Nelson (Nelson, 1988, p.319f. and 1992).

sparse in the literature. In spite of this fact I shall in chapter 2 survey what nevertheless has been said about financing innovations and point to possible elaborations.

One such obvious elaboration is to use financial theory to show how financing high risk projects takes place. In chapter 3 I take a closer look at one part of modern financial theory - the information and economics literature - to see if it provides a microfoundation for a theory.

Regardless of the results of this enquiry it is necessary to relate microeconomic discussions to the special case of innovations because, there are some characteristics of innovations and the innovation process which are necessary to take into account as they affect financing behaviour. In addition, it is useful to explain the characteristics of the innovation process in further detail to point out the precise object that needs to be financed and to make clear my view of what is a realistic innovation theory. This is the topic of chapter 4.

Next, in chapter 5, the characteristics of innovation are related to financial requirements. In the chapter I shall reveal who the needs for finance vary over time in an innovation project and consequently how there are different requirements that effect financial institutions depending on the development of the particular project.

Chapter 6 continues the discussion on financing innovations by particular institutions. Neither markets nor hierarchies are sole mechanisms of allocation in any economy; financial intermediaries are important in that respect in all countries and continue to coexist with both markets and hierarchies. Chapter 6 explores specific features of financial intermediaries to explain how these institutions actually work and behave when faced with financing innovations. Even though different kinds of institutions are dealt with, the emphasis will be on banks because they are by far the most common form of intermediary and financier of corporate investments.

In chapter 7, some of the points in the theory are illustrated by outlining relevant characteristics of the financial systems in selected countries. This is not meant to be an adequate analysis of the credit systems and capital markets of the different countries. It should rather be regarded as an illustration of how the innovative capability of nations can be limited or supported by the functioning and institutional set-up of financial systems.

In chapter 8, current trends in the development of financial systems are discussed. Possible effects of these trends are pointed out with special emphasis on the effects on innovation financing.

Whereas chapter 7 and 8 are in-between chapters in the sense that they are simultaneously micro and macro oriented and deals with indicative facts of archetypical systems, chapter 9 and 10 are purely empirical- and country specific. In these chapters I shall analyze the Danish system of innovation financing. The purpose is two-fold. Firstly, the chapters can be seen as illustrations of several aspects of the theoretical discussions. Second, they serve as concrete points of departure for policy discussions.

Finally, in chapter 11, the main results are summarized and possible policy implications developed.

Chapter 2. The current state of the art and its development until now

"The current state of the theory does not allow one to go much further than suggesting plausible taxonomies and empirically testable conjectures." (Dosi, 1988c, p.47)

2.1. Introduction

As the above quotation by Dosi suggests, this is an area which leaves economists with a lot of work to do. In the history of economic theory there have only been a few contributions linking finance and innovation. Even though it is intuitively obvious that it takes capital to conduct innovation projects and firms subsequently evaluate their innovation activities financially, innovation theory has tended to disregard financial aspects. Vice versa financial theory has tended to disregard the specific purpose of the investment to be financed. Why is this so?

One explanation is the sparse research into the relationship between real and monetary phenomena in general.[1] In addition, innovation theory has been marginalised in relation to the core of economic theory except for the past couple of decades. Lately, increased interest has been directed towards the relationship between finance and innovation, and empirical studies have started to appear. Although limited in depth and scope, this increased interest reflects a growing recognition of the deep involvement of firms in financial markets and the large, and increasing, costs of the R&D activities.

This chapter presents a brief survey of previous contributions on the relation between finance and innovations and sums up the state of the theory. This is necessary in itself because very little has been said on this issue in economic theory. The use of this chapter in subsequent discussions is twofold. It intends to point out some shortcomings and merits of the

---

1 This is reflected in - to some extent - different and independent areas of research. Joan Robinson, Keynes and later the post-keynesians argued for the importance of the interplay between monetary and real phenomena, but still this artificial division is common in economic analysis.

existing literature, and it serves as a source of inspiration for further theoretical developments.

The current state of the theory reflects that it lacks a solid foundation and a holistic, integrated view of financing innovations. Apparently this can be ascribed to the relatively recent development of theories on innovation. This may have hampered the development of a comprehensive and integrated theory.

However, in this chapter, I shall point to some previous contributions, one of which is directly focused on innovation financing and others which indicate the building blocks for further theoretical development. More precisely four contributions are dealt with all of them by famous economists of the early nineteen century. These particular authors are chosen because they represent four different aspects of economic theory which are highly relevant for the present problem. Schumpeter dealt with innovations and also their actual financing. Elements from innovation theory are indispensible for a theory of innovation financing. Keynes hardly mentioned technological development, but he is important in this connection because he pointed out the impact of fundamental uncertainty. Veblen claimed that a competence mis-match and differencies in logic between the industrial and the financial sphere are hampering industrial development. Hilferding is included in the quartet because he rightly points out the importance of interaction between the borrower and the lender.

These four aspects are those on which the survey has also focused in the recent works. Naturally, there are discussions which are only mentioned without really elaborating upon the issue. In subsequent chapters I shall return to those discussions. However, the contributions in recent years are still scarce and scattered and there is a great need for integrating and developing useful ideas in these contributions.

Although the chapter will not be in a strict chronological order I shall begin by discussing some of the writings by a selection of the great economists from the first half of this century. The emphasis in the first section will be on the contribution by Schumpeter because his contribution is the most directly related to a possible theory of financing innovations, whereas other economists deal with the more general topic of financing investments or the relevance of financial structures. The survey presents a selection of the major, influential contributions rather than being an account of everything which has been said. The method employed is the extensive use of qoutations to show that innovation financing was actually discussed in the early contributors. Secondly, I shall give a brief introduction to the areas of economic theory most relevant for the development of a more comprehensive theory on this issue. Thirdly, I shall point to some of the empirical studies conducted. Finally, I shall sum up by giving a few hints on how to proceed in building an adequate theory.

2.2. The theory of the role of finance in innovation in retrospect

2.2.1. Schumpeter - the grand old man of the theory of financing innovations

Schumpeter is the one "classical" theorist who addresses the question of financing innovations most directly in his writings[2]. But Schumpeter has a very broad innovation concept which modifies the term "directly".[3]

In Schumpeter's view the process of innovation is the prime mover of capitalistic development; development being something qualitatively new caused by endogenous, spontaneous and discontinuous changes in the channels of circular flow (Schumpeter, 1912/1934, p.63-64). The innovation process is thus a discontinuous process. On the other hand Schumpeter is not insisting on a theory of revolutionary innovations. Rather the evolution is a result of a combination of revolutions and small steps, which constitutes a wide range of events and influences (Schumpeter, 1939, p.181).

---

2 He also agrees that "money matters". In fact he insists (at least in 1912/1934 although modified in 1939) on the endogenous, integrated role of money in economic theory, as opposed to the Walras theory.

3 Thus, he lists a number of broad cases that characterize innovations (Schumpeter, 1912/1934, p.66) and claims that "innovation" covers "any doing things differently" in the realm of economic life" (Schumpeter, 1939, p.59) or "we will simply define innovation as the setting up of a new production function" (ibid., p.62). This innovation concept is, not unrealistic although analytically useless. Innovations are often a by-product of actions, which were not taken with the intended purpose of finding "new combinations". In other instances an effort is made in deliberately combining existing knowledge in new ways or developing new knowledge.

For expository purposes[4] Schumpeter developed his well-known circular flow scheme, which is in contrast to his development concept. In the circular flow state the economy is reproducing established routines, habits and norms. All capacity and money is utilized for this reproduction and Schumpeter denotes this "Wieser's principle of continuity" (Schumpeter, 1934, p.9). For our purposes there is no need to go further into a detailed description of the circular flow model (see Schumpeter, 1934, pp.3-55). What is important in this connection is that deviations from circular flow are made possible by the credit system.

According to Schumpeter, the entrepreneur is the driving force in the process of innovation, but it is a prerequisite that he can convince the banks, or the "capitalists", to provide him with credit for the financing of the innovation. In fact, this function is important enough to be the "differentia specifica" in the system (Schumpeter, 1912/1934, p.69). The creation of purchasing power by credit from the banking sector is necessary for financing innovations, because in the routinized circular-flow system all capacity is absorbed for reproducing circular flow.[5] The entrepreneur must argue that he can repay the loan as a result of commercially successful new combinations.

> "it means entrusting him with productive forces. It is only thus that economic development could arise from the mere circular flow in perfect equilibrium. And this function constitutes the keystone of the modern credit structure. Hence, while granting credit is not essential in the normal circular flow,...it is certain that there is such a gap to bridge in the carrying out of new combinations. To bridge it is the function of the lender, and he fulfills it by placing purchasing power

---

4 "...it is true we make an abstraction, but only for the purpose of exhibiting the essence of what actually happens", (Schumpeter, 1934, p.9).

5 The effect of more credit is increased demand, and as no new means of production are produced, this means increases in prices on means of production. The elimination of this credit inflation can be resolved if the entrepreneur repays the borrowed money though it may happen that he does not succeed in selling the produced goods in a sufficient quantity or to a sufficient price, or that the innovation project fails before there is anything sellable produced. The lender will then carry a loss, and if this is covered by additional credit e.g. from another bank, the result can be a permanent inflation (1912/1934, p. 109-111). Schumpeter thus considers the lenders' judgement of the borrower to set the limit of credit expansion.

created ad hoc at the disposal of the entrepreneur. (Schumpeter, 1912/1934, p.107)

This borrower-lender interaction is a question of judgement of credit worthiness on the one hand and, on the other, of "personal weight" ..."the only man he has to convince or to impress is the banker who is to finance him" (ibid.p.89). Let us now take a closer look at Schumpeter's view of the lender.

Like Keynes, Schumpeter distinguished between technical risk and commercial risk (1912/1934, p.32). As it is the capitalist who provides the credit it is he who bears the risk. The degree of aversion with the banker towards running a risk will determine the amount of available capital for carrying out new combinations (unless it is the entrepreneur who furnishes the capital).

> "riskiness...makes it more difficult to obtain the necessary capital and thus forms one of the obstacles entrepreneurs have to overcome and one of the instances of resistance of the environment which explain why innovations are not carried out smoothly and as a matter of course."(Schumpeter, 1939, p.79)

Schumpeter emphasizes the importance of a close contact between borrower and lender in the screening and monitoring function of the banker[6]. Thus, he

> "should know, and be able to judge, what his credit is used for and....the banker must not only know what the transaction is which he is asked to finance and how it is likely to turn out, but he must also know the customer, his business, and even his private habits, and get, by frequently "talking things over with him", a clear picture of his situation. But if banks finance innovation, all this becomes immeasurably more important." (ibid. p.90).

Schumpeter is aware of the high risk associated with innovations and he recognizes that the majority of innovation projects are never carried out and "of those who do,(carry them out) nine out of ten fail to make a success of them". A security can ease access to credit for these high risk projects (1912/1934, p.100).

In summation, Schumpeter provided an enlightening and original contribution to the theory of financing innovations. One can only wonder why the many "Schumpeterian" innovation theorists have largely ignored the "differentia specifica" in Schumpeter's innovation theory - the importance of credit for the financing of new combinations.

---

6 One dimension of this borrower-lender interaction is the possibility of applying the entrepreneur concept to the lender. If this is so the lender is leading or supporting development by inventing financial innovations. Although scattered throughout Schumpeter's writings, I find that there is evidence that supports such an interpretation. Other interpretations along this line, are by Minsky (1990) - especially p.52,61 and Vercelli (1985). Thus, Schumpeter notes that "The banker, therefore, is not so much primarily a middleman in the commodity "purchasing power" as a producer of this commodity" (1912/1934, p.74). In addition, Schumpeter's favorite reference case - the railway in the U.S. (1939, p.197f.) - is precisely an example of new combinations within finance that made the product innovation and diffusion possible. Notably specialized merchant banks developed as did the institutionalization of the Wall Street Stock Exchange. Other financial innovations appeared, most of them due to the large investments in the diffusion of railroads in the U.S. Thus, the fifteen largest railroad companies invested more than 5 billion dollars during the 1850s and 1860s, and this was well above their self-financing abilities. On the other hand, there is no in depth treatment of this aspect and within a passage he deemphasized the importance of the specific form of credit instruments (1912/1934, p.109), although this does not mean that he rejects the importance of new *combinations* of credit instruments. The banking system in pre-war Austria was dominated by universal banks which participated actively in the development of industry and had a close interaction with industry (for a thorough discussion on this, see Teichova, 1988, p.9ff.). Therefore, Schumpeter is likely to think of the banker as an entrepreneur to some extent. On the other hand, he strongly emphasized that a bank must be an independent agent without any stake in the project it is to examine, and he is thus not in favor of an integration of banking and industry (Schumpeter, 1939, p.92).

2.2.2. Putting money into focus - the works of John Maynard Keynes and successors

John M. Keynes emphasized the role of money in production in an entrepreneurial economy. Two points were especially novel compared to previous theories. First, he demonstrated that the role money is such that the economy does not converge towards full employment equilibrium. Second, he shows that uncertainty due to financial relations has real effects.[7]

For our purposes the latter point is the most interesting. In particular - although Keynes has been criticized for a too short perspective and a too high level of aggregation (see e.g. Vercelli, 1985, p.40) - two aspects of his theory are interesting in this connection. One is the relationship between the borrower and the lender and, the second interrelated, aspect is the effect of this on the aggregate stability of the banking system.

To illustrate the former, let us begin with a quotation from "General Theory":

> "Thus we must also take into account of the other facet of the state of confidence, namely, the confidence of the lending institutions towards those who seek to borrow from them, sometimes described as the state of credit."(Keynes, 1936, p.158)

The other facet he refers to is the state of confidence in investment decisions of the entrepreneur. Many of the macro concepts introduced in the General Theory have their micro counterparts. Thus, the "state of affairs", which is a macro economic concept describing the general business climate, is an aggregation of "animal spirit", or in other words, the state of risk aversion. He illustrates how processes at the micro level are important to the macro

---

7 He was actually one of the first to indicate that there may be a problem with credit rationing: "So far, however, as bank loans are concerned lending does not - in Great Britain at least - take place according to the principles of a perfect market. There is apt to be an unsatisfied fringe of borrowers, the size of which can be expanded or contracted, so that banks can influence the volume of investment by expanding or contracting the volume of their loans, without there being necessarily any change in the level of bank-rate, in the demand-schedule of borrowers, or in the volume of lending otherwise than through the banks. This phenomenon is capable, when it exists, of having great practical importance" (Keynes, 1930, pp.212-213). Gurley and Shaw (1955, p.531) restated the argument, which has had a large impact on theory.

level (but he truly fails to incorporate any analysis of technology or meso-level structural change).[8] In particular he discusses the processes of borrowing and lending:

> "Two types of risk affect the volume of investment which have not commonly been distinguished, but which it is important to distinguish. The first is the entrepreneur's or borrower's risk and arises out of doubts in his own mind as to the probability of his actually earning the prospective yield for which he hopes. If a man is venturing his own money, this is the only risk which is relevant. But where a system of borrowing and lending exists, by which I mean the granting of loans with a margin of real or personal security, a second type of risk is relevant which we may call the lender's risk. This may be due either to moral hazard, i.e. voluntary default or other means of escape, possible lawful, from the fulfillment of the obligation, or to the possible insufficiency of the margin of security, i.e. involuntary default due to the disappointment of expectation." (Keynes, 1936, p.144)

He then proceeds to relate this framework to the risk premium assessment of the borrower and the lender, and he notes that during a boom, estimations of the risk premium tend to be low.

In conclusion, Keynes provided a framework for incorporating borrowers and lenders risk[9]. Furthermore he pointed to the basic uncertainty in economics and the non-neutrality of money. Unfortunately his successors only gave brief and desultory references to the problem of finance in economic change in general, not to mention the particular case of financing of technological development. The Keynesian theory mainly focused upon

---

8 Apparently he did not elaborate on the problems of financing technology. However, in "Treatise on Money" he mentions the technological development and the power of the banking system in relation to the investment decisions of the entrepreneur. "...the pace, at which the (...) entrepreneurs will be able to carry their projects into execution at a cost of interest which is not deterrent to them, will depend on the degree of complaisance of those responsible for the banking system. "(Keynes, 1930, p.96).

9 This framework was later used and extended by Minsky (1975).

Keynes's liquidity preference theory[10] and thereby attention was directed towards the role of money as opposed to credit[11].

2.2.3. Hilferding - relationships between industry and banks

Like Schumpeter, Rudolf Hilferding (1910) argues that the relationship between the borrower and the lender is an important feature of capitalist development. The perspective is, however, different from Schumpeters'. Hilferding considers the bank -industry relationship to be an inherently asymmetric developing relationship. He argues from a macroeconomic perspective that the tendency (law) of the falling average rate of profits makes industry increasingly more dependent upon external finance from banks. The banks use this fact to dominate industry.[12]

The argument, and its assumptions, may be criticized for several reasons (see e.g. Wellhöner and Wixforth (1989)). The main weakness is that Hilferding is not at all clear in explaining the macroeconomic conditions for how bank-industry relationships may develop and affect the single banker-entrepreneur interplay.

This deficiency has not been resolved yet. Although the bank-industry relationships have been studied in recent years, the link between the micro level of analysis and the study of the impact of the surroundings on these micro processes largely remains an unexplored field of study.

---

10 A Post-Keynesian tradition insisted upon the interdependence of money and real forces in determining economic development (With people like P. Davidson (1972, 1978), Weintraub (1973), Leijonhufvud (1968), Clower (1965), Minsky (1975, 1986, 1989)). This maintenance of financial institutions in the analysis and the argument that "money matters" is, however, a too general formulation for analyzing the role of finance in technological change, but it does indeed put focus back on the financial aspects of economic development as especially forcefully argued by Minsky (1975).

11 The Modigliani-Miller article had a tremendous influence on economic theory, and the thoughts are still discussed although it was directed to a very limited case and generally now rejected. An issue of the Journal of Economic Perspectives, (Vol.2, No.4, Autum 1988) solely treats the extensive discussions on this theorem. One of the most serious mistakes of the approach taken in the Modigliani-Miller theorem was to disregard the purpose of the investment that need to be financed. Gurley and Shaw(1955) refocused the financial intermediation in the process of credit creation and the importance of the financial system was underlined. However the Modigliani-Miller theorem which argued for the irrelevance of financial structures in perfect markets, gave economists a pleasant excuse for neglecting the points made by Gurley and Shaw.

12 He is thus part of a marxist tradition speaking about a merging of finance capitalists and industrial capitalists.

2.2.4. Institutional economics - features from the writings of Veblen

A key element in institutional theory is the view that the evolution of society is a result of the interaction between progressive technological development and regressive institutions/institutional inertia. This view has frequently been called "the Veblen-dichotomy"[13], and Thorstein Veblen is an important exponent of institutional economics, from which a theory of innovation financing has some heritage.[14]

According to Veblen the two sides of the dichotomy are very different. On the one hand technological development has a certain logic characterized by idle curiosity, workmanship, inducement through a pure cause and effect, and an impersonal way of organizing work. The "machine process" is characterized by a distance from institutions such as habits and old ways of thinking by workers and their superiors (Veblen, 1904, p.310-311).

On the other hand institutions are habits which reflect former modes of thinking, not the future ways of creative organization and thinking. Large firms have vested interests in the established way of producing. Veblen saw this as an essential regressive institution. The behaviour of capitalists have a negative effect upon production to an extent that made Veblen use the term "sabotage" (Veblen, 1919, p.82) and claim that production could easily have been much larger were it not hampered by incompetent management.

> "..it is an open secret that with a reasonable free hand the production experts would today readily increase the ordinary output of industry by several fold,-variously estimated at some 300 per cent. to 1200 per cent. of the current output. And what stands in the way of so increasing the ordinary output of goods and services is business as usual." (Veblen, 1919, p.83)

---

13 Ayres (1944, 1961) and Forster (summarized in Journal of Econimic Issues, dec. 1984) made substantial contributions to the development of the dichotomy in a more sophisticated, and less deterministic, picture.

14 Other important contributors include Myrdal, Galbraith, Mitchell, and Commons. Especially Galbraith was, like Veblen, interested in the dynamics of the capitalist system in general and the financial system in particular. But the connection between finance, technological development, and institutional theory has been almost forgotten until recently.

The distinction between technicians and economically oriented managers is important to Veblens' argument. He points out that increased specialization has accelerated the division between industrial management and business management. Business managers, "the businesslike captains of finance", have increasingly lost the feeling for industrial production to the detriment of the society as a whole.

> "The result has been a somewhat distrustful blindfold choice of processes and personnel and a consequent enforced incompetence in the management of industry, a curtailment of output below the needs of the community, below the productive capacity of the industrial system, and below what an intelligent control of production would have made commercially profitable." (Veblen, 1919, p.78).

As a result intermediary institutions develop, by Veblen termed "consulting engineers" (ibid., p.80). The purpose of these is to advise investment bankers about the possible industrial and commercial soundness of potential investments. However, Veblen argues that the process of judging a firm soon became a matter of "standardized bureaucratic routine" and he denotes the intermediaries undertaking these judgments "lieutenant of finance" whereas

> "the captaincy having been taken over by the syndicated investment bankers and administered as a standardized routine of accountancy," (Veblen, 1919, p.81)

Veblens analysis is valuable in pointing out the importance of differences in logic in the financial and industrial sector, respectively. More generally, institutional economics is thus a necessary ingredient in a theory on financing innovations, in that it points out the importance of informal institutions, in addition to the formal institutions.

In this respect Schumpeter may be seen as also having institutional considerations[15]. In the circular flow system, society is in a routinized state due to strong informal
institutions (like habits, conventions, etc.). But new combinations (innovations) break up these routines and the inertia, and cause development. In his later writings (1943) Schumpeter takes into account the institutional set-up of society in a broader sense.

2.3. Contemporary contributions of direct relevance to innovation financing

The discussions in section two on the classical contributions illustrates four different kinds of theory which are useful for developing a comprehensive theory. This reflects my basic conviction that adequate theoretical developments must combine several different elements of theory to sufficiently cover relevant aspects of financing innovations.

Below I shall first mention some of the general subjects that are necessary ingredients in the innovation financing theory cocktail. Secondly, I shall present some recent contributions focusing directly on innovation financing.

2.3.1. Related theories relevant to a theory of innovation financing

It's natural, when talking about financing innovations it is natural to start with financial theory. However, traditionally, financial theory has tended to assume rational, maximizing agents with perfect foresight, operating in a perfect market. Happily, some parts of financial theory have moved away from this theoretical set-up. This applies to the "information and economics"-literature, which deals with the interplay between for example a lender and a borrower under imperfect information and as a consequence credit rationing.

---

15   Elliott (1983, p.288-89) notes e.g. that "Schumpeter was much more explicit than his contemporaries in specifying institutional aspects of his argument. Indeed, one is tempted to say that Schumpeter was more successful, in a limited way, in synthesizing an analysis of institutional change with economic theory than were institutionalist critics of mainstream economics in the early twentieth century."

The basic ideas about inefficiencies of financial markets started with the "Lemons problem" initiated by Akerlof(1970). He showed how asymmetric information might induce disruption of the function of the markets (and cause underlending) and this Lemons principle has been applied to the literature about financial markets. In fact Gurley & Shaw also found that credit rationing is used by banks rather than raising interest rates when they are faced with uncertain investment projects, (1955, p.531). Some of the most important examples are Leland & Pyle (1977) and Stiglitz and Weiss (1981).

Within this tradition in recent years numerous articles have been published. Some of them deal with ideas that overcome the weaknesses of the main body of the literature. Gertler (1988) surveyed parts of the literature (In chapter 3 I shall return to this part of financial theory).

The micro foundation of a theory of innovation financing can, however, not be based on this line of argument. The reason is that there are still reminiscences from neoclassical financial arguments at the heart of these theories and that implies operating with risk rather than uncertainty. This is incompatible with an understanding of the financing of innovation because innovations are inherently uncertain. Therefore one has to turn to the literature dealing with the consequences of uncertainty and to innovation theory to look for a micro foundation. This claim may be an exaggeration. Actually valuable theoretical deductions can be found in this literature in spite its dubious micro foundation. An integratal part of this theory must be the theories of industry-finance relationships, because this relationship is crucial for reducing information and competence dependent barriers to innovation financing.

At a higher level of aggregation the capability of the financial system[16] to support industrial and technological change is an important subject of

---

16 Financial systems can be defined as institutional arrangements for the transformation of savings or credit to investments, and for advising firms. Therefore, financial systems may differ in the way this transformation is undertaken and in the institutions undertaking it. More specifically financial systems are different in the division of labour between financial institutions, the degree of concentration of these and their size relative to the economy as a whole, the instruments used in the financial sector and the relation to the corporate sector - including the classical distinction of capital structure of the firms and degree of selffinancing.

analysis[17]. I maintain that variation in structure of financial systems makes a difference to their capacity for solving different tasks with respect to financing innovations. It is crucial to take into consideration this difference, when governments intervene in financial markets. Not only must the functionings of the national and international financial systems be taken into account, but the national systems of innovation and industrial development must also be an integratal part of the analysis, as well as the specific interplay between financial systems and national systems of innovation (Christensen, 1992).

International comparative studies is one way of approaching this subject. These comparisons have mainly focused upon comparing financial systems in five major countries: The U.K., the U.S., Japan, France, and Germany. Zysman (1983) is an important contributor in this group. Others are Cox (1986), Mayer (1988), Hu (1990), Rybzinsky (1984, 1988), and Frankel & Montgomery (1991). Mowery (1992) provides an interesting historical account of how the finance - industry relationships developed in the five countries during the first half of the century. Neave (1991) evaluates the different types of systems from a transaction cost economics perspective. Stiglitz & Greenwald (1992) and Stiglitz (1991) consider if financial institutions are effective allocation mechanisms seen from an information and economics point of view.

Works on national systems of innovation are sparse although gaining increasing interest. Nelson (ed.)(1992) and Lundvall (ed.)(1992) are main contributors to an empirically based analysis and a conceptual, theoretical discussion, respectively. McKelvey (1992) compares different approaches to the analysis of national systems of innovation. The linking of analysis of financial systems and national systems of innovation has not yet been developed to a great deal (Christensen, 1992).

---

17 Some valuable international comparisons of corporate financing have emerged lately and are still an important and productive research area. Especially a program at CEPR, Stanford is dealing with this question, but also Mayer (1988, 1990), Franks & Mayer (1990), Edwards & Fischer (1991), Alexander & Mayer (1990). See also chapter 7 of this thesis.

2.3.2. Contributions dealing explicitly with innovation financing

If a lender should characterize a "good, attractive borrower" it would be a firm with a large solidity compared to the size of the loan. In that case the lender is usually confident in a sufficient return. A large firm is often able to meet solidity requirements whereas a small firm may have difficulties in creating sufficient collateral. For start-ups the magnitude of the problem is multiplied. Moreover, uncertainty changes over time. Therefore, different financial sources with different risk profiles are relevant for a firm during its development. Consequently, an adequate theory of innovation financing must include a time dimension, i.e. considerations on the changing character of financial barriers as the product/firm develops.

2.3.2.1. The importance of firm size and life cycles

Firm size and product life cycle in relation to innovation financing is discussed in various contributions. Eliasson and Granstrand (1981) point to the screening function of financial institutions, the role of government and in particular the question of firm size. Is the financial system discriminating against small firms due to the large risk? They point out that equity participation rather than loans is the way to finance these investments. Small firms often lack the necessary amount and quality of finance and management expertise, but, on the other hand, a large part of innovation activity - especially down stream activity - takes place in large firms.

Storey (1990) identifies several aspects by which small firms differ from large firms, and he relates various stages of growth of the firm to which kinds of debt and equity financing are typical. He finds that in addition to traditional small firm features such as risk of default and volatility, small firms may be characterized by information deficiences both regarding amount and quality compared to large firms. Furthermore, he maintains that there is likely to be a conflict between the organization and personality of the small firm and its management, and the corresponding culture in banks.

Like Eliasson and Granstrand, Roy Rothwell (1981), and Rothwell & Zegveld (1983), argue that small firms may be very capable of innovating

41

but, in addition to other small scale disadvantages, they lack capital to fund high-risk innovations. Penrose (1980) points out that small firms may not only be met with a relatively higher rate of interest, but also banks may restrict the amount of credit they can obtain at any rate. In other words, credit rationing is frequently used.

Prakke(1988), on the other hand, thinks that the focus on large firm R&D, being a measurement of innovation, and the question of firm size has been over-emphasized in this matter. He employs a product life cycle model to show how the sources of financing change over time and how uncertainty and financial requirements are inversely related. Kline & Rosenberg (1986) are in agreement with the product life cycle view and add that product life cycles have become shorter and financial risks greater due to increased development costs.

The great risk associated with investments in new technology and new firms is one of the arguments for government funding of these investments. Governments need not employ the same profitability requirements as private financing institutions (Arrow, 1962), and social gains from increased employment and it is argued that vigorous growth in the prosperous, new technology based firms, legitimat government intervention. On the other hand opponents to government intervention argue that market forces will allocate resources in the most efficient and socially desirable way. Thus, there is no reason why a government institution should do any better in judging a project than a private agency. Grossman (1990) reviews this discussion and relates it to economic theory. Rothwell provides a thorough discussion on the role of government in innovation funding, as does Fölster (1991), OECD (1988,1990), and Garlato (1986).

2.3.2.2. Learning and the development of borrower-lender relationships

Another important impact of time is the possibilities of building up long-term relations between firm and financier. The purpose of such relationships is to reduce informational asymmetries and inadequacies, which are particularly pronounced in innovation financing. The propensity to establish such long-term relationships varies between institutional set-ups of financial systems. Christensen (1992) focuses on this aspect of learning by interaction between a borrower and a lender in different types of financial systems.

Another article along this line is Dosi (1990). He starts off with an evolutionary innovation theory in which learning and selection are crucial properties. Different structures and performances can be related to differences in emphasis on learning and selection. The influence of financial structures on innovation is thus dependant on the influence that the financial system exerts on learning by firms and selection of firms and technologies. Financial systems are discussed employing the distinction of credit-based and market-based systems and a trade-off is indicated to. This trade-off concerns the choice between evolutionary viability and efficiency; i.e. financial systems have to take chances and finance/explore unknown possibilities. This, however, is often in contradiction to the efficiency of the particular financial institution and, consequently, may result in conservatism in the financial system.

Prakke (1988) also incorporates the importance of learning in his article, and Sharpe (1990) shows how the learning processes on the lending side actually may have undesirable effects on the allocation of capital because it is difficult for high quality firms to break established relationships before they have built up a reputation. Haubrich (1989) points out that borrower-lender relationships may be a method for reduction of monitoring costs and Clements (1985) consider the impact of the environment on these relationships. Several observers have argued that current trends in the financial markets - notably deregulation and the development of information technology - have made former long-term relationships between banks and their customers disappear (e.g. Engwall and Johanson, 1990). I shall return to that issue in chapter 8.

There are many reasons why lenders and borrowers build up relationships and learn from each other. One way of approaching this subject is by visualizing the purpose of the relationships as a way of reducing transaction costs. Coase (1937) introduced this analysis which has gained tremendous recognition and use after Williamson (1975,1986) developed it further. In a transaction cost approach, markets would yield the worst conditions for learning processes compared to hierarchies. Williamson extended his original analysis to include the in-between - intermediaries - which are important to the present analysis. Even if conceptually clarifying and illustrating the approach does have some inadequacies. For example, an assumption in transaction cost economics is that agents act opportunistically. However, one of the reasons for the borrower - lender relationship is precisely to avoid opportunistic behavior through the build up of mutual trust.

Other approaches to the analysis of the nature and reasons for learning processes are those of, for example Arrow (1973,1974) and Lundvall (1985,1988). Although not explicitly linked to finance these kinds of theories may be used in relation to borrower - lender interaction.

2.3.2.3. Financial innovations and system development

A third aspect of time is the evolution of the financial system in relation to the technological development, or in other words the creation of financial innovations as a response to new technologies and vice versa creation of new technologies as a response to new possibilities of financing. This mechanism is dealt with by Reed and Moreno (1986) and Santarelli (1986) who, inspired by Dosi, Schumpeter and Nelson & Winter, analyze technological development as a continuous, endogenous process, where the interaction between the financial and industrial structure determines the capability of the national system of innovation. The technological development takes a course, which will restructure the existing financial structures. Financial innovations are thus closely connected to technological innovations, each of them being a condition for the other if the dynamics in the system are to be maintained.

In another article(1987) Santarelli argues that changes in economic activity and the direction of technological change affects risk aversion and contributes to the selection of the most efficient firms. Innovating firms may fear are inability to repay loans, and the availability of external financial sources is therefore a determinant for investments in R&D. The ability of financial systems to adapt to changing conditions and different directions of technology is crucial for supporting technological development financially.

44

"In fact, during the phase of emergence of a new technological paradigm, a financial system able to identify the driving forces of the process and willing to face the uncertainty connected with the innovative activity represents a factor that enables and accelerates the emergence of TC(technical change). It is an enabling factor when it allows the system of firms to set in motion the vector of innovation. It is a factor of acceleration when it provides further financial backing whenever the vector of innovation has been set in motion (diffusion)". Santarelli(1987, p.42)

2.3.2.4. The venture capital industry

A relatively large branch of literature has dealt with venture capital. This is reflected in Journals specifically oriented towards venture capital (e.g. "Venture News") and the forming of organizations of venture capital companies (e.g. EVCA - European Venture Capital Association). In addition, numerous books and articles have dealt with venture capital[18]. Often articles with a content close to innovation financing finish with a short section about venture capital even though venture capital is only a minor fraction of total innovation financing.[19] One of the original discussions of how the development of venture capital (in its original sense) occurred is in Bullock(1983).

2.4. Empirical studies

The nature of the subject makes empirical studies extraordinary difficult. For example, how can we examine the firms' perception of the financial barriers, when we cannot investigate firms which are closed down or have changed strategy due to problems with financing? The lack of a comprehensive theory does not make empirical studies easier. Furthermore, to what extent there is a financial barrier to innovations will always be a matter of interpretation. On the one hand financial institutions would,

---

18 The style and quality of these books and articles in wide ranging. Some are rather romantic and they differ widely in their level of abstraction.

19 Prakke (1988) refers to figures for 1981 where US venture capital funds totalled less than one-tenth of one per cent of pension fund assets. Since then there has been a large growth in the industry and the impact of the special character of the venture capital funding should not be underestimated.

presumably, claim that there is plenty of idle capital for good projects, and on the other, firms will complain about lack of finance for their projects. Thus, ideally, one has to investigate the problem from the side of both the borrower and the lender.[20]

To my knowledge there has only been a few empirical studies which have focused directly on innovation financing. Most studies are deal with corporate financing in general, or with venture capital companies, or they analyze the government funding of R&D[21]. In the U.K. the MacMillan Committee (1931), the Bolton-committee (1971) and the Wilson-committee (1979) were set up with the purpose of looking into this problem with special attention directed towards small and medium sized firms. ACOST (1991) is another valuable U.K. study of conditions for small firms. Piater (1984) summarizes some of the empirical investigations in the EEC, concluding that in all of these studies the lack of finance was emphasized. In general the few empirical studies carried out neglect the lending side, i.e. the lender's perception of whether there are reasonable projects to be financed. In Denmark this is also the case. On the firm side a few studies (although limited in scope) have documented the problem (Håndværksrådet (1983), T.Bak-Jensen (1982), NIPS (1991), Håndværksrådet (1992), DTI (1992), Nelleman (1990)). In Sweden Edenius and Bäckstrand (1989) and NUTEK (1991) made two of the few studies on the lending side and Gandemo (1989), Utterback (1988/1991), and IVA (1989) made surveys on the borrowing side. Landström (1991) investigates the interaction between entrepreneur and financer in the informal venture capital market in Sweden. A similar study on the Danish market is made by Koppel (1992).

2.5. Towards a theory on innovation financing - what needs to be done?

Many elements to a theory have been mentioned in this short review, each of them having their own qualities. Because of the relatively new status of the subject there has not been the incentive to synthesize the relevant

---

20 In chapter 9 I shall elaborate somewhat more on the methodological problems in empirical investigations.

21 See for example OECD (1988, 1990a, 1990b) who compares R&D programs in different countries.

thoughts into consistent theoretical constructions. This mix, and especially the connection between a) the micro-understanding of the relation between lender and borrower and b) the general understanding of technological development and the development of financial institutions, is important for the development of a theory on the role of finance in innovations. The survey throws light on elements for further development.

More specifically, there are some building blocks for a theory present, which need to be worked on and developed. Thus, one has to specify the special features of innovative investments on both the demand and supply side. This means exploring the financial requirements, technological investments, and the development of the firms on the one hand and on the other looking closer into risk aversion towards technological investments, the competencies for judging these and the ability of the lending institutions to generate financial innovations to meet new borrowing needs. Useful tools may come from: -

i)   financial theory - the branch which explicitly stresses imperfect information, imperfect loan markets, interaction between a borrower and a lender and credit rationing. In particular, this the information and economics literature.

ii)   innovation theory - the branch dealing with the importance of institutions and learning. An application of some of this theory to the interplay between borrowers and lenders is also important.

iii) institutional theory - the two parts of which are primarily occupied with a) the impact of uncertainty and informal institutions. The Carnegie-Mellon tradition has a strong position here but the traditional considerations by Keynes and others are still valid when it comes to describing the behavior of entrepreneurs and financiers under uncertainty. b) he institutional theories focussing on the interplay between formal, macro institutions and micro economic behavior.

In addition, one could add that studies of the organization of financial systems and innovation financing in different countries provide useful material for the inductive part of theoretical development as well as possibilities of verification. This applies to both the present architecture of allocative mechanisms of financial systems and the past industry-finance relationships.[22]

By no means is this an easy task. In the words of Dosi:

> "In fact, the relationship between financial structures and industrial evolution remains one of the most challenging, difficult, largely unexplored, fields in dynamic analysis. "(Dosi, 1988c, p.48)

---

22 "The Banking Project" at the Department of Economic History, Uppsala University, Sweden has made a most valuable contribution concerning research into the history of bank - industry relationships. Håkan Lindgren (1991, p.5f.) reviews the research done in that project.

Chapter 3. Credit rationing and asymmetric information

3.1. Introduction

In chapter 2 we indicated that there is likely to be "a fringe of unsatisfied borrowers", as Keynes denoted this phenomena. These potential borrowers are denied access to credit even though they may be willing to pay the ruling market price for loans. Thus, credit is rationed according to non-market criteria - the interest rate is not clearing supply and demand on the market for loans as a conventional model would have suggested.

There are various reasons why, and ways that, this rationing takes place. I shall get back to these later in this chapter. At this stage I shall only refer to an aspect of the borrower-lender relationships introduced in chapter 2. An important feature of such relationships is that information about the risk characteristics of the borrower and his project is usually asymmetrically distributed. Borrowers are likely to know more about the probability of default than do lenders. The asymmetry of information eventually leads to credit rationing and some projects, which may have been worthy of investment, are not undertaken.

Some parts of financial theory have recognized that there are imperfections in financial markets[1]. The "information and economics" literature, which is an expanding and vast part of financial theory today, analyses precisely these problems, i.e. deterrent effects on loan markets due to asymmetric information in borrower-lender relationships. In addition, related literature points out other loan market imperfections than information imperfections as a source of credit rationing.

---

1 Basically, the literature on credit rationing can be divided into two: one part concerns rationing due to various loan market imperfections (started by the "availability doctrine" in the early 1950s. This doctrine was primarily macroeconomic oriented but it started a discussion on the microeconomic level of credit rationing) and another part is based on imperfect information. The latter, more recent, literature will be focused upon in this chapter.

Apparently, this is a suitable micro foundation for a theory of innovation financing, as was hinted of in chapter 2. Therefore, in this chapter I shall examine the literature and look for theoretical results, which are valuable for a theory of innovation financing[2]. The overall impression attained from this inquiry into the information and economics literature is that in itself it is insufficient as a micro foundation, although some inspiration is indeed arrived at. In the following sections I shall point out the short-comings as well as the merits of these models when these are assessed from an innovation perspective. This procedure also gives us ideals relating to the direction in which a further search for elements of a theory should take place.

This chapter starts by briefly mentioning some of the original articles, that triggered off the literature. Second, I shall clarify what is actually meant by "credit rationing" and "asymmetric information" because the use of these terms is not unambiguous in the literature. Third, the basic principles of this family of models will be presented and a discussion carried out on how financial markets function in comparison with both a conventional perfect market theory and a model with credit rationing and asymmetric information. Fourth, to illustrate further how the models within this tradition function I shall present one of the most famous and influential models. The fifth section is a summing-up of main short-comings of the models. The sixth section brings us a step further towards a theory of innovation financing in that it points out some recent developments within the theory, which take some of the short-comings into account. Finally, I shall sum-up by relating the findings to requirements of a theory of innovation financing and I shall involve another, related, recent branch of literature as a way of highlighting features of the literature.

3.2. The intellectual heritage

The history of information and economics literature, goes back only some twenty years. In this literature, the basic ideas about inefficiencies of organized financial markets started with the "lemons problem" initiated by

---

2 As a consequence of this focus upon the possible micro foundation the exposition is mainly focused on the assumptions and basic principles of the literature, but specific results will be introduced towards the end of the chapter.

Akerlof (1970).[3] With the example of the "lemons" in the market for used cars, he showed how asymmetric information disrupts the functioning of the market (and causes underlending) and this lemons principle has been applied to the literature on financial markets.

One of the early followers of Akerlof was Arrow (1973), who also considered the quality aspect of the function of markets. He points out, that asymmetries of information will be a deterrent to the functioning of markets through the now well known principles of adverse selection and moral hazards (these concepts will be explained later). An effect of these mechanisms is increased information gathering, but not in the terms of the pure market. Rather than on anonymous buyers and sellers and price signals, qualitative information is gathered on identified individuals.

Arrow regards information as a category of goods, which has not been given much attention in economic theory. The emphasis that general equilibrium theory puts on prices is especially misplaced, according to Arrow. Instead, economic behaviour is, to a large extent, governed by non-price variables. Even though Arrow's contribution is important in what might broadly be phrased "information and economics-literature", the ideas in his paper have not had the impact on the future development of the theory they deserved.

In further development of the theory some economists have accepted the idea of incomplete markets but in other respects they are still working within a neoclassical framework. In the Lakatos-sense the hard-core assumptions are maintained while the auxiliary assumptions are modified. More specifically, the hard core assumptions are unlimited rational, maximizing agents whereas the auxiliary assumptions are that there is some degree of risk. Uncertainty and bounded rationality rarely enter the models. Unlimited rational agents are certainly a questionable assumption (especially

---

3 Akerlofs' motivation for writing was a discontent with the state of the theory in explaining important issues like involuntary unemployment, discrimination in the labour market etc. and in the narrow-minded way economic theories were developed by the dominating (neoclassical) school of thought. Rather than limiting theory to deal with well-established - but unrealistic - assumptions, there was an urgent need to incorporate elements from sociology, psychology and anthropology, according to Akerlof (see the introduction to Akerlof: "An economists book of tales", 1984).

when the focus is upon agents involved in processes of innovation), so why not stop here and continue to bounded or procedural rationality models? The reason we still need some elaborations of this branch of literature is that the information and economics literature does present us with some useful theoretical results. In addition, it has attracted great attention and some of the considerations of the theory are sound enough. These will be introduced below together with the basic principles and a few further comments and references on the theoretical genesis.

3.3. Conceptual clarifications and the nature of loan markets

The headline of this chapter "credit rationing and asymmetric information" involves two concepts which needs to be clarified.

In general terms the former can be defined as a situation in which the rate of interest on loans or the non-interest terms of loan contracts does not adjust as they would have if a Walrasian market clearing mechanism existed. Moreover, banks discriminate between apparently identical borrowers; i.e. some borrowers obtain loans on terms similar to those that other, rejected, applicants were willing to accept.[4]

Assume that the supply function for loans shifts leftwards in figure 3.1., for example as a consequense of a central bank tightening of monetary policy. Market equilibrium for loans would then shift from A to B. If banks choose not to use the interest rate r to clear the market, and instead use non-interest means to tighten supply of loans, then the demand will shift to S_2 and equilibrium will be established at a lower quantity of loans at C.

---

4 Jaffee and Stiglitz (1990) review some different definitions of credit rationing employed in the literature.

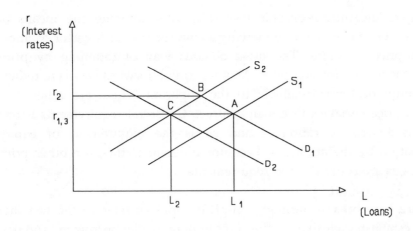

How do we explain this phenomena? In my opinion at least five issues must be considered in a further discussion of definitions of and principles of credit rationing. One is the level of aggregation the rationing is undertaken on and a second is the means of rationing. A third is the causes of credit rationing. A fourth, related to sources of rationing, is the time horizon used in rationing. Is it a temporary or permanent phenomena? Fifth, and finally, the effects of credit rationing and asymmetric information must be made clear. Let us examine each of these subjects in turn, but leave the discussion of effects to be carried out under the heading "basic principles".

Credit rationing, or rather credit control, on a macro economic level has been the most frequently debated form of the phenonemon and it has been subject to many theoretical and empirical investigations. A change in monetary policy by the authorities may have pervasive effects on conditions for firms to borrow in a bank. Thus, the authorities may use price regulations to restrict credit, for example by increasing the interest rate banks have to pay on loans in the central bank, or they may use quantitative regulations, such as loan limits. Both measures will, most likely, have an effect on corporate borrowing. I shall leave this subject with the above, few comments, because it is not highly relevant for our purpose right now. I shall only point out the interdependence between general conditions for the banking system and the spill-over for terms and possibilities for borrowing. In chapter 6 I will return to this subject.

Turning to the microeconomic level of credit rationing the means of rationing can be explained by viewing a loan contract as a vector of price- and nonprice variables. The most obvious way of rationing by price variables is to raise interest rates. Another straightforward way is to reduce the amount of funds available to the applicant. There are other, less obvious, price variables in a loan contract. Collateral requirements is one often used way of rationing and so is the requirement of equity participation by the applicant. Fees, for different fsctors, are other price variables as are profit sharing requirements.

What are here broadly termed non-price variables refer to the fact that lenders establish exclusive relationships with particular borrowers, and that lenders classify borrowers into groups of specific types.

The multiplicity of different means of restricting credit makes empirical investigations difficult. The appropriate means of rationing is likewise difficult to determine, in particular as the means are often used simultaneously. In general, the degree of competition between banks is one parameter affecting decisions to ration through price or non-price variables. Intense competition between banks may induce an upward stickiness on interest rates. Interest rate changes are generally not used if an applicant is judged as particularly risky[5] [6].

But why does credit rationing come about in the first place? I shall try to answer this question by referring to a number of market imperfections which explain what the causes of credit rationing are. Implicitly in this discussion I shall deal with the question of whether the time horizon of rationing, ie. if it is a permanent or temporary phenomena.

In my view a major quality of the literature on credit rationing is the rejection of the unrealistic, but still widely popular theories, which maintain,

---

5 In spite of this fact I do not totally neglect the importance of rationing with price variables in practice. With price variables introduced the question of timing of price- and nonprice variables arises. Do banks tighten both interest rates and nonprice variables simultaneously or do they move in opposite directions? Harris(1974) shows that the former theory is valid in the U.S.

6 Later we shall test empirically whether Danish banks use increases in interest rates towards risky projects or if they prefer to ration credit.

that price movements equilibrate supply and demand also when dealing with financial markets. As indicated in figure 3.1. financial markets do not function in the same manner as described by theories of markets for physical goods on which this way of thinking is based. There are several problems with the conventional perfect market theory.

First of all, the aggregate supply for financial markets is not a fixed quantity as in the market for say cars. It is possible to create credit out of nothing, and likewise credit can disappear for instance as a consequence of a confidence crisis, or intervention by the National Bank. The mere fact that credit is regulated on a macro level and the uncertainty about future monetary policy may cause banks to ration credit.

Second, different expectations on the demand side confuse the perception of what the "goods" on the market actually are. Loan contracts are usually made in nominal terms, and therefore borrowers with expectations of high inflation rates in the future, will view a contract as a bargain, compared to the borrower with low inflation expectations, regardless of the expected returns of their respective projects.[7]

Third, and most important, there is no general clearing mechanism in the market for credit. The direct application of traditional models would suggest, that interest rates should equilibrate the demand and supply for loans and provide information to the agents about changes in supply and demand. However, I will question this mechanism. Banks are likely to adjust interest rates sluggishly to changes in characteristics of the borrower or to abstain from using them at all.[8] This behaviour is rational for several reasons.

First of all there may be legal restrictions and institutional controls such as requirements for advance notification of changes in interest rates, which

---

7 This problem could of course be alleviated if real interest rates where the measurement in loan contracts.

8 Moreover, interest rates are not the only factor determining cost of capital, which is the relevant measure when profitability in a project should be predicted. Tax etc. is important as well and usually other factors are a natural part of a contract.

may impose advertisement costs and administrative costs on banks[9]. These costs may exceed expected proceeds from adjusting interest rates. Second, interest rate ceilings or quantitative restrictions can limit possibilities for rationing credit through interest changes.[10] Third, social, or moral considerations may cause banks to avoid a too large discrimination between applicants. This may also harm relationships to customers (Driscoll, 1991, p.31). Fourth, banks may harm its existing customers by financing a product or process development that would outperform those by the established customer firm. Fifth, it may not be rational to let the risk perception be reflected in variations in interest rates. Banks may wish to protect the work done by assessing the risk characteristics of the borrower and the borrower may wish to protect his reputation or possibilities for borrowing elsewhere. Therefore neither of them is interested in making the interest rate reflect risk judgement and in particular they are not interested in judgement becoming public.[11] Sixth, credit rationing or degrees of interest rate changes or differentiation may also be imposed on specific classes of borrowers. For

---

9   In the literature such reasons for credit rationing are often referred to as disequilibrium rationing. In contrast credit rationing in a fully deregulated market is denoted equilibrium rationing.

10   In order to argue that such regulations will induce credit rationing it is necessary to make certain assumptions restricting the degrees of freedom of how borrowers behave. For example, access to other sources of funds such as the foreign capital market should be limited, substitutability between the organized loan market and other forms of "grey" markets should be limited, etc.

11   If the borrower changes status quantity rationing will also take place rather than price adjustments. A new borrower or a new demand for funds will undoubted impose extra monitoring and information costs on the lender, and therefore the bank will prefer lending to an established customer even if their projects have the same expected risk (Goodhart, 1989, p.165). In addition, price adjustment may have deterrent effects on the borrower. Banks function as a kind of social accountants, because they classify borrowers into categories according to their credit worthiness (Stiglitz and Weiss, 1989). If a borrower wishes to obtain extra finance, but is met with a higher interest rate due to extra risk then he might choose not to obtain the loan. This is because agents or the market (other lenders and trading partners) will perceive the changing conditions as a decrease in credit worthiness, and the borrower risks loosing something more valuable than extra finance, that is his reputation. The agents know that neither borrower nor lender is willing to give information about the worsened position of the borrower, and therefore reactions on the market will be strong to this kind of information. Due to this reaction the quantity of loans will be rationed both by borrower and lender in the first place. If the information about the worsened position of the borrower becomes public, reactions on the market are likely to limit the quantity of loans to the borrower rather than price.

example, applications for small amounts of loans may be rationed because costs of screening and monitoring is approximately the same for all contracts.

The most important reason, however, is that loan markets, even if fully deregulated, are characterized by information imperfections. Basically these problems arise because of another fundamental difference between financial markets and markets for physical goods. In markets for ordinary goods the exchange of goods for money takes place more or less simultaneously whereas a loan contract is only a promise to deliver in the future. That promise is not always kept. The impossibility of full information in screening and monitoring borrowers makes it irrelevant to use interest rates to equilibrate supply and demand for loans, as will be explained below.

This lengthy discussion on the concept of credit rationing indicates a confusion in the literature on the use of the concept. In order to avoid to contribute to this confusion in the following pages I shall by "credit rationing" understand a situation where borrowers are denied credit in spite of a willingness to accept the price variables in the loan contract. The reasons for this rationing most often relate to informational imperfections in combination with other loan market imperfections. But even in fully deregulated and "perfect" loan markets informational imperfections would induce credit rationing in our sense[12]. These informational imperfections are explained in more detail below.

The second concept to clarify is that of asymmetric information. This refers to a case when borrowers and lenders do not have equal access to all available information. Information is not only limited but also asymmetrically distributed. The lender is even not able to reveal some part of the relevant information regardless of his effort. Thus, the borrower is likely to know more about the technical and perhaps even about the commercial risks of his project[13] and, of course, also about his own moral attitudes towards taking excessive risks and his willingness and ability to

---

12 Thus, I employ an "equilibrium rationing" explanation for credit rationing.

13 Sometimes the commercial risk is better assessed by the lender. It may also be the case that the lender is more capable of project management and therefore is better at judging for example if the organization is properly geared to the project.

redeem payments on the loan. The latter kind of information is inherently disclosed to lenders whereas the estimation of the former may become more certain through search efforts by the lender.

Broadly speaking, asymmetric information is treated in three manners in theories on credit rationing under asymmetric information.

One is that there are some parts of the relevant information, the lender does not have costless access to. This applies to, for example, the evaluation of the outcome of the investment project and therefore the conditions for pay back of the loan may not be made dependent solely on the reported outcome of the project. This principle has been named "the costly state verification principle". (Townsend,1979)

Another asymmetry in information is that the lender cannot distinguish good borrowers from bad. Opportunistic behaviour among some borrowers may lead to high risk of default in some projects. (Jaffee and Russell,1976)

A third form of asymmetry is that firms may deliberately undertake risky projects, while this choice is not revealed to the lender. (Stiglitz and Weiss,1981)

What kind of asymmetric information as the reason for credit rationing is important when considering measures to overcome the problems? When such measures are discussed I shall explain which kind of asymmetry I refer to whereas in other cases I shall refer to asymmetric information in general, i.e. the three cases above in combination.

3.4. Basic principles and reduction of asymmetric information

There are two main explanations as to why interest rates are not used to clear loan markets and why asymmetric information may have deterrent effects on loan markets. These arguments refer to the principles of respectively moral hazards (or "adverse incentive effect") and adverse

58

selection. The basic principles of adverse selection and moral hazards can be further illustrated[14] as out below:

Assume a fixed contract between borrower and lender in an uncertain investment project, where monitoring and bankruptcy is costly. Furthermore, the expected outcome is assumed to be positively correlated with the risk of the project. In that case the downside risk to the borrower is limited compared to the potential upside gain. This has to do with the nature of the loan contract. The borrower can only loose his collateral in case of default but he may achieve a profit if his project succeeds, whereas the lender may loose all his investment. Consequently the borrower may have an incentive to change the risk characteristics of the project to a more risky one. The lender will then have a larger risk of loosing his investments but the borrower can still only loose his collateral although potential profits have increased[15]. Higher interest rate charges may then attract projects with a higher risk but a lower mean of expected rate of return.[16]

The moral hazard mechanism can be illustrated by a comparison of two investment projects with the following likelihood of different returns:

---

14 From Goodhart (1989,p.161).

15 In addition, the principle of limited responsibility means that borrowers see default as a perfectly acceptable way out of a bad project.

16 From this it is obvious that the argument applies to debt markets only. However, as with the debt markets also the equity markets can malfunction due to lemons problems. If there is asymmetric information about the real value of a firm the possibility of raising external funds by issuing new shares may be limited (Myers and Majluf,1984). In some cases firms may have an incentive to misreport the results of their investment projects, and this faces the lender with a cost of monitoring the borrower.

	Return	Probability
Outcome of		
Project 1	0	1/3
	15	1/3
	30	1/3
Project 2	0	4/5
	40	1/5

How do firms choose investment project if the payment to the bank (D) changes? The example shows that Project 1 appeals to the firm if D<15, as 1/3(0) + 1/3(15-D) + 1/3(30-D) > 4/5(0) + 1/5(40-D).
If the bank tries to raise interest rates above 15 - that is if 35>D>15 then the high risk project appeals to the firm.
If D exceeds 35 none of the projects is profitable.

Similarly there may be an adverse selection effect from raising interest rates. Assume again that to ration out bad borrowers a bank raises interest rates, how would potential borrowers react? Some borrowers with safe projects would view the rise in interest rates as unacceptable because it detoriates possibilities of a resonable profit. Safe borrowers would then withhold their projects whereas suppliers of lower than average quality projects would still have an incentive to undertake their expected high-yielding, but risky projects. Borrowers with low risk projects may leave the loan market and the average project become more risky. Risk premium will then increase, causing still more safe projects to leave the market etc. Therefore, interest rates are not used to clear the market. Instead credit rationing is imposed.

The effects of credit rationing resulting from asymmetric information are impossible to stipulate with accuracy. As explained in chapter 1 it can only be shown ex post which projects should have been initiated and which should not. The desireable level of credit rationing is thus difficult to determine and even if it was possible, how should one argue that the right projects have been rationed. What is desirable for a single bank may not be the be desirable for society as a whole. For example, the single unit is likely to use realized profits as criteria for success whereas there are other considerations to be made at the aggregate level.

A frequent practice when rationing credit is to classify borrowers into particular classes like small businesses, innovation projects, projects with a long time horizon, projects within certain industries, etc[17]. Although it may be individually, privately rational to ration credit to these kinds of borrower it may be socially rational to induce such projects. Consequently government intervention or special institutional arrangements are established to mitigate inexpedient effects from denying credit to these groups.

Even if an optimal level of rationing is an arbitrary concept, both from an individual point of view and from a social point of view it is beneficial to reduce asymmetric information induced credit rationing. There are several ways to do this.

One is to require larger collateral from the borrower. However, in several cases this option is not appropriate as shown by Stiglitz & Weiss (1981, p.402). In addition to Stiglitz & Weiss' arguments the question can be asked as to how much collateral is worth, because it is often rigid in its use and specifically tied to one kind of production. Increasingly production is knowledge based and this fact makes it even more difficult for firms to provide collateral.

Another method used is to require the borrower to put an equity stake in the project. This will signal that he also views the project as safe. Usually this equity can only be a small fraction of the total amount necessary, because if the borrower had most of the required capital he would not be on the loan market at all. However, just a small fraction may serve the purpose of signalling high project quality.

---

17 Correspondingly potential borrowers classify lenders also as do depositors. The borrowers' perception of how willingly one specific bank enters high-risk projects may vary a lot. Depositors similarly consider if the bank is safe and if it will yield a satisfactory interest rate and service.

A third way is to increase the screening and monitoring competence within the financial institution. This can be done by specialization or increased efforts to accumulate, store and use what was learned from previous contracts.

Fourth, and related, the lender can collect information on the applicants in addition to what is presented by them. In that case rational lenders will search for new information until marginal expected return from having additional information is less than the costs of searching.[18]

Finally, lenders can establish close, long-term relationships with the borrower in order to avoid opportunistic behaviour, to reduce monitoring costs, and to increase monitoring effectiveness. The institutional set-up of the financial system will determine how these functions are undertaken and how effective they are.[19]

Below I shall give a short description of one of the classical models within this tradition[20], in order to give a better understanding of the set-up of these models and to have a basis for discussing the limitations of them. Even though the model is to some extent chosen as a representative for the tradition, there are of course a multiplicity of models and there is rapid development of new thoughts, which are not possible to capture here. Nevertheless, the thoughts expressed in the model below could be taken as general illustrations of the way of reasoning.

---

18 This general statement needs to be modified though. For example, the financial institution does not know how much it reduces the risk before it has the information. At that time it has already paid for collecting it. Moreover, there may be other, long term, motives for searching, e.g. the aforementioned wish to expand screening competence, or a wish to know more about the applicant for the purpose of doing more business with him in the future, or to suggest cooperation with another of the banks portfolio firms.

19 This is one explanation for why financial intermediation occurs: the costs of information, and the variations in costs of monitoring, verification etc. explain why institutions for providing these services exist. The differences between financial institutions reflect comparative advantages in different modes of information processing and combination. The possibility of economies of scale in these activities is the reason for the existence of banks. In chapter 6 and 7 I shall get back to these issues.

20 Other classical articles include Jaffee & Rusell (1976), Leland & Pyle (1977), Townsend (1979), and Myers & Majluf (1984).

3.5. A traditional model of credit rationing under asymmetric information examplified by the Stiglitz & Weiss model

The paper by Stiglitz & Weiss is inspired by the model by Leland & Pyle (1977). Leland and Pyle consider a financial market where informational asymmetries are particularly pronounced. Borrowers have inside information about their project and about their rectitude. In addition, there is often a reward for exaggerating the positive elements of the project, and the true character of the project can be costly or impossible to reveal. Through a description of the adverse selection principle on financial markets, they show that venture capital markets may be inefficient.

Stiglitz and Weiss(1981) (SW) is one of the best known articles in this tradition. As opposed to Leland & Pyle they do not operate with the assumption that the probability distribution of the outcomes of the projects is known to the borrower and the lender. To demonstrate the adverse selection effect S&W set up a model, where a bank faces a number of projects, but it is not able to determine the risk of the projects. The outcome of the projects is denoted R and the probability distribution of the outcomes . It is assumed that risk increases with R. The risk will be measured by the variance of and the bank will prefer projects where the satisfactory outcomes are most concentrated in the . The borrower is borrowing an amount B, and the interest rate is r. Collateral is denoted C.

The assumptions are that the collateral is fixed; lender and borrower are risk neutral; the costs of the projects are fixed; the projects are indivisible.

The borrower can be said to default on the contract if collateral plus return does not exceed payment obligations:

$$C + R < B(1+r)$$

To the borrower the net outcome of the project is

$$J(R,r) = \max(R - (1+r)B, - C)$$

And for the lender:

$$p(R,r) = \min(R + C, B(1+r))$$

The borrower thus must fulfill the contract ($B(1+r)$) or pay what he is able to ($R+C$)

If there is a adverse selection effect, from raising interest rates for high risk projects then the interest rate must be showed to function as a screening mechanism for projects. If it does there will be a minimum value of   for a constant interest rate. Let us denote this value λ. The firm will only borrow if $>\lambda$

The nature of the loan contract makes the profits of the borrowing firm a convex function of the return on the outcome of the project as there is a limited downside risk to the borrower (only collateral and reputation is lost in case of default), but large upside potentials (gains above interest rates charged in case of success are comparatively large). (fig.S&W 1)

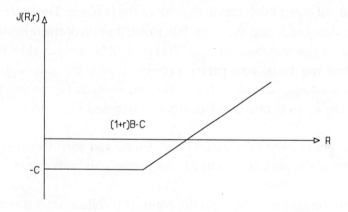

From the banks point of view S&W illustrates its return in this way

The return for the bank is a concave function of the return on the project because payments to the bank will increase with increasing returns for the firm until a certain point where payments level out; the bank can only hope to get the initial amount plus interest rates back. It does not receive a share of extra profits from a succesful project.

64

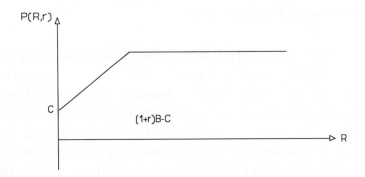

Drawn in the same diagram the critical value λ can be shown

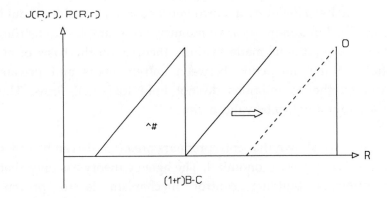

The area λ shows in the region in which both ordinary and high risk projects apply. If the bank increases interest rates above this, λ increases. The return for the bank increases, but so does the firms required outcome for the project, shown as the line O. So the increase in interest rates will increase returns for the bank, but at the same time an increase in interest rates above r will attract high risk projects (because the outcomes R are an increasing function of the risk of the project), whereas low risk applicants withdraw from the market and this will have the opposite effect on returns. In other words there is an adverse selection effect, but whether this will counterbalance the increase in returns for the bank from raising interest rates is an open question.

3.6. Short-comings of the models

The models discussed in this chapter, examplified by the model by Stiglitz and Weiss, suffer from several weaknesses. First, they are one-period models, designed to reveal the a priori incentive structure of lender-borrower interaction. However, the time perspective is extremely important in borrower-lender relationships. Repetitive contracts and long term relationships have several impacts on the informational problems described by the models. One such impact is that a mutual confidence may be built by knowing the other party. Trust is not incorporated in the models even though a mutual confidence may mitigate problems with moral hazards[21]. Instead agents are chracterised by opportunistic behaviour and are maximizing rationally. However, a borrower-lender relationship should perhaps be described in a more positive manner. For example, Landström (1991) rejects the assumptions made in these theories on the basis of an empirical study of the interaction between entrepreneurs and private investors. At least the assumptions do not hold for small firms. The assumptions are found not to be valid because

> "Studies have shown that entrepreneurs are often driven by other motives than purely economical. The agency theory assumes that the principal building control mechanism is to prevent opportunistic behaviour from the agent (i.e., a "negative" relationship between the principal and agent). The relationship between the private investor and entrepreneur has a more "positive" character, where the interaction is based on support and mutual trust. In many cases the control mechanism functions as a dysfunctional factor with lowering trust between the principal and

---

21 Trust is essential not only in the interaction between borrowers and lenders but also more broadly to credit arrangements. Sampson (1981, p.17) points out this fundamental feature: "Behind all its global responsibility and impersonal style banking is still a "people business" as this gathering makes clear. Economists may talk about the macro-economic functions of the international capital market, but down in the marketplace itselt there are real people trying to impress and persuade other people, worrying about their bank's balance sheet and writing off their bad depts. It may be the most personal business of all, for it always depends on the original concept of credit, meaning trust. However complex and mathematical the business has become, it still depends on the assessment of trust by individuals with very human failings."

agent, which impedes open communication etc." Landström (1991, p.26).

Another impact is that the screening ability may be improved by long term relationships, and monitoring costs may decrease. Later I shall come back to the information effects of long term borrower-lender relationships. The consequenses for the theory is that there is a need to work with a multi-period model, allowing for the effects from learning and former relations-hips. The trouble is that the models are too focused on describing states of nature as opposed to the process that leads to this state. In association, former relationships and former performance of a firm may contribute to a build-up of a reputation, which will releave the lender from some of the screening process.

Second, the effect of the institutional set-up of the environment is rarely taken into account. This set-up differs across countries which makes it necessary to differentiate the presumptions of the models. For instance the notion "lender" needs a clarification in order to capture these differences. Many models define the scope for the analysis as the loan market[22] (while others concentrate on the equity market, e.g. Myers and Majluf (1984)), which is perfectly legitimate, but even within the loan market there are large differences between types of lenders. An example, which shows that the legal framework is also important for the borrower-lender interaction, is the commercial bank which is engaged directly with borrowers e.g. with an equity stake in the firm or participation on the board of directors, versus the bank, which is prohibited from undertaking such direct investments. In the former case the lender will have both possibilities and incentives to

---

22 Some models analyse the choice between debt and equity (see MacKie-Mason (1989) for an article within this tradition, which gives an overview and a discussion of the choice of financing source), but both debt and equity is supplied in several ways (and often as a mix), and each of them may have its own informational con-straint. This is particularly relevant in light of the international trends in financial systems today, as despecialization, diversification etc. change the profile of financial institutions. In addition there is not always an equal choice between debt and equity. For example, the industrial structure in Denmark, with many small and medium sized firms, would not leave firms with an equal choice between methods of finance. The stock market is irrelevant to most Danish firms due to their small size and informational constraints in introduction to the stock exchange. Even the Over The Counter exchange has not eased external finance constraints for Danish firms.

monitor the borrower closely whereas this task may be harder for the lender without these connections with the borrower[23].

Another example is the extent of risk spreading. For some projects and in some countries government agencies are lenders and there may be other assumptions for this type of lender concerning risk neutrality and pay-back performance criteria than for a private, financial intermediary. Another risk spreading instrument is securitization but this may cause free rider problems unless incentives for monitoring and screening are established.[24] In addition, it is important to consider if there are alternative sources of financing than banks.

Third, they are very stylized models with limited references to actual situations and empirical verifications. There is certainly a need to develop the empirical side of the theory and this may also encourage a reformulation of the models to less stylized versions[25]. For example, behind the adverse selection argument is an assumption of a positive correlation between risk and return. But this relation need not be linear. There may be discontinouties in the risk/return relation and consequently a gradual increase in the interest rate may not cause safe, low rate of return projects to leave the loan market.

---

23 In fact, one could argue that the models are not making themselves clear if they do not define the meaning of "external finance" for investment projects. If the lender is to some extent integrated with the borrower, then it may be wrong to uphold the sharp distinction between them in the models.

24 The article by Diamond (1984) could be applied to the securitization case. He points out the importance of delegating monitoring of a lender because a bank could disclose information on true states of the nature of outstanding loans to depositors. Similarly, the security issueing organization could keep information on the development of the diversified entities of the securitization portfolio and this would cause free rider problems and disincentives to monitoring.

25 Vasan (1986, p.2.27 and 2.61) reviews the empirical studies of credit rationing up till 1985. Among the few, recent empirical investigations on credit rationing are Fazzari, et.al.(1987), Vasan (1986), and Berger and Udell (1989). Vasan (1986) finds that "..at certain points in the business cycle, banks tend to rely more heavily on customer relationships, and place greater emphasis on intended loan uses, in deciding on loan requests. This is a logical response to the information asymmetry inherent in the lending process, and appears to result in a combination of non-interest rationing and non-price rationing. Our results suggest that unestablished and ostensibly small borrowers are the customers who should be affected most severely by this rationing."

Fourth, even though there is strong opposition to the assumption of perfect foresight in the theories, they do not incorporate true uncertainty in a Knight/Keynes sense. That is, the uncertainty concept in most models, including that of Stiglitz and Weiss, is basically risk. Some models assume a known probability distribution of default of the projects, e.g. Leland & Pyle (1977), while others, like Stiglitz and Weiss (1981), drop that assumption, but still there is no considerations on unknown and unforeseen possibilities. In the model above, for example, there is an assumption of fixed costs of the project. In a highly uncertain project one of the uncertainties is surely about the actual ex post costs of the project; an uncertainty stemming from unforeseen costs in the development or marketing of the product. The relevant knowledge for screening and monitoring a set of borrowers is actually not revealed to the lender, but in fact it is often tacit to the borrower as well.

Finally, like most other agency theory, there are only considerations of opportunistic behaviour by the borrower. The borrower-lender relationship is viewed just like a landlord tenant relationship. The principal - the bank - is likewise able to cheat, and it would be just as appropriate to establish incentive structures for the principal to behave in accordance with the interests of the agent as vice versa. Furthermore, the incentive structures are described, not explained. In other words the models are functional explanations. They are unable to explain how the incentive structures develop. Rather their function is explained.

3.7. Extensions of the models

3.7.1. Introductory remarks

The development of this theory has followed Stiglitz & Weiss in 1981, and various aspects of the theory have been expanded and applied to different examples and empirical tests. However, even though some of the points of criticism above have been dealt with, the problems are far from being solved. One of the most serious shortcomings of the theories is the lack of time perspective in the models. A few suggestions of how a two period model would look have however been made.

Below I shall briefly present important results from a few two-period models made in the past decade. Even though it is a step forward to extent the models to more than one period the models are not that succeful in capturing important aspects of borrower-lender interactions. Taking the point of departure for granted (meaning that my first point of criticism - the lack of trust in such relationships - is disregarded) an alternative way of developing this aspect of the models is suggested below using game theoretical considerations (which have become increasingly popular in the past few years). But even this exercise is not enough. In particular the shortcomings are enhanced when the models are used on financing innovations. The last section of this chapter carries that point further but it also points out some merits of the literature in this tradition.

3.7.2. Two-period loan agreements

In fact, Hellwig (1977) was one of the first to present specific features of long-term relationships between borrowers and lenders. Stiglitz & Weiss (1983) extend their own model to two periods and Moore (1987) allows reputation effects from repetitive relationships as does Diamond (1989).

Results from these theories are mainly concerned with the effects on incentives in the first period together with the possibility of bankruptcy and cut off of credit in the second period by the firm and the bank respectively. It is assumed in the models that the lender recovers nothing if the borrower goes bankrupt. The borrower avoids his obligations from the first period but is denied access to credit in the second period as a consequence of his default. If he does not default the lenders' decision problem is whether he should punish unsatisfactory outcomes in the first period by cutting off credit (or raising interest rates) or whether he should extend credit further. If he extends credit he risks throwing good money after bad but on the other hand he may increase the likelihood that the borrower will eventually be able to repay the loan from the first period. The threat of cutting off credit or restricting terms on credit may discipline borrowers to act honestly and not take undue risks - even in the first period. But if the borrower expects the lender to extent credit and perhaps use a "salami-tactic" to succesively make the lender extent credit then this threat will not have the effect of reducing opportunistic behaviour.

If we reverse the picture borrowers may also discipline the bank by a threat to change bank connections. This threat is only valid if the project seems prosperous or if the borrower has a reputation as a stable and good customer. With this statement I have introduced a third party in the borrower-lender relationships which is competition between lenders. Just as borrowers seek potential funds, lenders compete for good borrowers, and the degree of competition from parties outside the established or potential borrower-lender relationship affects the character of that relationship. This point is rarely taken into account by the models (it should perhaps be added to my list of criticism points above) not even the multi-period models in this tradition consider this aspect. Hellwig (1977) does however point out that established relationships tend to disclose competition from other, third parties because the lender in the first period has a cost advantage to others. This advantage stems from the fact that potential further loans will help borrowers repay earlier loans.

The incentives and reactions to information are very sensitive to mistakes and past performance. If a borrower makes a mistake in one period it may be interpretated as a signal of deliberately acting opportunistically and access to credit will be denied. Moreover the history of the borrower may counterbalance such reactions. If the reputation of a borrower is positive he is likely to have a wider range of potential funds and more scope for mistakes without serious consequences. Diamond (1989) adds by modelling the case in which the lender will have incentives to monitor borrowers to avoid moral hazards. His model allows for learning effects from repeated lending helping banks to classify borrowers into different types. Moore (1987) focuses upon detecting observation costs over time as a result of learning within the borrower.

3.7.3. Repeated borrower-lender relationships - applying game-theoretical considerations to the models[26]

Given mutually potential opportunistic behaviour a borrower-lender relationship may be viewed as a game in which bahaviour is split into two[27]: Honest (H) and Opportunistic (O). In our case honest behaviour would for the borrower mean sticking to actions that would not harm his abilities to repay the loan. Honest behaviour would for the lender mean to render agreed upon non-price services, to give transparent informations on the real costs of the loan, and to support the firm with credit when the firm is liquidity constrained or othervise in financial distress.

A prisoners dilemma-game may illustrate incentives to take moral hazards or otherwise cheat. It is assumed that the benefit of cheating while the other part is honest is greater than if both act honest which in turn is greater than if both act opportunistically. The matrix show the benefits for the two parties.

Figure 3.3. A one-period prisoners dilemma

	O	H
O	1,1	4,0
H	0,4	3,3

If one of the parties cheat the other part will cheat in the next period and then the relationship will be dissolved. If the parties know that the game is only played once it is bound to result in that one, plausibly

---

26 As already mentioned some of my points of criticism also holds for repeated borrower-lender relationships and assumptions in game theory are not more realistic than in the information and economics literature (I shall abstain from discussing them here). The exposition is carried on though, not because I share the views behind game theory but because it illustrates how a possible extension of the models previously discussed might look like, and because a simple game may illustrate basic features of the relationships not subject to my criticism.

27 Game-theory is a vast and expanding branch of economic theory. Schotter (1980) surveys the literature upto 1980 and explains the basic principles.

both, of the parties act opportunistically because even though it is socially optimal to cooperate it is optimal to cheat at the individual level as 1>0 if you expect the other part to cheat and 4>1 if you expect him to be honest.

If the prisoners dilemma is repeated a large, but a priori determined finite number of times then both parties will benefit from coorperation, in theory until the last period. In that period both parties know that it is rational to behave opportunistically but it is likely that the cooperation is terminated before they reach that period. It would be rational to act opportunistically in the period before the last because benefits from cheating in one period equal benefits from cooperating in one period plus benefits from cheating in the last (when both are cheating) (4 = 3+1). Both parties know this. Afraid of being caught in the situation where the other party is cheating while the first party is honest (thus only acquiering 3+0 in the last two periods) the time for terminating the relationship is pushed towards its initial establishment . In Axelrod (1984) the games are repeated in a finite number of times but his result is cooperation until very near the end of the time horizon. This is, of course, a rational outcome of a repeated game seen over the whole of the time horizon but it demands an auxilling assumption that both parties know that it is rational not to cheat before the last period, and if they can agree upon that why not then also cooperate in the last period? It also demands that both parties should know exactly when the relationship is finite. on Applied to the borrower-lender interaction this result shows that although trust may be built up during the interaction an initial trust is also essential for a relationship to persist.

If the time horizon is infinite, however, cooperation will be maintained as long as the parties can benefit more from cooperation in two subsequent periods than from cheating in two periods (6>5).

This is only the two-party repeated game. Even a bad relationship would be maintained were there are solely these two parties in the world. In other words the incentive to maintain cooperation also rests on the potential benefits of alternatives. For example, if you behaved opportunistically in the previous period the potential benefits from a relationship with that party in the next period may be as shown in the matrix below

Figure 3.4. Repeated prisoners dilemma

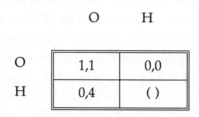

	O	H
O	1,1	0,0
H	0,4	( )

It is impossible to reestablish cooperation because the other party will certainly act opportunistically. Therefore, your benefits in period II are 1 (0+1) (which means you will cheat). Assume that a permanent alternative is to play the game with a third party offering the potential benefits.

Figure 3.5 Repeated prisoners dilemma with more than two agents

	O	H
O	1,1	3,0
H	0,3	2,2

In this case it would be rational to shift relationships either in the hope of gaining 2 (2+0) if you act honestly or, if you cheat, 3 or 1. However, if behaviour within the relationship in period I is obervable to outside parties it is doubtful if a relationship would be established, and if it is, the new partner is likely to behave opportunistically (and therefore there is no reason to shift as 1 = 1.

In effect contracts between a borrower and a lender have to be made in a way that punish opportunistic behaviour enough to maintain the cooperation. With this exercise we have demonstrated that the time horizon is crucial in models of borrower-lender relationships. In a one-period model the scope for charlatans is wide; cheating is beneficial in a single-period game. If the games are however repeated a finite number of times the relationship will inevitably break down before the end of the period. If the time horizon is infinite the parties are likely to maintain relationships. Time horizon is rarely mentioned in the models within the information and economics tradition however. Thus, we can now add another point of criticism to the list in section 3.6.

3.8. The information and economics literature in relation to transaction cost economics and a theory of financing innovation

This final section puts the literature in this chapter in perspective. In the section above information and economics literature was developed using recently popular methods in game theory. Another popular approach to the issues discussed here is transaction cost economics. Below this approach is compared with information and economics literature. Furthermore, a summary is made of why the literature is inadequate as a theoretical foundation for the analysis of innovation financing but nevertheless may be an inspiration for some points.

One criticism levied at the information and economics literature (in this section called agency theory is the focus upon the individual instead of the transaction. In particular transaction cost economics and incomplete contracting literature directs its attention towards the transaction and the allocation of control respectively.[28]

Some similarities are to be found in the behavioural assumptions. Transaction cost economics assumes agents to be boundedly rational and opportunistic. The information problems in the Williamson notion of bounded rationality and the asymmetric information in agency theory, are in some sense essentially similar. Incomplete contracting is thus a result of the bound on rationality imposed by informational constraints, and moral hazards are relevant due to opportunistic

---

28   Surveys of incomplete contracting literature can be found in Hart and Holmström (1987) and in Holmström and Tirole.

behavior with the borrower or lender (note that neither the information and economics literature nor transaction cost economics adapt Simons' concept of bounded rationality. In his concept there is also a bound in that the agents may be satisfying rather than maximizing and in Simons' concept agents may face computational limitations - i.e. they may not be able to process all the information available).

Even though focus in both theories is upon incomplete contracting, the approach is different. The agency theory mainly analyses contracting from an ex ante, incentive point of view, where the individual agent is the basic unit of analysis. In contrast, transaction cost economics focus upon the ex post structures of the organization which undertakes the transaction and the safeguarding and costs of the contract. Debt and equity are not regarded as financial instruments in the transaction cost economics approach, but rather as governance structures.

Another difference is the relative weight given to private ordering and organization form (Williamson,1988, p.572). Disputes are thus by and large neglected in agency theory, whereas transaction cost economics analyses dispute avoidance and mechanisms for processing disputes. Bankruptcy is for example more complex than assumed by agency theory.

One qualification of the transaction cost economics approach is that the purposes of the investment projects must be taken into account rather than assuming a fixed composite-capital set-up, and regarding debt and equity as financial instruments. In agency theory institutions are virtually non-existing, and microfoundations and behavioural assumptions are rarely discussed.[29]

To sum up, there is some appealing research within this area and the literature has merits valuable for innovation financing. In particular the literature directs our attention to the impact on loan markets of information incompleteness. The notions of asymmetric information,

---

29 In contrast a neo-institutional economics has emerged, trying to integrate historical economics and more precise "nano-economic" discussions, but that is another story not to be told here. It is though touched upon in the next chapter.

credit rationing, adverse selection and moral hazards highlight important features of the nature of loan markets which are also relevant to innovation financing. They also point to the relationships between a borrower and a lender although the specific character of these relationships is only described by incentive structures. On the other hand there are some straitjackets which hamper further developments and use of the information and economics literature. Specifically, it is unable to analyse the *process* of innovation financing. The approach is static and lacks an incorporation of time perspective. Furthermore, the institutional set-up is almost disregarded as is the purpose of the investments. The determinants of risk willingness of banks is another area with is not thoroughly dealt with and uncertainty is generally absent from the models.

Chapter 4. Innovation and uncertainty - implications for economic behaviour, coordination and financing

4.1. Introduction

Chapter 2 pointed out the poor state of the current theory of innovation financing. There is a great need for better theories on innovation and finance. Chapter 3 provided some theoretical discussions on this topic but the theories dealt with were evaluated as insufficient. In particular, they disregard the institutional set up and they failed to incorporate true uncertainty. In addition, the specific purpose of investments was generally not taken into account. These deficiencies motivate this chapter. In order to understand how to finance innovations it is important to understand the character of the innovation process.

Here the focus is upon how uncertainty affects individual behaviour. This is important in its own right in an effort to establish a theory of innovation financing. But it is also useful later because then we shall see how it affects systemic behaviour. I shall use the considerations in this section when discussing the behaviour of financiers towards innovation financing. In addition, it is useful to consider what should be used as an alternative if the theories in chapter 3 are inadequate as a microfoundation for a theory of innovation financing.

This chapter constitutes the necessary link between the previous discussions on lender-borrower relations and the decisions to finance innovations in that it presents some important features of innovations and the innovation process. Although it is not a digression from financing innovations, considerations solely on finance will be kept to a minimum in this chapter. In stead aspects of the innovation process which are crucial to an understanding of how to finance this process will be pointed out. In addition to the nature of innovations and the behaviour of innovators and financiers under uncertainty these aspects will involve the coordination of the innovation process. Various mechanisms - in particular institutions in a broad sense - prevent the innovation process from being totally random and this is important when it comes to financing the process.

The chapter is organized as follows. First, I shall give an outline of basic properties of the innovation process. It is argued that the innovation process is non-linear and the section provides a framework for understanding how financial requirements differ during the process, a subject dealt with in further detail in chapter 5.

Second, the market uncertainty and the technical uncertainty in innovations will be further specified with respect to origins and degree.

Uncertainty is a basic property in investment decisions, be it ordinary investments or innovation investments. Therefore, in the third section, the impact of uncertainty is considered. This is a wide ranging topic. More precisely the focus is on how agents decide, learn and behave under uncertainty. The purpose is to give a basis for later discussions on the behaviour of financier and innovator.

Another important feature of innovations, in particular in relation to financing innovations, is information exchange and information transfer. The theoretical models in chapter 3 focused on information. In the fourth section (4.5.) the impact of learning, uncertainty and information on innovation projects is introduced and related to the considerations in chapter 3. Its' purpose is to point out how the surrounding institutional set-up is important to the way information transfer and information exchange takes place and consequently the environment in which this transfer and exchange takes place is also important to methods and possibilities of innovation financing as well. Moreover, the discussion in that section shows that the systemic perspective is important not only in relation to how the institutional set-up of financial systems support technological development, but also in shaping the innovation process. Furthermore it is argued, that in spite of increasing internationalization, the nation state is still of importance to innovation processes. The point is that through coordination uncertainty in innovation is reduced. Two other aspects coordinating the innovation process are dealt with in section 4.5. First, it is argued that the innovation process is path-dependent. Second, the concept of development blocks is introduced to show how such a block may coordinate the innovation process.

The fifth, and final section sums-up the discussion and relates it to financing innovation.

4.2. General characteristics of innovation and the innovation process

So far innovations have been treated in a general manner. This concept is common throughout the literature, but it is appropriate to try to obtain a definition of "innovation". I shall furthermore give a first approximation of a characterization of the innovation process. In chapter 2 Schumpeters' innovation concept was characterized as broad but not unrealistic. In the following section I shall understand by innovation the development and introduction on the market of new products and/or the development and application of new methods of production.

A key requirement is a further definition of a "new" product or process. To whom is it new and how new does it have to be compared to the previously used process or product to be different from the old one? Demarcation lines are not sharp on these issues. I shall use the broad specification that new products are significantly different from those previously produced by the firm with regard to material, design, technical specifications and areas of use. New processes are characterized by an impact on the possibilities of producing new products or existing products more rationally. "Innovation" is related to the firm and its previous mode and range of production. A firm perspective rather than a market perspective is important, especially as a new introduction of products or processes in a firm creates both uncertainty within that firm and uncertainty with those who should finance the introduction as to how well the firm will manage the new situation.

The innovation *process* is dealt with in detail below, but a first, very general, approximate definition is the description employed by Dosi (1988, p.222):

"innovation concerns the search for, and the discovery, experimentation, development, imitation, and adoption of new products, new production processes and new organizational set-ups".

One only needs to go a couple of decades back to find a very poor state of innovation theory. Innovations were by and large considered the outcome of a "black box". What went on inside the black box - how the transformation of inputs to outputs took place - was disregarded[1]. Schumpeter considered innovations as endogenous to the process of economic development but even many years after Schumpeter technology was still viewed as fully developed at its first appearance. In addition, the absorption of new technologies was assumed to take place smoothly. Technological problems were reduced to the act of looking up in "the book of blueprints" to see what technique was superior in reaching whatever goals were set. The technique is assumed either to be embodied in the physical capital stock and how given inputs are combined (the technical coefficients) or to be totally disembodied. Technical progress is reflected in a change in technical coefficients, according to this traditional view (Amendola & Gaffard, 1988, p.2). In this framework there are rarely any reflections on where the blueprints come from; the innovation process is a diffusion process (often even taking place in logical time) and the economy adjusts instantly.

In contrast to this static, unrealistic view basic characteristics of the innovation process are now recognized which are much closer to intuitively plausible relations on theoretical grounds and also closer to the accounts of empirical investigations of the innovation process. Before proceeding to innovation theories, which emphasize uncertainty reduction, I shall give a short account of those characteristics which I find relevant to the present

---

1 The title of a famous book on innovation theory refers to this fact: "Inside the black box" by Rosenberg (1982).

discussion of innovation financing.[2] This account will supplement the brief definition of innovations given earlier.

In the mind of many people, and in many innovation studies, innovations are associated with radically new products. Thus, some studies focus on visible, radical innovations like computers, synthetic materials, etc. However, the physical end-product is only the tip of the iceberg. In fact, the major, resultant innovations are outcomes of a long process, which is characterized by much more gradual modifications than the impression one can get from focusing on end-products. Even Schumpeter, who is often regarded as spokesman for radical, discontinuous jumps, recognises a gradualism element in the innovation process:

> "what we designate as a big invention hardly ever springs out of the current of events as Athena did from the head of Zeus, and practically every exception we might think of vanishes on closer investigation. Cooperation of many minds and many small experiences acting on a given objective situation and coordinated by it slowly evolve what appears as really new only if we leave out intermediate steps and compare types distant in time or space....What is technically called a revolution never can be understood from itself, i.e. without reference to the developments that led up to it; it sums up rather than initiates." (Schumpeter, 1939, p.181)

The term "end-product" is not that fortunate because even after commercialization modifications continue as feedbacks from users, sales offices, competitors etc. are important inputs to further development of the product. Kline & Rosenberg (1986) emphasize this perspective by putting up a so-called chain-link model of the innovation process as an alternative to the traditional, linear model, which sees the process as a continuous, progressive development from research through development and production to marketing. As opposed to this model the chain-link model

---

2 There are, of course, differing opinions on what these characteristics are. Nevertheless, the general characters below are widely accepted in non-neoclassical innovation theories. Compared to other disciplines of economics there are only a few overviews of innovation theories. The few include Dosi (1988), Eliasson (1988) and Freeman (1982). Dosi, Freeman, Nelson, Silverberg, and Soete (eds.) (1988) is a collection of articles which cover a wide range of the frontier research within this area.

emphasizes feedbacks which help to formulate how to proceed. In other words all innovations even the most radical, involve elements of incrementalism.

Innovations are results of an open-ended, evolutionary process which makes it hard to date the start and end of an innovation in time and to see it as a single event[3]. They are often a result of small deviations from every-day routine activities and are often created by new combinations of existing knowledge. Application of an existing product, process or new knowledge to a new area may yield great effects and may contribute to further modifications of the original innovation. The modification/effect each have two aspects, which relate to the distinction between market- and technical uncertainty. A minor innovation in technical terms may have large economic effects, and vice versa great changes in the product may only marginally affect its performance in economic terms. For example, changing the colour of a car is a minor change, but may have - and actually has had (Kline & Rosenberg, p.294) - large economic effects.

On the other hand there is also a discontinuous aspect to innovations. This originates from the search for new process technologies or new products which may earn a quasi-rent at the market or add to the firms' general knowledge base. This kind of search and exploration is often less related to a specific firm or product (the extreme example being fundamental research and general education at universities), and discoveries are often non-linear.

However, even if not totally predetermined, searching is not totally random. The argument for this is twofold. First, the direction of searching is determined by the existing knowledge base in the firm and by exogenous stimuli e.g. from competition or other environmental influences. Innovation, in other words, does not take place in a vacuum. Rather it is partically

---

3 Recognizing the creation of innovations as a process implies a necessity of severe methodological considerations. Thus, patent statistics and databases of innovations are only static, one-time glimpses of a process which continues through time. Biologists have discussed an analogue problem when it comes to determine the level of pollution in a river. Using laboratory measurements would give a very precise analysis of the state of the water, but only at the time of taking the test and only of that particular quantum of water passing through. A few seconds later different water passes the place where the test was taken. Therefore, the method usually employed is to use the existence of prevailing water insects with different pollution thresholds as indicators of pollution.

rooted in the existing institutional set-up and the prevailing economic structure both at a firm level and at a macro level of aggregation. Over time the innovation process is cumulative in that the choice of technological solution to a problem builds upon the technology already in use at a general level. At the firm level (or organization or even country) solutions are sought in accordance with the firms' technological level (Dosi, 1988c, p.223). The environment of the innovation process changes itself as a result of the process (Amendola & Gaffard, 1988, p.3) and modifications of the environment may be a source of new technology (ibid., p.14)[4]. Second, there are certain guide-posts as to the direction of technological development as briefly mentioned above and further dealt with below.

As already indicated learning processes are important features of the innovation process be it learning-by-doing (Arrow, 1962), learning-by-using (Rosenberg, 1982), learning-by-interacting (Lundvall, 1985) or learning-by-learning (Stiglitz, 1987). These processes are important medias for the development of new combinations of knowledge and generation of new knowledge. As already mentioned knowledge is a social phenomenon and innovations are to a certain extent also characterized by some kind of direct or indirect interaction with other people and previously developed knowledge. According to Dosi (1988, p.224) knowledge is a precondition for solving an innovation problem, and it has at least three dimensions: It can be universal versus specific, articulated versus tacit, public versus private. Even though all six kinds of knowledge are relevant to innovation processes, knowledge in innovations is primarily specific, tacit and private. Therefore, information is not an ordinary commodity (with public appropriability), as Arrow (1962, 1973) points out. Knowledge may be very valuable to some but at the same time useless to others[5].

---

4   An obvious example of this is educational efforts. Other, less obvious cases, are organizational changes that are deliberately aimed at promoting innovations stemming from ideas of blue-collar workers and others involved in the production (see also chapter 4. Another consideration is the degree of coordination and steering of the innovation process. Even if the efforts need some degree of control, creativity may be lost if the process is over-steered (Freeman, 1982).

5   Zander (1991, p.109-126) provides a more thorough discussion of knowledge aspects of technology using Winthers' (1987) taxonomy.

To sum up, general characteristics of innovations are strong uncertainty, learning, incrementalism, technological and social dependency. A final point to make is to stress the sequential, cumulative character of innovation processes. These are inherent, general if not universal, characteristics of innovation. There are, however, some indicative stylized facts, which characterise the specific way the innovation *process* is taking place today.

An innovation created in one sector often has technical and economic effects in other sectors as well. However, there are differences between sectors as to how easy an innovation is to appropriate and there are even differences in what opportunities are present for technological development (Dosi & Orsenigo, 1988, p.15).

The second indicative fact relating to the innovation process is its increasing dependence on scientific inputs. These inputs often involve human resources and the use of special resources is more and more frequent (Amendola & Gaffard, 1988, p. 12)[6]. As a consequence the search for new combinations is formalised and organized in R&D-departments in large firms, government laboratories and universities to a greater extent than in earlier times. The search activity of the isolated individual has become less important (Dosi, 1988, p.222, and Freeman, 1982).[7]

Third, users are more important than earlier for two reasons. The market is now more segmented and, secondly, technological development plus great changes in the mode of production have made it possible to specify demand to an extent that it actually enters the innovation process as an input (Amendola & Gaffard, 1988, p.13).

---

6 In another paper (1989) the authors mention that the innovation process is in general hampered by a human resource constraint and a financial constraint. The former sets the innovation process off, but is gradually modified through the process and additional resources are needed (p.7) while the latter is regarded in a Schumpeterian circular-flow manner: additional finance is necessary for the innovation process because of the time lap between inputs and sales, and because all available capital is utilized. Additional finance in the form of credit or sharing sunk costs is therefore needed.

7 This development is not new. Both Galbraith and Schumpeter (1942) recognized that innovative activity was increasingly becoming concentrated in large firms' R&D-departments rather than with individuals or with small enterprises.

Fourth, and finally, I shall only briefly mention a couple of other indicative facts relating to the innovation process which will be discussed further in chapter 5: product life cycles for most products have become shorter; investments for the single R & D-project have become larger; the use of external finance has increased, and immaterial investments and cooperations between firms are becoming increasingly important. However, uncertainty may be the most important and fundamental characteristic of innovations, especially when considering possibilities for financing the process. Let us take a closer look at the uncertainty aspects of innovations.

4.3. Uncertainty in innovations

When considering uncertainty it is useful to divide the analysis into three parts: first, I shall deal with the reasons for uncertainty in product innovations and second, the degree of uncertainty in product innovations is discussed. Third, process innovations are focused on.

I have divided uncertainty into market uncertainty and technical uncertainty, the former being the uncertainty as to whether the project will be a commercial success and the latter relates to uncertainty on the technical accomplishment of the project.[8] Both market uncertainty and technical uncertainty are an increasing function of the radicality of the innovation.

4.3.1. Reasons for uncertainty in product innovations

Inherent in the innovation process[9] are reasons why it is an uncertain process - an uncertainty of higher degree than in ordinary investment projects. The character of this uncertainty can be split into a technical and a market - or commercial - uncertainty.

---

8   Freeman (1982, p.149) includes a third category by discussing general business uncertainty, which is the general state of business on which firms create their perception of what is profitable investments.

9 It must be emphasized, that by "the innovation process" meant is a general process, which is not related to a specific industry. It would of course produce a major bias if there were large differences between the specific nature of the innovation process in different industries (cf. Pavitt (1984)), but in the general description below the proposition is not particularly influenced by industry specific features of the innovation process.

The former stems from three main sources. First, the magnitude and number of technical problems in the development process is often difficult to predict. Although technical production plans have been made beforehand, new, and unforeseen problems often emerge during the production process[10]. These problems include uncertainty on the input side. Situations demanding unanticipated external expertise or physical materials may arise. This is likely to delay the process and make it more costly

> "....it is parthetic to watch the endless efforts - equipped with microscopy and chemistry, with mathematics and electronics - to reproduce a single violin of the kind the half-literate Stradivarius turned out as a matter of routine more than 200 years ago." (Polanyi, 1962, p.63)

Second, the design of the product often changes several times before the final stage. Third, the date of marketing the end-product is often unknown because of the above unforeseen technical problems and related organizational and production line changes. Moreover, exogenous changes may affect decisions to market the product. In effect the costs and time perspective of an innovation project are difficult to predict and most often underestimated.[11]

Market uncertainty originates likewise from three main sources. One is that the market value of the single end-product is unknown both because time has passed from the launching of the project to the completion and because users are not accustomed to the new product and may not be willing to pay the calculated price. Another cause of uncertainty is that from the

---

10 Kline & Rosenberg (1986, p.297) calls this a "false summit effect", referring to mountain climbing. What seems to be the top of the mountain is over and over again only a shoulder on the trail.

11 Svensson (1988) studied expected compared to real costs and time in 35 innovation projects in large, Swedish enterprises. Data from this study showed that on the average there were considerable overruns in time and also costs exceeded what was initially planned. Thus, 40% of the projects were delayed by between 30% and 50%, and costs were often exceeded by 20-40%. In 8 similar studies analyzing a large number of projects average time overruns were more than 50% and real costs exceeded expected costs by close to 100%. Freeman (1982, p.153) reports figures even more conclusive in pointing out that both costs and time of innovation projects are usually under estimated.

aggregated proceeds from sales and the timing of these proceeds. The number of entities sold before demand declines may be insufficient to cover expenses. Related to this cause there is uncertainty about the development of competing and/or substituting products.

Over time market uncertainty and technical uncertainty are not totally independent. Changes in market conditions, results from market research etc., may influence how the development of a product proceeds. Likewise technical problems or changes in design may have an impact on market uncertainty. Another example of this dependence is that delays and unforeseen cost in development may determine the necessary scale and consequently become a reason for market uncertainty. Therefore, a combination of thorough technical and market knowledge is a precondition for successful innovation.

This is, however, not an easy task. Coupling technical and commercial knowledge in practice often takes place between two separate entities in an organization or between the organization and another organization. Knowledge on a high level both on technical and market matters is unlikely to be held by one person, or sometimes not even by one organization. This is the background for why there may be a competence mismatch between a borrower and a lender. The complexity of assessing both market possibilities and technical perspectives separate judgements between two organizations sometimes with little overlap and little in common.

4.3.2. Degrees of uncertainty in product innovations

The time dimension is of the utmost importance to the degree of uncertainty in innovations and this applies to both market uncertainty and technical uncertainty. As the product "moves downstream", i.e. gets further in the development process, most technical problems are solved - the innovator approaches the summit, to use Kline & Rosenbergs' terms. Technical uncertainty is thus reduced substantially. Usually this process is not a gradual one. Major problems may hamper or even wreck the project for a considerable time until this "shoulder on the trial" is passed. After prototypes have been completed and production started, innovations continue because adjustments and incremental changes are important responses from both production staff and customers. Technical uncertainty is, in other words reduced but not eliminated.

Market uncertainty is only reduced slightly over time in the development phase. The reduction stems from a better knowledge of competing products, a better feeling for how the final product will look, and perhaps through market research undertaken. Later, when sales have begun, the innovating firm will, of course, have a greater knowledge of how the market reacts to its product.

In the next chapter I shall use these considerations of uncertainty over time in order to differentiate between financial requirements at different stages of product development.

In addition to time and stage of development the degree of radicality of the innovation affects the degree of uncertainty of innovations. Obviously there is more uncertainty in developing a new, non-polluting car than in reducing air friction on existing models. If innovations are graded according to radicality the following scheme is useful (Freeman, 1982, p.150):

Degree of uncertainty associated with various types of innovation

1 True uncertainty	fundamental research fundamental invention
2 Very high degree of uncertainty	radical product innovations radical process innovations outside firm
3 High degree of uncertainty	major product innovations radical process innovations in own establishment or system
4 Moderate uncertainty	new "generations" of established products
5 Little uncertainty	licensed innovation imitation of product innovations modification of products and processes early adoption of established process
6 Very little uncertainty	new "model" product differentiation agency for established product innovation late adoption of established process innovation in own establishment minor technical improvements

The above distinctions are perhaps too general. It is therefore important to determine to whom a change is only associated with very little uncertainty. A small product differentiation may cause considerable efforts of a highly uncertain character by engineers even if the change is apparently only minor to others. Thus, a small change in the design of an aeroplane wing may cost many millions of dollars and months of research. The scheme above is nevertheless illustrative for the point.

A third dimension to this has to do with the above second dimension, but is not identical. The degree of development of the underlying science and technology strongly affects technical uncertainty in the innovation process (Kline & Rosenberg, 1986, p.295). A well developed scientific base will presumably reduce costs and time of development and perhaps eliminate the need for further research.

Fourth, various institutional arrangements can be guide posts in an uncertain world. One example, which reduces market uncertainty substantially, is forward markets, or pure contract producing firms. Some subcontractors produce in this way. On the other hand, the uncertainty is not eliminated but rather redistributed by contracts. At the time of signing the contract the purchasing party will be more uncertain of the market value of the product he buys when the product is completed. He will take some of the initial risk. Other risk spreading arrangements can be thought of. Interfirm R&D corporation is one way of distributing risks and later I shall discuss others.

Fifth, consumption often follows certain patterns both as a result of a learning process[12] and because established patterns of consumption entail some inertia to new products[13]. If the innovation implies large deviations from established patterns of use, then uncertainty on how users will perceive the innovation becomes greater. Likewise there are technological trajectories and lock-in effects which determine certain paths for the development and use of new technology[14]. I shall get back to this point later and only note here that both market uncertainty and technical uncertainty increase the more innovations divert from established trajectories.

---

12 Pasinetti (1981, p.68-76) uses the Engel-curves to illustrate that consumption follows certain patterns. On the other hand, Pasinetti notes, in an economy where income rises learning becomes a crucial element because consumers have no experience with consumption at a higher level of the Engel-curve. Knowledge can be obtained by experiment and by external information. The latter depends very much on the institutional set-up of the society but even if information was perfect learning processes would be relevant.

13 For example, it is difficult to market a competitor to the longplay record because people are used to records and already have a collection of records and a record player. It took several years before the CD had a market share of any importance and still records are dominant on the market in spite of obvious quality and practical drawbacks. Another, slightly different effect of consumption is a market effect, leading to a gradual shift towards monopoly or oligopoly. An example of this is the competition between Beta and VHS-video systems. When VHS gained a small market lead share, demand shifted more and more towards VHS in a self-reinforcing way, because video machine producers choose to produce in the most common system.

14 One of the most cited examples is the QWERTY keyboard design (David, 1975). Even though a more optimal distribution of letters on the keyboard could easily be designed, the first step has large implications for the way subsequent innovations are undertaken.

Finally, the demand and actions of government affect uncertainty in innovations. If government policy is to give priority to certain areas such as environmental protection and perhaps introduce standards accordingly then innovations in resource and pollution reducing technologies are likely to have a market.[15] The overall degree of government actions thus affects uncertainty as well, provided these actions are not shortsighted and volatile.

4.3.3. Technical uncertainty in process innovations

The title of this subsection indicates that only technical uncertainty is relevant in process innovations. The reason for this is that process innovations relate to in-house requirements. Although this is the general pattern a modification is that some firms have specialized in production systems and production rationalization consultancy as well as producing items which can be applied to the existing production system in a firm with positive results. The market for such services is as volatile as any other market and a fraction of process innovations is therefore also subject to market uncertainty.

Implementation of new technology in the production process involves uncertainty in several respects. Compatibility with the existing machinery may be more problematic than anticipated, and technical problems with the functioning of new techniques may arise. Furthermore, there may be uncertainty as to whether the qualifications of the labour force are adequate for the optimal use of the new technique, and organizational changes may be required in order to gear the organization to the new situation.[16]

The degree of uncertainty in process innovations depends on the degree of radicality compared to existing processes in the firm, as indicated in the scheme above but also on the overall flexibility of the firm. Thus, uncertainty also arises in process innovations.

---

15 Rosen, Schnaars and Shani (1988) discuss this subject and compare different approaches for setting standards for technological products.

16 A Danish study (Gjerding et.al., 1991) showed that technical problems, over estimation of the ability of the employees to utilize the new technique, and re-organization of the work were serious and frequent problems (p.118).

It follows from what has been said that uncertainty differs between innovations but also that it can be reduced even if the innovations are high in the hierarchy of uncertainty developed by Freeman. This reduction is essential to possibilities for obtaining external finance because uncertainty is a major obstacle for financing innovations. However, only reduction, not elimination, is possible. If uncertainty was totally eliminated there would be no truly innovative activity. Thus, even sophisticated project estimation techniques (discussed in for example in Freeman, 1982, p.151f. and Coombs et.al., 1987, p.74f.) would not solve problems of estimating the outcome of innovation projects (this discipline is consequently not discussed in the present book).

But why should anyone engage in such uncertain activities and what motivates behaviour in uncertain situations? The next section tries to answer these questions by discussing principles of uncertainty and relating them to financing innovations.

4.4. The impact of uncertainty on economic behaviour and investment projects - basic features of uncertainty

4.4.1. Risk and uncertainty

One of the implications of Keynes' theory was a renewed interest in what could be termed fundamental uncertainty. This concept is in contrast to the Benthamite philosophy, which underlies neoclassical theory. According to that philosophy pain and pleasure are measurable and calculations of all kinds of economic activity including future activity can be made. In opposition to this view Keynes stated in a famous passage that

> "We are merely reminding ourselves that human decisions affecting the future, whether personal, political or economic cannot depend on strict mathematical expectations since the basis for making such calculations does not exist;" (Keynes, 1936, p.162-63)

In an extreme version of neoclassical theory there is perfect foresight and neither risk nor uncertainty is a problem. However, some degree of risk is usually incorporated and whereas neoclassical financial theory used to assume that agents are homogeneous and thus have the same perception of risks, there is now a drift in modern financial theory towards analyzing situations with heterogeneously distributed information, as we saw in chapter 3. The distinction between risk and uncertainty is nevertheless rarely made in spite of the intense debate on the issue in the 1960s and 1970s.[17]

1921 was the most important year relating to the development of this distinction. In that year two major works on risk and uncertainty were published. After several years of writing, Keynes published his methodologically oriented "Treatise on Probability", and Frank Knight published his "Risk, Uncertainty and Profit". In short, risk refers to situations where the probability of the future can be specified in quantitative terms whereas in uncertain situations future states of nature and the number of possibilities are unknown and therefore impossible to quantify.[18]

4.4.2. The nature and importance of knowledge

The concept of knowledge is central to all discussions on uncertainty and risk, on institutions, and on borrower-lender interaction also.[19] According to Keynes, knowledge may be split into direct knowledge and indirect knowledge. The former is possible to obtain without deductions on the basis of past experience whereas the latter is based on direct knowledge but through a logical relation to this - hence it is obtained "by argument" (Keynes, 1921, p.14). It is important to understand that knowledge is not

---

17 Some of the most active participants in this debate were Clower, Shackle and Davidson. There is even a journal entitled "Journal of Risk and Uncertainty".

18 Keynes defines his notion of uncertainty in op.cit. 1921, p.4. It is, however, not at all clear whether the term is used for situations where the nature of an action makes it unpredictable or for situations where the likelihood of different actions is calculable, but it is not possible to determine which one will be in effect. In his famous article in the Quarter by Journal of Economics 1937 (p.213-214) he restates his uncertainty definition using practical examples and here it is clear that the former definition is valid.

19 There has been a debate within the newly emerging evolutionary theories in economics on: what evolves? If there is any consensus in the debate it is that what actually evolves is knowledge (Boulding, 1985).

only tied to the individual. Direct knowledge is created in an interaction with the social environment and thus knowledge is a social phenomenon.

In a world with imperfect knowledge agents need guidelines for behaviour and they have to make predictions on which they are more or less certain. The principal guidelines for behaviour under uncertainty are institutions such as conventions, but they should not be seen as governing behaviour totally.[20] "Animal spirit" motivates some to undertake actions contrary to established conventions - provided they believe strongly in a positive outcome.[21] Such actions may contribute to a change in conventions and new conventions may change common behaviour.

To base formation of expectations, reaching far into the future on conventions may be inexpedient as there is usually some uncertainty as to the stability of conventions. Conventions are influenced internally, by changes in belief in the convention, or in other words, the co-existence of more than one convention on the same subject, and externally, by other institutional changes (Keynes, 1936, p.172). Routinized behaviour may change in periods of crises in conventions and the transformation from one convention to a new are dominated by learning processes which adjust old behaviour to the new situation. The old convention is usually not totally abandoned but some adjustments take place (Lawson, 1985, p. 921-923). To give an example, a bank may be successful in using standard operating procedures. But if the outcome of these procedures is eventually shown to be unsatisfactory because changes in external conditions make the procedures inadequate, then the bank will adjust routines to the new situation. If the new situation is radically different from previous situations, then discretionary, non-conventional behaviour may be the only option

---

20 Heiner (1983) argues that the very presence of uncertainty affects behavior in such a way that it may contribute positively to possibilities for predicting the future. Given a competence-difficulty gap in uncertain situations, agents will choose a conventional behavior because they have no routines and experience to cling to. Conventions are strong under uncertainty and therefore it is easier to make predictions as deviations from usual behavior are less likely, according to Heiner.

21 Individual entrepreneurship may have become less important in recent years but still it has a role to play in innovation. Schumpeter discussed the role and character of the entrepreneur as does Wärneryd (1988). The latter discusses definitions of an entrepreneur and surveys research on entrepreneurship, especially in psychology but also in economics.

available until a new convention has been established through learning processes.

In other words expectations are not formed totally individually. A too subjectivistic view excludes the impact of the social system and institutional framework in which the individual lives and obtains knowledge. Behaviour is not a random choice. Rather an individual limits him-/herself to the institutional and social context, which forms his/her reproduction sphere (Hutchison, 1978, p.210-212). In this sphere agents learn in different ways, with different intensity and with varying interaction with the surroundings.[22] Banks may for instance, have different interpretations of a given development and they may pay more or less attention to past performance or various economic indicators.

Perfect choices are not the ordinary case in real life. Agents are unable to behave rationally in all circumstances because they do not have all relevant knowledge, and if they had, they would not be able to process it all. In addition, and as a consequence, they would rather limit their search for optimal choices and stick to satisfactory solutions.[23] This is what Simon has denoted "bounded rationality" (Simon, 1982, p.131f.)[24]. A rational behaviour would, under these circumstances, be to concentrate on creating well-working procedures for obtaining a choice set and making a choice rather than focusing on a one-time selection of a solution.[25] Compared to the models in chapter 3 this is rather different. Although there is imperfect information in these models the bound on rationality is only the amount of

---

22 Johnson (1992) lists the knowledge increasing activities imprinting, roote learning, learning by feed-back and searching on a scale of increasing human interaction, and explains how institutions affect learning processes and how innovations are rooted in the institutional set-up of the economy.

23 Moreover, to search for optimal solutions demands that agents have a clear perception of what their optimum is, or in other words, they must have a clear strategy of where they are going and this strategy guides decisions on whatever choice they are confronted with.

24 Schackle (1967) talks about the origins of uncertainty as an "unlistability problem", which has a) cognitive limitations in quantitative and qualitative information processing; b) no clear picture of expectations and preferences; c) unsatisfactory outcomes of previous, similar decisions; d) problems of identifying possible actions and consequences.

25 This distinction is the one between procedural and substantive rationality, respectively. For an elaboration see Simon (1982).

information available to the agents. Computational limitations and satisfying behaviour are not taken into account.

As mentioned above, some theories, like those in chapter 3, incorporate unequally distributed information. However, they do not consider if this heterogeneously distributed information is treated differently between agents - or even if the same, equally distributed information is treated differently - due to differentiated behavioural patterns. The models in chapter 3 assume an universal, rationality[26], but in fact agents - including lenders and borrowers - differ in several respects which affect their behaviour.

To identify some examples, with the set-up in chapter 3 as a reference point, time horizons may differ between lender and borrower and indeed between different lenders. Their focus may be directed towards different variables such as security, interest rates, budgeting and, respectively, technical opportunities, implementation in existing production and product lines, etc. Their specialization may differ, even if they all belong to the group "lenders", and this will affect in which areas they are competent. The importance of the decision may differ, again both between borrowers and lenders and within the two groups. Thus, a small bank may carry out a more careful screening and monitoring of a firm than a large bank would, because the loan is a relatively larger share of its portfolio. Finally, a rather fundamental difference is that agents behave for a large part on the basis of past experience. Luckily we are not all alike and this also applies to our stock of knowledge. Consequently agents will have different rationalities because of differences in how far back they remember analogue situations and differences in how past learning and forgetting processes have formed their routines, opinions and ways of reacting to new situations. The primary reason for this fundamental difference is that agents are participating in different social networks and interact with different groups, individuals and institutions.

---

26 To the extent that these models differentiate rationality - they recognize e.g. that some borrowers may be dishonest - they take an average point of view by working with a distribution of aggregated risks.

4.4.3. Formation of expectations

Past experience and learning is essential in connection to the formulation of choice sets. Choices are rarely made totally transcendentally. Agents grade information according to past experience because they recognize patterns from the past, similar to the situation in question. After sorting out relevant information and deciding on a relevant time perspective, the organization of relevant choices and procedures for making a choice comes into effect. Due to a feed back mechanism agents learn about the effectiveness of these procedures (instincts, rules-of-thumb, habits, administrative rules, etc.) and adjust them accordingly. In the words of Katona (1975, p.44)[27]:

> Change in the environment -> Intervening variables -> Overt behaviour.

Two basic methods of forming expectations are relevant, according to Katona (ibid., p.48). One is simply a situation through which is similar to or analogue to a previous situation. Your confidence in expectations and behaviour will then depend on how many times you have been in this situation in the past and how since you were in that situation. The other method relates to the case in which the situation or the information you receive appeals to non-routinized behaviour. Then a search for information may begin and alternative choices will be considered more carefully. Such processes may be nessesary because the decision has great importance to the agent; the routinized behaviour is inappropriate in relation to your present group or reference group; that new information affects decisions substantially.

Entropy[28] is thus not only quantitatively important; the character of information is equally important as it affects agents disproportionately and unequally. A new information may motivate agents to do a "crucial

---

27 The writings of Katona (summarized in op.cit. 1975) provides an interesting exercise in the field of psychological economics and behaviourism. Concepts commonly used by economists without explanation, such as expectations, learning, information processing, conventions, and attitudes, are explained with the discipline of psychology as a reference point.

28 A designation of the quantity of information.

experiment", which is a non-routinized and irrevocable action, not formerly undertaken. Such an action may include an element of "potential surprise" (Shackle, 1974, p.41), or in other words, as actions provide information to other agents, whose response is unknown, a new, unforeseen situation will potentially develop. Innovations are typically crucial experiments as are decisions to finance developments of new products.

In the next section I shall examine how selected innovation theories deal with the problem of reducing uncertainty in innovations and point out some other properties of the innovation process which are important when financing innovations compared to financing ordinary investments.

4.5. Chaos or coordination

4.5.1. Introduction

The theories in chapter 3 were pleasant in terms of complexity of explanation, they are rather simple in their assumptions and their view of how agents behave. The discussion above on uncertainty, potential surprise, and non-optimising behaviour may seem to have reintroduced chaos into our analysis. There are, however, reasons why innovation processes are not totally stochastic. Thus, Dosi and Orsenigo (1988) argue that at different levels of aggregation there are mechanisms coordinating innovation processes in spite of true uncertainty.

In this section it is argued that innovation processes should be analyzed as dynamic, evolutionary processes. Key elements within these are the learning processes and coordination processes. Therefore, it is maintained, taking a closer look at their nature will bring us closer to an understanding of the evolution of new technology.

Four subjects are the main ingredients in what follows.[29] First, elements of learning processes are discussed with the borrower - lender interaction as a reference point. Then coordination processes are discussed in three

---

29 This broad topic calls for a much wider range of subjects to be fully covered. For example, the coordination effort of governments. However, for the present purpose a partial analysis is sufficient.

perspectives. One of those perspectives is the systemic one, meaning a further specification of the context innovation processes take place within. The nation state is the primary subject of analysis in that section. Another coordinating factor is the degree of path-dependency of innovations. Theories on this subject are reviewed. Finally, coordination is discussed in a development block perspective.

4.5.2. The nature and importance of learning processes in borrower - lender interaction

The focus upon knowledge in section 4.4. and before naturally leads to a discussion on learning processes because such processes are one important source of growth of knowledge. The character of different kinds of learning processes was pointed out in section 4.2. and I shall now demonstrate that learning is also important in finance. In particular, I shall elaborate on how financiers and entrepreneurs learn when they interact in a close relationship. But what is a "close relationship"; what is actually learned in the interaction, and why should a firm or a bank be interested in sustaining the relationships?

4.5.2.1. Conceptual clarifications and theoretical considerations

There are of course different opinions on what a relationship is and what "close" actually is. One important criteria, which I shall use in the following, is that some kind of repetition is essential to the relationship if it is to develop. The new exchange situation (of goods, information, money) does not necessarily have to be like any other former exchange. The relationship can take various forms. It could for example be ownership, participation in management, formal or informal contracts, relations based on personal acquintaince, etc.

Industry-bank relationships do, of course, change over time and between projects. The mutual dependency is influenced by increased competition in the financial sector, changes in the self financing ability of the firm, establishment of financial departments in firms etc.

101

On the lender side, specific knowledge will be generated about the technical aspects of projects and the industry in general. On the other side, the borrower will learn about prices of funds, different financial instruments and financial innovations relevant to corporate finance. In addition the fund raising ingenuity, that Schumpeter and Penrose (1980,p.37-39) characterized as essential to the entrepreneur, will improve.

4.5.2.2. Why are bank-firm relations persistent phenomenon?

The interaction between lender and borrower will tend to be stable for several reasons: first, confidence between borrower and lender is necessary for the interaction to develop qualitatively. Obviously asymmetric information may induce credit rationing if the borrower takes advantage of this asymmetry. It is natural that the lender does not have the possibility knowing as much about the project as the borrower - not to mention the moral rectitude of the borrower. The degree of moral hazards will then determine whether the borrower will try to exaggerate positive qualities of the project.

But even if there are no asymmetries in information, opportunistic behaviour might give one of the parties an advantage. For example it could be an advantage for the borrower, if he succeeded in convincing the lender that their true and common knowledge about the negative sides of his project is wrong. This makes confidence in the other party's conception and fair use of information important. In addition there must be a confidence in the actual fulfillment of the contract after it has been entered, a confidence that can only be increased through experience, or through the reputation of established firms (Arrow, 1974, p.19).

Second, the very transmission of information is easier when relationships have been established and ways of communication, which are understandable by both parties, have been worked out. Once established through a process of learning, one is unwilling to pay the cost of building up new relationships implying a new series of learning processes.

> "A communication system has some cost of initial investment
> which is irreversible. In particular, a communication channel

is used to greatest capacity when it has an optimal code for transmitting messages. This "code" need not be interpreted literally; the term refers to all patterns of communication and interaction within an organization, patterns which make use of conventional signals and forms which have to be learned. Once learned, however, it is cheaper to reuse the same system than to learn a new one; there is a payoff on the initial learning investment but no way of liquidating it by sale to others."[30]

A prerequisite for efficient information exchange is common channels and codes of information, effectively distributed and understood. The specific channels and codes will reflect the cultural, geographical and organizational differences between the borrower and the lender. Thus, there may be difficulties in the ability to process information. For instance the borrower might have difficulties in decoding information about the different instruments and prices on finance, whereas the lender might not be able to decode information on the technical substance of the project put forward. One response to this problem might be to increase the number of receptors, but this raises two other problems: that of minimizing costs and that of coordinating information and knowledge. Therefore the interaction must lead to ways of pooling the information in a manner suited to the receivers organizational structure and ability to process informational signals. The more specialized the organizational design, the more effective the receiving and processing of information. Less flexibility is, however, the negative side of this trade off.

Third, there might be other culturally related reasons why alternative relationships do not appeal to companies already involved in a relationship to a bank. In the banks budgets and financial management of the firm are given high priority when judging a project, while technical competence for judging the project is rare. Decisions about loans are often taken without any close relationship to the firm and to the possibilities of the project in the long run. Instead they rely on actual and past figures from the firm. On the other hand, especially small firms focus too much on the technical

---

30 Arrow (1974), p.19

possibilities of the project and have no firm grasp of financial management. Therefore, establishing new relationships may be difficult. Established relationships will be kept when satisfactory exchange of information (through learning processes) has developed together with an establishment of competence on both sides. The establishment and maintenance of relationships between users of financial services and producers of these services is facilitated by a social and cultural coherence.

Finally, there will be a mutual irreversible dependence between the lender and the borrower once the application of loans has been accepted. If the project does not show the expected performance, the lender has an interest in keeping the firm solvent, by additional loans and perhaps by influencing or participating in management, in order to keep the firm able to pay the annuities on the loans in the long run. From the company point of view there may be an advantage in being closely tied to a bank, because of the long term security for finance.

Many advantages resulting from these stable relationships could be mentioned besides the alleviation of information problems. The development of the relationships is not only a development and accumulation of knowledge about a single project of innovation. As the borrower becomes better at articulating financial needs concerning investments in technological change, the lender might be able to develop financial innovations to meet these needs.[31]

On the other hand, there is a danger that these stable relations might result in inertia and a resistance to change. Decentralized methods of obtaining finance might be less than socially optimal, if some part of the borrowing

---

31 Arrow has described a dilemma concerning information and innovations. On the one hand it is important to give information about the project to raise funds, but on the other hand competition poses a limit on the information flows - the innovation must have a degree of secrecy. To overcome problems of ability of judging the technical and market aspects of an innovation in new, small firms, it has been a practice in some Danish banks to require to place a person from a large company producing the same kind of product on the management of that firm. This shows both that information is more important than secrecy in innovations, and that the established relationships to larger firms go beyond a one-time decision on a loan.

were to be automatic using standard lending procedures[32]. In addition there may be economics of scale in information gathering and monitoring in a centralized, organized market with special agencies for mitigating informational imperfections.

The behaviour of banks and the effect of mitigating informational asymmetries is not only an outcome of the isolated bank-firm relationships. The effect of actions taking by the banks are also highly dependent upon the strategic factors governing industry, such as the links between suppliers, large firms, customers and finance. One way of looking upon these links is through the concept of "development blocks", which is dealt with in section 4.5.5.

4.5.3. The systemic perspective

The discussions above have primarily referred to a non-specific context. But the innovation process and learning processes are not only governed by inherent characteristics. They take place within external boundaries which are of some important to the processes. One important boundary is the nation state[33]. There has recently been an increasing recognition of this fact, reflected in the amount of studies focused upon, or using the concept "national systems of innovation"[34] and in the use of the concept by policy-makers[35]. On the other hand increasing internationalization in recent years

---

32 In Denmark the mortgage institutions have been successful intermediaries by using standard lending procedures with a interest rate premium at only 0.3% (recently increased losses has forced them to make more careful credit judgement). Ray & Hutchinson (1984, p.138) advocate increased amounts of multivariate loan evaluation techniques in order to improve profitability.

33 Lundvall (1992, p.2) points out that the concept of nation state has two dimensions: a national-cultural and a etatist-political. An ideal, abstract, and somewhat unrealistic state is characterized by both dimensions.

34 Actually the first study with this focus dates back a long time in history (List, 1841). More recent studies include Freeman (1987), Nelson (1988, 1992), Porter (1990), Lundvall (1988), FAST (1991) and Lundvall(ed.) (1992). McKelvey (1991) compares some of these studies. In none of them, but Lundvall (ed.) (1992), is the role of finance treated thoroughly although its importance is recognized.

35 Thus, the TEP-program, launched by OECD in 1988, concluded that it is important to understand the nature and diversity of national systems of innovation when designing technology policies (OECD, 1991)

can be said to make the concept of a *national* system of innovation to some extent more irrelevant.[36] According to some observers (e.g. Ohmae, 1990) the world is now more or less borderless and competition global. Let us proceed to some arguments for and against the view that the nation state matters as a determinant for the scope of innovation processes, the purpose being to establish a framework for discussing the role of finance in national systems of innovation at a more aggregated level than the single firm[37].

Transnational innovation activity is a very common feature of many, especially large, firms. Increasingly large firms have become multinational and foreign direct investments are part of the everyday picture. In addition, international joint ventures on R&D or product design have appeared in many industries and trade has been liberalized substantially. In general, cross-border technology transfer has increased.

There are other, broad developments which point to a lesser importance of national borders. Politically and economically many industrial nations have converged and efforts are being made to accelerate this process (cf. the single European market, which may develop into a political union). As a consequence a firms' home base market is no longer that different from markets abroad and technologies used in major industries are approximately alike. Moreover, why discuss the nation state as the particular relevant limitation to technological transfer? Could the innovation process just as well take place in certain regions or in certain industries across borders? Storper (1991, p.37) thus recognizes the importance of cultures, rules and institutions for the innovation process, but he argues that these factors are also highly differentiated at the regional level.

---

36 One can discuss how an innovation system should be defined. In any case it should include more than the R&D system as has been the approach in some studies. Rather the system includes a wide range of institutions, production structures and linkages between them.

37 There are of course, differences as to how open countries are and which subsystem of the national system of innovation is the most important. In Lundvall(ed.) (1992) we "assume that differences in historical experience, language, and culture will be reflected in national idiosyncrasies regarding the: internal organization of firms, inter-firm relationships, role of public sector, institutional set up of the financial sector, education and training, R&D-intensity and R&D-organization", and "....important is the relationships between the elements", (Lundvall, 1992, p.13).

Carlsson and Stankiewicz (1991) in addition describe the innovation process as a part of a larger system, which forms a so-called technological system defined as a network of agents interacting in the economic/industrial sector under a particular institutional infrastructure and involved in the generation, diffusion, and utilization of technology. Technological systems are increasingly international although there are still reasons for a geographical, cultural and political proximity. But, according to the authors, there is no reason to believe that national borders necessarily coincide with technological density and diversity. These are properties of regions rather than nations, says Carlsson and Stankiewicz referring to Silicon Valley and Route 128. Whether the technological systems are international, perhaps even global, national, regional or local depends on for example the technological and market requirements, the capabilities of various agents, the degree of interdependence among agents, and the stage of development of the technology.

The above can be taken as arguments against the importance of national borders as a co-determinant for the scope of the innovation process. The following are the central arguments why the nation state still affects to innovations. First, the general propositions above need to be modified because their validity varies with the technology and industry in question and it differs over time as to how strong a case could be made. Thus, it is plausible that complex technologies with many, specific inputs such as tacit knowledge and advanced demand patterns, require a higher degree of proximity between users and producers, thereby alleviating problems with communication costs through common cultures, language and geographical proximity. Likewise, it should be expected that proximity is more important in early stages of the development of a technology while more distant relationships are sufficient in downstream, or even standardized, technologies (Lundvall, 1988). Distance is, however, not a complete argument for the nation state as a boundary for the innovation process. The argument could equally well be applied to regions or local areas. On the other hand, even if counter-examples are easily found, the general picture is that language, culture and business norms to a large extent coincide with national borders.

Second, legislation, standards and other regulations, are primarily national, and this is important to firms when choosing their innovation strategy. Even if liberalized public procurement is often directed towards domestic products the overall government technology-, industrial-, and economic policy also affects the innovation process.

Third, and related to the second point, paths for exploration are defined through a historical process of interplay between demand patterns and the domestic production structure. The existing range and specialization of products produced in a country largely reflects this process, and it is not as easy to switch path as it is to import goods.

Fourth, some of the knowledge valuable to innovations is produced in public laboratories, universities and other parts of the education system, which is primarily national. Limited mobility across borders of the labour force is another argument for the effect of the nation state on innovations.

Finally, the institutional infrastructure is to a large degree national in character. Among important institutional factors are the division of labour between financial institutions, the function of financial institutions, conditions for establishment on the market, different risk spreading arrangements, and the ways that relevant information is produced and distributed.

The nation state is, and will continue to be, important in framing the innovation process[38]. This is likely to result in the direction of technological development being more predictable and therefore uncertainty may be reduced by the national character of the innovation process. However, there are certainly some parts of the system which are international and increasingly so. One subsystem that have been profoundly internationalized recently is the financial system. In a later chapter I shall deal with this process and discuss if it is still relevant to talk about a national financial system and if increasing internationalization effects to financing innovations.

---

38 Recent events in Europe certainly put a questionmark on this statement. Is the nation state as coherent an entity during crisis? The answer must, of course, be differentiated according to how heterogenous the people within the nation are with respect to religion, language, history, standard of living, etc.

4.5.4. Path-dependency of innovations

As already mentioned innovations do not take place randomly. The point of departure has a great impact on where the process is going and several theories have contributed to an understanding of the innovation process as path-dependent. Although these theories all describe path-dependency they are not rivals but rather complementary, their main differences relating to the level of aggregation considered.

Thus, at a macro level "techno-economic paradigms" (Perez, 1983) and "technological paradigms" (Dosi, 1982) set the stage for technological development. The former concept refers to a dominant technological style with an inherent logic which affects the entire economy and production in both a technological and economical way. Interrelated technical, organizational and managerial innovations prove superior in terms of the relative cost structure of inputs to that of production and thus affect production universally (Freeman, 1988, p.10). The technological paradigm concept, introduced by Dosi, refers to an identification of the needs to be fulfilled and the scientific principles and material technology to be used for the task. The paradigm is both a set of exemplars of the basic artefact to be improved and a set of heuristic. Perez's concept covers in some sense an aggregation of several technological paradigms in Dosi's sense.

At a still lower level of aggregation a "technological trajectory" (Nelson & Winther, 1977, Dosi, 1982) is the actualization of the promises contained in the paradigm obtained by pursuing "the movement of multidimensional trade-offs between technological variables that the paradigm defines as relevant.. and economic variables" (Dosi, 1982, p.85). Using another vocabulary Sahal (1981,1985) views the innovation process in a similar manner. His terms are "technological guideposts" and "innovation avenues" indicating that a dominant product, method or design determines possible pathways for innovations. A similar meaning, but with different term, is to be found in Rosenbergs "focusing devices" (1976). Finally, the "lock-in" concept (Arthur, 1985, 1988), is used to describe how a firm may be irreversibly locked into a specific technology or standard regardless of cost, thus determining future developments. An example often used is that of the QWERTY keyboard. It could be added that as past technologies are embodied in equipment utilized for present day solutions to technological problems the paths possible for technological development are limited.[39]

In a way the different theories relating to path-dependency can be seen as analogue to the above distinction between incremental and radical innovation. A certain path-dependency for technological development helps reduce uncertainty although there is still room for considerable uncertainty inside the path used and uncertainty as to when the paradigm or trajectory changes.

4.5.5. A development block perspective on how to create dynamic transformation power and innovations

Another method of coordinating of the innovation process uses development blocks. The concept of development blocks originates from Erik Dahmén (1950, 1988a). According to Dahmén the fundamental properties of a development block are complementarities and structural tensions. Furthermore, a distinction is made between development blocks which may be identified ex ante and blocks only identifiable ex post.

Complementarities refer to strategic growth factors within industry each being a precondition for the other if a balanced growth is to result. For example, advanced computer software demands a complementary hardware to be fully utilized. Structural tensions are disequilibria, or "imbalances" between factors in a block, indicating that action must be taken to fill a gap e.g. between demand and supply of capital to the entrepreneur. This stimulant of entrepreneurial activity may "complete" the block and make it develop. Dynamics can develop from either a "positive" or a "negative" transformation pressure (or a mix of these). The former relates to a situation where opportunities for new markets or other kinds of activity are the driving forces, and the latter represents a situation where there is a need to restructure and adapt to new circumstances. A development block may even be created by a positive transformation pressure if an entrepreneur, or a

---

39 Some opponents of the theory of path-dependency (e.g. Amendola, 1988) claim that innovations induce even more possibilities of new innovations and new directions of technological development. The scope for new combinations becomes greater. Even if appealing the argument disregards the fact that new combinations, even if actually more numerous, is likely to take place within certain paths.

110

group of entrepreneurs, identifies a new market ex ante, and creates brand new areas of activity. On the other hand uncompleted blocks could be identified ex post and stimulate activities directed towards eliminating structural tensions (Dahmén, 1988, pp. 4-6).

At the macro level a diversity of uncompleted blocks would be an advantage for the economy, because they facilitate large possibilities for restructuring and shifting activities from crises ridden areas of production. This is particularly important in economies without the coordination powers for promoting new development blocks ex ante.

This perspective (or a somewhat similar one using the same concepts and referring to Dahmén) has been adopted, explicitly or implicitly, in some recent studies of industrial development.[40] There are, however, differences between definitions of what a development block is and often definitions of the concept are imprecise. Consequently one has to ask who are the actors in the blocks, how is the block defined, what tensions produce the dynamic forces and how are the institutions and organizations within the block interrelated?

In order to answer these questions I shall define some conditions for the dynamics in transformation of development blocks by listing some important strategic factors in a block. The first of these is entrepreneurial activity which could be undertaken by an individual, a firm, government or a cluster of firms. The second is the suppliers and users connected to this activity. Third, the entrepreneurial activity, the suppliers and the costumers will have some kind of socio-economic rooting. This wide concept includes in this case the education and training system (or more broadly the "knowledge base" of the economy), natural resources and government policies.[41] Again the implication is that innovation activities are not completely random. The historical tradition for production and consumption, the natural and human resources and the prevailing

---

40 For example Dalum et.al.(1991) and Edquist & Lundvall (1991). In a sense also Porter's (1990) "diamond" can be taken as an implicit development block.

41 Actually the list also includes informal institutions such as conventions on ethical issues, the business climate, the pattern of consumption and the propensity to innovate, but they are not incorporated in the model as an independent factor.

technological trajectory will be guidelines for search will take place. Fourth, a supply of capital is needed for innovation activities.

In the following text I will define a "development block" as a linkage-intensive, potential or actual, part of the production structure, where the linkages to and between the entities below are essential to the dynamics of the system.

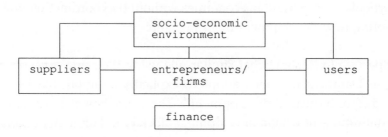

Dynamics are induced by an imbalance between entrepreneurial activity and the environment in which it takes place. These may also come from changes in the environment such as new standards, changes in terms for competition etc. A presumption for action towards equalising these imbalances is that they can be properly identified. In my model one decisive factor for this, is the distances between the strategic factors or in other words the intensiveness of the linkages between these factors. The closer the entrepreneur is to the users, the better possibilities he/she has for learning about unfulfilled needs; the closer his contacts are to the bank, the better his possibilities for finance and economic advice; the closer he is to the suppliers the better knowledge about production capacity, etcetera.

Even though the imbalances are crucial to industrial change, they must not be too large. If one part of the block is too underdeveloped compared to the others, it might prove impossible for the block to develop as a block - or in other words it is difficult to produce anything if one of the factors is missing.[42]

---

[42] As hinted upon in the introduction, this also shows, that understanding the *process* of industrial and technological change also implies thinking over what did not happen. Why are some of the apparently natural areas of production not as strong as one should think (why do Denmark e.g. not have a strong block in bicycle production?).

An important part of any development block is the financing of transformation from one stage to another. It takes capital to equilibrate the structural tensions. Even though a substantial uncertainty remains as to where and how the development block is actually developing it is, from the financiers point of view, less risky to finance a cluster of firms within the same "block". Development blocks may, therefore, be a way of coordinating the innovation process which also facilitates financing. The Japanese "Keiretsus" (explained in chapter 7) may be regarded as a development block including industrial firms, subcontractors and a financial institution.

4.6. A summary of lessons from uncertainty in innovation

With this chapter we came closer to comprehending what the process that should be financed actually is. We found that the specific character of the innovation process has implications for the financing of the process. In particular it is important to assess the varying degrees of technical and market uncertainty when financing innovations. This is not an easy task. It is not possible to obtain full information on the future development of the process and the search for information is weighted against potential outcomes of that information.

A natural reaction when faced with uncertainty is to apply conventional behaviour and this may hamper innovation financing. However, the innovation process is not totally chaotic. It is suggested here that at least four reasons for coordination of the process reduces uncertainty and thus induce innovation financing. These four coordinating factors are the stability of borrower-lender relationships over time, the environment in which the innovation process takes place - in particular the national system of innovation, the path-dependency of innovation, and the development block perspective.

What is evident from the discussion of uncertainty in innovation in this chapter is not only the importance and character of uncertainty in innovations but also that the impact it has on innovation projects varies over time. Whereas one kind of uncertainty is particularly important for some innovations at some point of time, another kind of uncertainty may be relevant at other times. This fact is extremely important to recognize because it has great implications for the financing of that process. Consequently it is dealt with in further detail in the subsequent chapter.

Chapter 5. Financial requirements for the firms' innovation processes

5.1. Introduction

The focus on uncertainty and decision making under uncertainty in chapter 4 was motivated by the substantial difference in uncertainty between innovations and other investments. This is but one of the special features of innovations. Below I shall carry the discussion in chapter 4 on the innovation process further by relating some of the basic properties of the innovation process to its financial requirements. In particular, the emphasis on the *process* is important.

Thus, the purpose of the chapter is to investigate what the needs are for financing the innovation process discussed in chapter 4. The starting point is the overall claim that analysis of financial requirements for innovation processes has to be dynamic in the sense that needs and potential sources for finance vary over time. This approach has important implications. It means that financing innovations should not be dealt with in a too general manner. Rather the above mentioned differences should be specified and the uncertainty of the innovation process analyzed in chapter 4, related to a dynamic perspective where the focus is upon the development of a firm or a product.

A useful way of analyzing the differences in the financial requirements of a project over time is to employ a product life cycle theory and relate it to finance. This is done in section 5.2.

From this theory it almost follows, that the conditions for a small and a large firm are not the same. It is crucial to understand differences in financing possibilities between a large and a small firm - both in order to implement appropriate policy measures, and to understand which innovations are possible to undertake. The importance of firm size is discussed in section 5.3.[1] Having determined some characteristics of the firm, which have an impact on opportunities for obtaining finance, I turn, in section 5.4. to consider implications for strategies of the firm.

As an aggressive strategy, such as aiming at developing radically new products, implies different degrees of uncertainty, the possibilities of obtaining external finance depend on which innovation strategy the firm employs. Likewise the amount of collateral it is possible to provide depends on the choice made. Thus, the following discussion of innovation strategy will shift perspective from that for a principally single-project to a firm-strategic perspective.

The summation up in section 5.5. outlines some required features of financial institutions, if they are to support innovation. The chapter illustrates why financing the innovation process is different from financing industrial development in general, and has implications for the capability and design of financial institutions and financial systems.

5.2. Product life cycle and financial requirements

5.2.1. Introducing the coupling of product life cycle and financial requirements

An innovation project is not a single event but rather a continuing process with different content and varying degrees of uncertainty over time. During the innovation process there are differences in the need for capital and the sources of finance vary over time. Management thus faces different problems depending on the maturity of their project.

To illustrate this I shall present a stylized innovation project[2] divided into four stages:

---

1 A somewhat detailed discussion of this subject is provided because it is important in the Danish context, as we shall see later.

2 In chapter 4 linear modelling of the innovation process was rejected as unrealistic. It could perhaps be argued that the present version of the innovation process could equally be regarded as linear. However, feed-back mechanisms and incrementalism are integrated in the analysis.

1. Commencement/early stage
2. Start up
3. Expansion
4. Mature growth

Obviously, inspiration comes from the well known theory of product life cycle which is developed in a large number of versions.[3] This is, of course, a general description of the innovation process and financial needs, and, obviously, in the real world, there are many deviations from this typical process. Many firms or projects never get any further than the start-up phase, and many firms do not want to expand. There are national differences in the way the process is financed, and in intensity of the contact between firms and financial institutions. The pattern for a large and a small firm is not similar, and the strategy of the firm affects the project agenda. Reservations could be expanded. One clarification is important to make before proceeding. In many articles it is not made clear whether the life cycle is for a branch of industry, a firm or a specific product. Here the term project is used because it involves a combination of product innovation and process innovations over time.

In this context one could perhaps talk about a "financial life cycle". The stages in the life cycle are, of course, overlapping and thus not strictly well-defined. Likewise, the time-span on the product life cycle may vary between industries and change over time.

Three subjects are discussed in relation to the stages above. First, the definition of the stages, or in other words a project agenda is listed in table 5.1, and subsequently some of the characteristics of a product innovation process are explained. This explanation uses results from chapter 3 and 4 as a framework - especially with respect to uncertainty. Second, the most important financial sources are related to different stages. Third, the kind of and intensity of borrower - lender interaction (explained in chapter 3 and 4) is addressed.

---

3   A recent one is Cainerca et.al.(1992) while a more classical reference is Abernathy & Utterback (1978).

The table below gives an overview of the three subjects which are addressed in this section and it differentiates them into the four stages of development.

Table 5.1.: Financial issues at different stages of the product life cycle

Stage	Early	Start-up	Expansion	Mature growth
Project agenda	Project planning, 1. market research, advisory network	Additional competence, set-up of production, sales, and organization	2. generation products, 2. market research, develop econ. of scale	Diversification, reducing cost, consolidation
Financial sources	Personal funding, government grants and loans	government grants and loans venture capital, bank and mortgage credit	Banks, venture capital, trade credit	Stock market, pension funds, banks, LBO, MBO
Lender-industry relations	Advisory aid with government institutions, entrepreneurial learning	Network, personal contact, cultural learning	Information, distribution, communication, system build-up, stability	Diversification of financial sources

The abbreviations in table 5.1. are further explained during the discussion below on how project agenda, financial sources and borrower - lender relationships changes over time.

5.2.2. Project agenda and uncertainty

In chapter 4 uncertainty was stressed as the most decisive factor in innovation processes. Reasons for technical and market uncertainty are explained and factors reducing uncertainty was pointed to. On the firm level of aggregation there are strategies for reducing uncertainty in innovation as well. Obviously these measures are determined by the potential problem and degree of uncertainty in various stages of development. Figure 5.2. below illustrates the development of technical and market uncertainty as well as sales and financial needs.

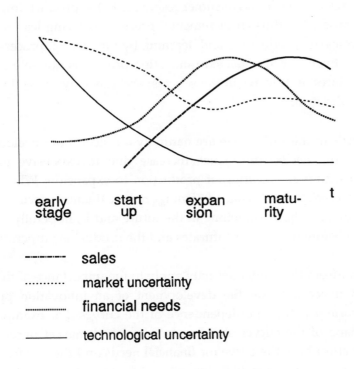

early start expan matu- t
stage up sion rity

----------- sales

.... market uncertainty

.... financial needs

_____ technological uncertainty

In this model market uncertainty is substantial when the project is initiated due to the large time lag between starting out and commercialization and even longer to break-even. Sunk costs are a potentially deterrent to the project. As the design converges towards its dominant version, market research is undertaken and when potentially competing products are introduced on the market uncertainty is gradually reduced. When the first sales are done and reactions from customers perceived, market uncertainty gets even further reduced. However, an expansion and large scale sale may reintroduce uncertainty on whether the project is commercially successful. Finally, in maturity, market uncertainty is reduced to a persistent level which is impossible to eliminate.

Technical uncertainty will decrease, but is likely to persist even after introduction on the market as explained in chapter 4. The reason is that the innovation process is rarely a predetermined, detail-planned process throughout all of its stages. During the process changes are made for

119

example as a result of user- or consumer responses to the product. Improvement of the product is thus an incremental process involving learning-by-doing processes in production and learning-by-interacting processes in consumption. Even a well-managed innovation process is not able to take account of failures and delays in the process, and this may cause financial pressures on the firm.

Financial needs in the early stage are naturally a function of development costs.[4] Later, the needs for finance increase due to expensive market research, marketing and gearing of production to expansion. When sales have reached a certain level retained earnings reduce financial needs. Break-even may, however, be at sometime in the future and is, hopefully for the firm, reached before the market saturates and the product is outperformed.

Lessons learnt from the model not only apply to the importance of the role of time and uncertainty on the development of an innovation project. Equally important is the interdependence of the curves. For example the level and shape of the curves showing technical and market uncertainty significantly affect both the curve for financial needs and the one for sales. The sales curve, in turn, affects the shape of the curve for financial needs, and the initial level of the different curves strongly affects the others. These levels are determined by the characteristics of the specific innovation project in question with respect to the features discussed in chapter 4.

Kay (1988, p.282f.) examines some of these characteristics in relation to the stages of the innovation process. He finds that product- and firm specificities of R & D increases during the development of the project as does cost levels and the associated financial resource demands. Time-lags and uncertainty, on the other hand, decrease as a project develops over time. This has implications for the costs of innovating which may be a barrier to entry in themselves.

Kline & Rosenberg (1986, p.301) note that development costs in innovation have increased substantially. Furthermore, lead times are long and

---

4 Obviously the share of internal funds is likewise determining the level and shape of the financial needs curve in figure 5.2. Development costs includes expenses for setting up a business plan.

technological change is more rapid than ever. In combination with shortened product life cycles and a large scale of financial commitments the risks of long-lived plant and equipment increases financial risks and makes precise timing crucial. A "fast second" imitator may, thus, be better off than an innovator because he avoids some of the technical problems in early stages, according to the authors.

5.2.3. Different financial sources funding different stages?

The long and uncertain time-span between initial investments, commercialization and eventually break-even requires that financial institutions employ a certain time horizon if the financial pressure on the firm does not make it change innovation strategy or give up the project.

Specificities of the product make the evaluation of the technical uncertainty very difficult for financial institutions. The degree of specificity changes over time as the basic R&D is usually non-specific. On the other hand it is difficult to observe any direct link between this research and commercial success, and consequently financial institutions rarely finance R&D. This is rather a task for large private enterprises, private entrepreneurs, or governments.

In early stages of an innovation project uncertainty and failure rates are very high. Even after some time the uncertainty is often too large for financial institutions. Due to this uncertainty financial institutions rarely enter the process at an early stage[5].

The numerous sources of funding in table 5.1. indicate that an innovation project is sensitive to fluctuations on the financing side. Early in the project external investors are rarely directly involved due to the substantial uncertainty, high rate of failure, and lack of competence to evaluate projects. Later, when technical uncertainty has been reduced, the potential investors

---

5 It is not unusual that firms are advised to modify the radicality of the innovation because it would otherwise not be able to attract external capital. It is also usual that firms uses a "salami-tactic" when negotiating with a financial institution. This is a way of involving the financial institution piece-by-piece by initially putting only a part of the actual project forward and subsequently asking for a gradually larger part of the necessary finance.

still face a high market uncertainty. Furthermore, firms at that stage often have a high debt/equity ratio[6]. If these firms apply for additional capital for immaterial investments in for example human capital, exploitation of learning processes in production and consumption (marketing, market research, product development), and other investments which are impossible to provide collateral for, it enhances financiers' reluctance to provide credit or equity.

The period just before commercial expansion is crucial for innovation projects, and many projects actually fail at this stage due to lack of external capital.[7] This illustrates, that the project is not any stronger than the weakest link in the financing chain.[8]

When the project has proven viable a new pool of funding sources are available to the firm. Thus, trade credit is a commonly used form and even later pension funds or stock market introduction may be considered. Methods of exit such as management buy-outs may also be an option.

5.2.4. Intensity and kinds of interaction between the lender and the borrower

The financier-firm relationships may deserve a few comments, because at first glance the many different sources of external financing seem to indicate, that the borrower-lender relationships (referred to earlier) is not as stable as maintained. But financial institutions are not only suppliers of funds. They also form links between the firm/entrepreneur and other sources of finance, and they are important to the corporate sector as advisors. Government institutions may provide firms with funds, but they also educate the entrepreneur in the early stages and encourage him to establish a network with investors, advisors and perhaps also with

---

6 D/e ratios would almost follow the financial needs curve in figure 5.2.

7 In France the national guarantee fund SOFARIS realized this, and extended its guarantees to immaterial investments. This step has had a positive impact on the possibilities of financing innovations in small companies (Derian, 1990).

8 Nevertheless, there have only been few attempts in government policy programs to link the financing of each of the stages.

customers and other firms. This network is essential to the firm as it alleviates informational constraints and reduces uncertainty in the project.

Venture capital companies may also invest in the start-up and supply the firm with additional competence, but the financing of growth often takes a joint involvement of several funding sources, and the venture capital companies often work as intermediaries in regard to these other sources.

Likewise banks can ease access to other sources of finance, e.g. the stock market (especially in Germany). In particular, small and medium sized firms may be facing an informational barrier to obtaining financing through introduction on the stock exchange. Consequently a bank often guarantee the introduction[9].

The measures of intensity in interaction between the lender and the borrower are, of course, ambiguous, but in general, the first contact with a financial institution, be it a government agency, venture capital company or bank, involves a strong element of information exchange. In addition, the need for close contacts with lenders or investors is essential when the firm requires extra external capital for expansion. In maturity the retained earnings from sales may reduce the financial needs. Diversification of financial sources can reduce contacts with the single investor, and initial investors may be bought out. If the firm decides to be listed on the stock market, the suppliers of funds may become mainly anonymous, and interaction limited.

Apparently such relationships are only relevant when talking about external finance. However, also within a firm similar relationships may develop. When the innovation manager, the R & D department, or the technical staff come up with ideas suggesting technical improvements or new products, these suggestions will have to be approved by financial management. The interplay between the R & D director and the technical management within the firm has similarities to those interactions with external financial institutions.

---

9 These general considerations must of course be differentiated when applied to real world analysis because there are large institutional differences between countries with respect to the role of financial institutions (see chapter 7 on this).

One important difference is that a rejection is irrevocable in the "hierarchy" internal of the firm, whereas a firm with external sources has the option of several financial institutions. The latter is more of a market relationship. Other differences relate to the size of firms, so let us turn to this subject now.

5.3. Firm size, innovation and possibilities of obtaining external finance

> "In fact, it should perhaps be noted that the reality of the problem of financing SME's will never be "solved" in the sense that it will "disappear". This is due to the nature of the problem itself, arising as it does from the action of market forces in allocating relatively scarce capital between competing uses."(Maxwell, 1990, p.10)

The mere size of the innovating firm has implications for the possibilities of obtaining external finance. There are several, interrelated, arguments for this claim. First, I will point out that some innovations are impossible to undertake for a small firm. The complexity or size of a project may exclude some firms from considering a project. Even if small firms make an above average inventive effort they are not necessarily innovative to the same degree. The reason is that expensive development work is easier for a large firm.

> "The relative performance of large firms is apparently better with respect to innovations than with respect to inventions, and Jewkes accepts that their role in development work (which is usually far more expensive) is much more important. Thus, it may be reasonable to postulate that small firms may have some comparative advantage in the earlier stages of inventive work and the less expensive, but more radical innovations, while large firms have an advantage in the later stages and in improvement and scaling up of early breakthroughs. (Freeman, 1982, p.137)

Freeman (op.cit.) gives the extreme example of Apollo XI where more than two million different components where used. Even much smaller projects would obviously be impossible to undertake for a small firm.[10] There may be other related disadvantages of small scale. In-house training of the labour force may be very costly if done on a small scale and establishment of a viable R & D department with a diverse amount of specialists and R & D projects may equally be difficult for the smaller firm. If financiers stress the knowledge base of the firm when screening innovation projects these small-scale consequences are likely to be a major disadvantage when external finance is needed.

Second, the performance of a small firm varies much more than that of a large firm. Thus, the volatility of growth rates and profits decreases with increasing firm size. Presumably, this reflects a wider range of products and customers in the large firm, as opposed to a higher propensity to have a single customer, single product in the small firm. Consequently, the small firm is more sensitive to unexpected changes in its environment. In addition, such changes are more likely to occur. Compared to that of a large firm the demand for its products, the turn-over and the required outlays in a small firm are large compared to its capital base, whereas the large firm has a more incremental development (Storey, 1990, p.8). Stages in the development of a firm do not, in other words, indicate a smooth development for a small firm. Rather the stages can be seen as a sequence of changes in the nature of the business. As the project agenda changes the firm faces a range of new challenges of managerial character, challenges to resources, to organizational change, to external relationships, and market assessment.

These transitions are highly risky because they involve major changes in many aspects of the firm and financiers may be reluctant to take a risk of changing a consolidated stable business into a new high risk firm. On the other hand, an injection of external capital is essential when taking a step further on the growth ladder. This was also found in a number of case studies of small firms in the U.K. and the U.S. (ACOST, 1990).

---

10 Variations between industries are important in this respect. For example, in some industries there is a limit below which it is difficult to make a successful innovation. This applies to the chemical industry, aerospace, nuclear energy and several others. In a Danish survey it was found that in the most research-intensive industries it is mainly small firms who lack capital whereas large firms in the least research-intensive industries lack capital for large investments in process innovations (Kristensen, 1991, p.101).

"A fundamental problem they faced was the lack of synchronization between their current flow of funds and the prevailing needs for investment in R & D, particular for new products. The development of the technology base typically involved step changes in the level of funds to be committed, and current levels of turnover could not cope with this. In general, bank finance was not appropriate because it required the security of marketable assets which risky innovative activities cannot supply. The only way for the firm to surmount this barrier was through an injection of external funds." (ACOST, 1990, p.19)

Third, there is a higher risk of default in small firms. This has to do with a large ratio of expenditures on a single innovation project to the capital base of the firm and it has to do with the sensitivity and step-wise growth rate described above. To this sensitivity might be added, that the small firm usually has a smaller management team. In some start-ups it is only the owner. This makes the firm very reliant on the skills of a few persons and consequently, the firm is also sensitive to unexpected changes in management. Moreover, financiers often stress the competence of management when screening innovation projects and this is not without reason. Running the volatile development of a small firm requires skillful management and adequate organizational changes to new situations as does producing a creative environment able to foster new ideas and innovations to sustain competitiveness and growth in the firm. Small firms may not be particularly successful in this respect as they may not have the same management resources and are not as flexible in reacting to major changes in markets as the larger, multi-product firm.[11]

Fourth, there are greater asymmetries in information when a bank is dealing with a small firm. A larger firm will usually have a past record to rely upon or it may have a certain reputation. Some information on large firms is even publicly available. Both the technical and the market uncertainty may be more difficult to assess in a new, small firm, as there is little experience to

---

11 The ACOST report points to lack of strategic thinking by management and lack of available external funds as major barriers to growth in small U.K. businesses.

126

build upon. Therefore, in the judgement of the small firm is management itself important.[12]

Fifth, small firms are met with requirements of higher interest rates, higher demands for collateral and credit rationing.[13] In addition to the greater uncertainties described above, I shall mention two other reasons for this. One is that there are initial costs for a bank if it enters an engagement. These costs are mainly associated with monitoring and administration. Therefore, a large loan will yield a larger profit for the bank compared to the fixed costs. Small firms thus often hit the lower limit where financiers invest. The other reason is the limited market power a small firm can mobilize when negotiating with banks.[14] The consequence is that small firms have to undertake projects that have a higher profitability than do large firms and some areas of production are then inaccessable to small firms. It is an open, but interesting question, if some small firms actually deliberately chose risky projects because they need higher profits, and thus, creates a self-reinforcing high risk - high interest rate circle.

---

12 This emphasizes the importance of entrepreneurial fund raising ingenuity in small firms (Penrose, 1980, p.37-39,220 and chapter 4). In addition to the entrepreneurial personality, also a difference in mentality between the small firm manager and the larger firm manager may hamper possibilities for obtaining finance because small firm managers tend to view rules and procedures in financial institutions as bureaucratic and slow compared to his own flexible and fast responding firm. The organization and speed of response in the large firm is more like that of a bank (Storey, 1990, p.11).

13 Hall,G. (1987, p.55) summarizes a review of various empirical studies by stating that "There is little doubt that, compared to large firms, small firms are usually required to pay a higher rate of interest and offer a higher level of security. This reflects, partly, the greater risk inherent in the small-firm sector and, partly, the endemic conservatism of bank managers. The latter, furthermore, are inefficient at undertaking financial appraisals." It is however, unclear if the latter explanation - that banks are inefficient - is true. It may well be that it is perfectly sound to be tougher on small firms due to their high failure rates. Thus, ACOST (1990, p.1) state that "Smaller firms do suffer disadvantages in raising external risk capital, there is a definite equity gap, but the extent to which less advantageous borrowing terms faced by small firms reflect rational risk assessment by lenders remains unclear;".

14 Maxwell (1990, p.11) reports recent studies that show that small businesses in Ireland have to provide collateral in the ratio of 3:1 to cover bank borrowing. The similar figures for the U.K. are 1.5:1 and for the U.S. 1.2:1. In addition, the small firms have to pay an extra interest rate of 3.75%

Although some government programmes aim at supporting small firms these firms often lack the knowledge about the possibilities and they lack the skills and capacity to see clearly what the content of the different programmes are and fill out applications. These shortcomings were pointed to by the Bolton Committee in 1971:

> "The role of institutions is important, however, and it is unfortunate that small businessmen and to some extent their professional advisers, have a lamentable ignorance of the sources available to meet specific financial needs."

In addition to the external funds the advisory system is especially important for small firms since they are likely to need external advice for making a business plan and for adjusting the firm when moving to another stage in development. However, often the set-up of this system is not adequate for the problems that small firms are facing. If set up in a sectoral manner the advisory system may not be able to meet the needs of small firms whose problems are often integrated and non-specialized compared to those of a large firm.

Futhermore, another difficulty with innovation financing in small firms stems from a general problem of competence mis-match between the borrower and the lender. On the one hand firms (especially small firms) have little knowledge about ways of financing innovations, and they tend to focus on the technical possibilities of their project instead of on financial management. In financial institutions, on the other hand, decision makers are reluctant to achieve project- and branch specific knowledge and to use that information as a criteria for judging a project. Instead, emphasis is placed upon past balance sheets, solidity, regularly budgets, liquidity forecasts etcetera, or in other words financial management.[15] The large firm is closer in culture to the financial world as they often have a separate financial department and the organization may be more similar to that of a bank.

---

15 Dunning concludes in a report to the Bolton Committee that imperfections in the market mainly stem from an information gap and inability of financial institutions to spot potential winners.

At least two other features of typical small enterprise development is worth mentioning. One is that a protection of innovations against copying is important to the incentives to extent the knowledge base of the firm. Legal rights to innovations are protected by the patent system. However, a patent is expensive and small firms often lack financial resources to acquire patents. Furthermore, external financing of patents is difficult because financiers estimate a low value for a patent - especially if the innovation which is protected is very specific. The second small firm growth feature I would like to mention is the likelihood and desirability of remaining independent. The transitions mentioned above are costly and expenses are often not only beyond what is possible to cope with internally but also exceed what is possible to raise externally. The consequence is often that the firm is acquired by a larger firm able to reconstruct and gear the firm to the new development phase. There are pros and cons of a takeover. The pros are that a new organization and management in addition to more capital may be exactly what is needed to carry the firm on. On the other hand, the new, parent company may fail to incorporate the organization and management of the firm they acquired in its own organization (ACOST, 1990, p.30). Moreover, take-overs may prevent firms from establishing reputation and customer relationships.

Although small scale disadvantages may be predominant there are also advantages in being a small firm. Mueller (1972, p.201-3) thus argues that information transmission is a major advantage of size (of hierarchies) because a large firm with internal funds is able to keep information within the organization. If the information is appropriable this is important compared with the case if entrepreneurs are separated from the sources of financing. However, responsibilities for supplying R & D units with capital rests with the top management, and the flow of information upward through the hierarchy may easily loose quality and quantity. Thus, the question of size is a trade-off between loss of ownership of information or loss of content. Williamson (1975, p.144 f. and especially 1986, p.131 ff.) elaborates on the question of firm size in relation to organization and information.

5.4. Innovation strategies and financial opportunities for the firm

5.4.1. Choices of innovation and financing

It has been suggested in this chapter that demand for finance depends not only on which stage of development the firm/entrepreneur is in, and on such factors as firm size, but also on choices made by the firm. The ambitions to develop within the firm also affect which innovation strategy is employed and consequently opportunities and needs for further financing. Both opportunities and needs for finance are affected by the degree of internal financing, if the firm has any options.

In addition to opportunities and needs for finance the financial strategy of the firm is important in financing innovation in firms. The strategy has to be compatible with innovation strategy in order to achieve a smooth innovation development. Financial strategy is affected by the financial and regulatory environment such as the type of financial system and legislation, and it is affected by the resources initially in the possession of the firm. Furthermore, it is affected by the organization in the firm with respect to the role and compatibility of corporate goals of owners versus management. For instance, there may be a question as to whether the firm wants to grow at all[16], and if it does, what strategy does it follow to reach its goals[17]. This question calls for considerations of selected areas of the strategy of the firm.

---

16 The most important reason for not wanting to grow is probably a desire to remain independent. Expansion often requires capital expansion and external investors may want to get an equity stake which is frequently a controlling one if the total needs for finance are to be covered. Other reasons may be a fear of a too radical change in company culture if it becomes growth oriented to a larger extent.

17 Speaking of the intentions of the firm it is relevant to point to a classical discussion, which has been called managerialism. In short, the key question in this context is: who is the firm? The owners may have an interest in large dividends or a capital gain, whereas managers may wish to expand the firm, just to mention one example of possible conflicts of interest between managers and owners. This is, of course, only provided that there is a distinction between managers and owners, which has increasingly been the case.

Although some of the strategies below exclude each other in a specific area of production there may be different strategies in the same firm at the same time, because some products may be developed with one strategy and some with another. In line with Freeman (1982, p.163) and Kay (1988, p.288) (who adopts Freemans framework), I shall relate innovation strategies to financial opportunities and -problems. Before that a few remarks on internal financing are appropriate.

5.4.2. Internal versus external financing

Investments in general are mainly financed internally, and this is even more so when talking about innovations. As discussed, in start-ups there is a huge uncertainty and this keeps external investors away. Small firms/entre-preneurs, however, have only limited resources, and external finance is necessary at some stage. Large firms have better possibilities for obtaining external finance, but they are usually also better equipped for financing innovations themselves[18]. If the firm is large and has some reputation and several projects, then the continuous financing of the firm rarely separates supplies of funds between those meant for high-risk projects and those meant for every-day financing of activities. Funds for innovations are then allocated according to rules-of-thumb in the firm or according to what the present innovation strategy or -projects are.[19]

Possibilities for internal and external financing are likely to have an impact on the innovation strategy of a firm. Thus, a firm with large capacity for internal financing enjoys more freedom to pursue the innovation strategy, it wants, regardless of conditions and prices on credit, whereas the possibilities on the market for external capital may influence the innovation strategy of a firm without this capacity. Although a firm may see advantages in one strategy the lack of possibilities of raising funds may hamper the firm in its choices.

---

18   In the report to The Bolton Committee it was pointed out that small, fast growing firms in the Committees' sample financed investments equally from external and internal funds, which is an over-average ratio of external finance.

19   Thus, some firms calculate with profitable products - "cash cows" - paying for the risky investments - the "wild cats".

5.4.3. Offensive product development strategy

An offensive innovation strategy may be suitable when there are large advantages of being first-in on the market. The strategy aims at getting a technological and market leadership. Therefore, property rights and lags on competitive responses and imitations are important factors to take into account, when deciding on this strategy (Kay, 1988, p.288). Using this strategy a long time horizon is often necessary, and this enhances the danger of irrelevance of the product when it finally is ready for introduction. By then, a competing or similar product may have conquered market dominance or the conditions on the market may have changed as a result of public regulation, changes in consumer preferences etc.

The long time horizon in itself has some financial implications, as previously discussed. In addition, it is likely that a number of failed development projects is necessary before a new product is developed and this poses extra financial burdens on the firm. Even if these failures are productive in the sense that they contribute to sophistication and improvements of the final product and accumulation of skills within the development department, then it is difficult to, a priori, legitimate failures to external investors.

An important prerequisite for this strategy is either a research and development department or easy access to relevant basic research[20]. This enables the firm to develop products from ideas generated internally and to incorporate information from outside into the product development.

5.4.4. Imitative product development strategy

This title may sound a bit like a contradiction in terms. But the point is that firms with this strategy eliminate some of the large uncertainties "upstream" by developing or redesigning products, which have been introduced by others.

---

20 In any case it is usually not possible for a single firm to do all the basic research which is relevant. Consequently, firms have to use fundamental research from elsewhere like universities and government research institutes (Freeman, 1982, p.172).

The financial institutions are likely to be more prone to finance these firms as both technical and market uncertainties are reduced substantially, time horizons are short and activities product specific.

5.4.5. Process development strategy

To develop the production process strategy is aimed at reducing costs increasing product quality, or precision in delivery. Large-scale, specialized production equipment is necessary as is a certain stability of the market. If the firm has limited production to one or a few products it will be sensitive to market fluctuations.

Although the development of a firm with this strategy is usually gradual the investments in production capacity are concentrated and large. For high technology the implementation may take a considerable time (Gjerding et al., 1990).

5.4.6. "Learning-to-learn" - the competence developing strategy

The notion of "learning by learning" was introduced by Stiglitz (1987). The important thing to understand about the concept in this connection, is that the strategy of the firm is not aimed at specific products. Rather it attempts to make the firm a "learning machine". This is done by improving general skills and competencies in the firm and gearing the organization to be flexible enough to switch between products. Processing and collection of information becomes important in this strategy as does human capital (Eliasson, 1990)

Flexibility in development and production is the key competitive factor in this strategy as it enables the firm to produce efficiently in small scale. But this competitive advantage could be eliminated if there were stability over time on the market. Then, fordist modes of production would outperform the competence developing strategy.

Financial institutions are, in general, unable to evaluate the competence development strategy even though the strategy has become increasingly widespread (Cohen and Zysman, 1988). In theory, it could be an advantage that the production base is immaterial and thus not tied to an end-product, which may be subject to market fluctuations. On the other hand, human capital is worthless as collateral, and impossible to tie to the firm infinitely[21]. Furthermore, investments in organizational changes and general competence build-up are likely to be viewed as irrational by financial institutions if the investments do not have any direct relation to potential incomes. Immaterial investments also create problems for financial institutions in case of default as the assets of the firm are tied to the employees and their ability to cooperate. Apparently this process has been going on for a long time. Thus, Veblen wrote in 1919:

> "...the continued advance of the mechanical technology has called for an ever-increasing volume and diversity of special knowledge, and so has left the businesslike captains of finance continually farther in arrears, so that they have been less and less capable of comprehending what is required in the ordenary way of industrial equipment and personel." (Veblen, 1919, p.76)

5.4.7. The dependent strategy

Some (especially small) firms may choose to be connected to a larger firm, group of firms or government institution. Subcontractors usually only make minor, incremental innovations, often on the request of the dominant firm, or they adjust to changes in specifications.

The financial uncertainties are small when following this strategy. Often the product is determined and sold well in advance of the actual production. A financial backing is necessary, though, since subcontractors usually have to give trade credit.

The matrix below summarizes the discussion on innovation strategy and finance.

---

21 Relationships between the firm and key personnel should in fact be important for external financiers when they have to assess intangible investments. A close relationship and traditions and social conditions for not changing job frequently ties personnel to the firm on a long-term basis. For example, in Japan traditions for life time employment in the same firm makes it more likely that financiers would take into account the human capital in firms.

I   =   offensive product development strategy
II   =   imitative product development strategy
III   =   process development strategy
IV   =   competence development strategy
V   =   dependent strategy

Table 5.2 Type of innovation related to financial risk

Type of innovation	Product	Process
Financial risk		
High	I	IV
Low	II	III/V

5.5. Summing up - requirements for innovation financing

In general financial institutions engaged in corporate financing perform
three important tasks in the process of financing innovations. First of all
they do the initial screening of projects, that is selecting those projects which
they judge as worthy of investment or credit. Secondly, they monitor
projects once they are started. Thirdly, they undertake actions according to
the monitoring of projects.

From the discussion of the innovation process above, it is possible to deduce
certain key factors that financial institutions have to take into account when
screening projects. One of these is the large technical uncertainty of
innovation projects. The magnitude of this uncertainty is of course
dependent upon when the financier is entering the project, but before prototypes are completely developed and tested on potential customers there
will be an uncertainty about the duration and costs of developing the
product and consequently on the needs for additional financing. This
uncertainty is usually very difficult to judge for the financier unless 'he' has
developed special technical knowledge about the area in question, or is
specialized in lending to a limited branch of industry. One way of dealing
with this problem is to use external technical expertise to evaluate the
technical difficulties in the project.

Another uncertainty is the problems of predicting future possibilities for
selling the product. Usually some market research is performed at an early

135

stage, but it is nevertheless necessary for financial institutions to screen projects on their future sales prospective. In innovation projects the uncertainty will be even greater as customers have to be taught to use new products (or to use a product in a new way). The market research may reveal a need for the product, but an uncertainty remains on how long it will take before users will demand the product in a quantity sufficient for generating cash flows in excess of repayments on loans. The estimation of the "death valley" point where the product is ready for final marketing and sales, and the estimation of costs for learning in consumption[22], is important when screening projects and competence is required to rightly assess the costs of marketing a new product and a feeling for the market needs, competing products and barriers of entry.

I have already touched upon another special feature of innovation project screening. The time perspective in innovation projects is often different (longer) than in ordinary investment projects, and a correct assessment of exactly how long it will take before -and if - the project shows profitable is an important part of what could be termed good banking. Different financial institutions have different pressures on them for showing profits in a short term perspective and this may influence the propensity to enter innovation projects.

Due to the special character of innovation projects there will inevitably be some information that the lender is not able to obtain. Therefore, the innovation projects will usually imply even more asymmetric information than ordinary investments. Consequently one aspect of screening projects is to consider how much, if any, information the borrower is disclosing, and to what degree he is acting opportunistically, e.g. by taking greater risks than agreed upon or using the funds for other purposes. Another aspect of judging the entrepreneur/management of the applicant firm, is to ensure a sufficient competence in the management to carry the project through.

---

22 This learning is not a linear function on the money spend on promoting the product. It is also necessary to take into account, that some products or processes may meet moral or ethical opposition. Examples are numerous: nuclear power, irradiation of food, transplantation of human organs etc. not to mention the general fear of technological unemployment and the opposition to making society and every day life too technically sophisticated.

Finally, and related to the screening on the skills and honesty of the management, financiers need to judge the value of internal human resources and costs of further immaterial investments. In innovation projects the knowledge base of the firm is an important asset, but it is a volatile, non-physical asset, which is often firm specific, difficult to sustain in the future, difficult to evaluate and therefore regarded as worthless as collateral.The monitoring of an innovation project may take the form of a mutual learning process as the financial institution learn further about the technical and market conditions of the particular branch of industry, whereas the industrial firm learn about economic management by being supervised and regularly delivering budgets and status reports. In case the project does not fulfill the business plan, actions may be taken. The various forms of these actions include stopping supplies of funds, advising, demanding changes in management or adding external competence.

These special roles of financial institutions in innovation projects have some implications for what an efficient - understood as supportive for innovation projects -financial institution is.

To sum up, financial institutions supporting innovations must have a time perspective with a horizon long enough to prevent "short term pressure" on the projects. In order to reduce problems with asymmetric information it is an advantage if the financial institution has some knowledge on the market for similar products, the branch and the technical trajectory. These potential problems may also be reduced by a close relationship between the lender and the borrower. Because of rapid changes in technology, and industry in general, flexible institutions able to adapt to changing conditions in industry and the macroeconomic changes will have an advantage. Due to increased complexity of economic problems, (e.g. as a consequence of internationalization) and project management, firms need specialized advice, which in turn may demand a certain degree of specialization from financial institutions[23]. Furthermore, an important aspect of supporting innovations

---

23 This is though a very general statement (discussed again in chapter 7), which may deserve a few modifications. For example, there is often a wider range of problems in small firms and decisions are concentrated on a few persons. Therefore, a too specialized system of advising will complicate support to these firms. On the other hand, large firms may demand a wide range of financial products in the same financial institution. Finally, to be too specific in one specialized institution, may make financiers disregard the interplay of

in the long run is an organization, which allows knowledge created through the financing of innovations to be accumulated for future use.[24]

However, as indicated in table 5.1. there is to some extent a division of labour between financial institutions and this division is not random.[25] Some financial institutions are appropriate for financing a certain kind of technology or a certain stage in the development of a project while others are relevant as financial sources at other stages. For instance, it may be more important to have a close relationship with a borrower in the early stages of a project when information exchange is greatly needed and the applicant have no reputation to build upon.

Some financial institutions induce such relationships better than others. Likewise, some financial institutions may be better at assessing technological uncertainty than others, for example as a result of specialization on a particular industry. This division of labour may be an advantage if institutionalized in some way or another. On the other hand, a too sharp division of labour may be inexpedient to financing the innovation process. If firms have to raise funds from different institutions their application may be rejected and possibilities lost of exploiting benefits from a long term relationship to a lender.

Thus, the characteristics of the innovation process have several implications for the financing of that process. Especially as the high degree of uncertainty has been shown to influence decisions on financing innovations. In the next chapter I shall elaborate on the decisions to finance innovations and the, just mentioned, characteristics of financial institutions, which are used as criteria for evaluating different kinds of institutions and instruments as to how effective they are in innovation financing. In a sense, focus of the analysis shifts from a demand (for capital) side to a supply side.

---

different problems.

24 It is tempting to include a property termed risk willingness. But risk aversion is not any objective, neutral and easily defined concept. If the financial institution has an optimal screening of projects they can hardly be termed more or less willing to take a risk.

25 Even within a group of financial institutions there may be a division of labour. For example, Danish venture capital firms are divided into one or two firms, financing innovations and the others financing traditional projects and restructurings.

Chapter 6. Deciding to finance innovations

"...not only the availability of financial ressources is important but as far as innovations are concerned quite more important is the behaviour of financial agents." (Falciglia, 1986, p.8).

6.1. Introduction

In the preceding chapters a framework was established for understanding the nature of financial markets, borrower-lender relationships, the innovation process and its financial requirements seen from the firm. Although a number of ideal (taken as the ability to finance innovations) features of financial institutions were deduced from these discussions it was not considered if and to what extent financial institutions are able to live up to these requirements.

In this chapter the financier is at the centre of analysis as opposed to the previous focus upon the innovator. Thus, the emphasis is more on financing rather than innovations. Above I have discussed important features of the innovation process; now a discussion is required of some of the key issues in financing the innovation process - both in a general form, and in a more restricted sense. I shall try to get closer to a theoretical understanding of what determines decisions to finance innovations.

Previously a distinction was made between financing in markets, hierarchies, or the in-between, through a financial intermediary. This means that the transformation of funds from initial suppliers to ultimate users is channelled through market transactions in securities, internally between corporate divisions, or through various lending and borrowing arrangements. All three usually co-exist in financial systems because they each have their respective advantages. A discussion of these advantages is provided in section 7 of this chapter. In transaction cost economics the only criteria for such an evaluation is cost efficiency. I shall argue in that section that other criteria are important as well and I shall use those criteria to evaluate how different kinds of transactions are undertaken and how institutions perform.[1] This is, in fact, a comparison between specific characters of financial institutions and the requirements listed in section 5.5.

Even if markets and hierarchies are dealt with, the focus is mainly on intermediaries in this chapter, and especially in the first part of it[2]. This is due to the large impact of intermediaries in financing new technology and because of later application of the theory developed. Last, but not least, intermediaries are better at dealing with very uncertain investments like innovations as will be argued in the section after this introduction. In order to talk about efficiency in transactions it is necessary to discuss what the specific transactions are. Therefore, in the first section I shall discuss the role of financial intermediaries in financial systems in general and in financing innovations in particular.

In chapter 4 and 5 it was argued that uncertainty is one of the most important factors governing behaviour in innovations. Thus, although the single financier is the prime subject of analysis in this chapter, treating the environment in which the financier operates is essential. In section 6.3 a suggestion is developed on what determines risk willingness in financial institutions. Implicit in that discussion is that the degree of uncertainty profoundly influences the inducement to finance high-risk projects.

Time horizons in investments are both a determinant of risk willingness and simultanouesly are influenced by risk willingness. In section 6.4 there is a discussion of whether there is a conflict between the required time horizon in investments in innovations and the incentives for managers to take such time perspectives in their investments.

Financial institutions do not necessarily take risks even if the determinants of risk willingness apparently are present. Just like the inducement to

---

1 Transaction cost economics is here not used as a theoretical framework but rather for expository purposes. A discussion on the limits of transaction cost economics is contained in Lundvall (1991).

2 A large number of different kinds of intermediares exist. In the first sections of this chapter I shall concentrate the exposition on banks and then extent the analysis to other types of institutions in the latter part. The complex and extensive discussion on government funding of R&D and innovations is left out (see Grossman (1990) for an overview of the arguments). Instead it is mentioned in chapter 9.

innovate in the firm depends on the strategy (as explained in chapter 5) of the firm, the strategy of the financial institution determines whether it participates in risky arrangements. In section 6.5. a discussion of how different kinds of behaviour may influence decisions to finance innovations is presented.

Using the discussion in chapter 4 on micro economic behaviour a discussion is presented in section 6.6 of how to model risk willingness in banks.

Finally, before a brief summing up, I extend the analysis to a higher level of aggregation and consider some developments in financial institutions and technology, which affect the topics of this chapter.

6.2. Why financial intermediation? - financing by institutions, markets or hierarchies

6.2.1. The ability to handle different transactions in institutions, markets and hierarchies

In chapter 4 Heiners' argument (1983) about uncertainty as a reason for stereotypical behaviour was considered. Even though uncertainty may well make agents behave conventionally and rule bound, innovation often excludes this possibility as there sometimes is a lack of established routines to cling to. Financing innovations is an uncertain activity and agents recognize this in advance and take appropriate measures to reduce or compensate for the uncertainty.

Thus, while making a contract initial uncertainty on what is to follow is substantial. But recognizing that the contract is "incomplete" at the outset in the sense that not all possible future states of nature are taken into account makes agents ensure that contracts can be adapted to changing conditions.

The purpose of investment determines the degree of incompleteness of contracts and the likely needs for ex post adjustments. For example, as was explained in chapter 4, the degree of asset specificity has an impact on whether there is a secondary market for the assets and consequently how

141

worthy they are as collateral. The large proportion of human capital in production is one example of such specific assets which will induce a high degree of discretionary contracting. Another example is the one-time type of transaction. If a certain type of transaction occurs frequently, the skills to evaluate its likely outcome cost effectively are often available or are generated over time, while the unfamiliar kinds of transaction may incur greater costs for screening and monitoring than anticipated (Neave, 1991, p.27). Learning by doing is, in other words, important as a means of reducing costs in transactions in that some kinds of transactions may be subject to standardization of screening techniques while other, less frequently occurring transactions, may need discretionary treatment.

Whether one or another kind of transaction is regularly occurring or not depends on the specific institutional surroundings. The traditions and production structure of the national industry are thus contributing to what are the most common kinds of transactions. Financiers are likely to be reluctant to enter unfamiliar transactions unless they are relatively certain on the outcome or, the outcome seems to be well over average. Competition may force banks to minimise operating costs and this is only possible in familiar transactions[3]. On the other hand, entrepreneurs face costs of searching for the best and cheapest financier. In order to minimise these costs entrepreneurs are likely to explore well known sources and accept the first feasible arrangement they find. Inherently there is a tendency towards inertia when both financiers and firms are reluctant to explore all available possibilities as they would have were they operating unbounded and rationally in a full information society.

Capabilities to handle these different kinds of transactions differ according to which type of financing or in other terms governance mechanism is chosen. In general, the more transactions are characterized by uncertainty and discretion the more screening and monitoring capabilities is needed (Williamson, 1988). Furthermore, the more uncertain the transaction, the stronger the need for ex post adjustment of the initial contract because only

---

3 Another strategy is to specialize in order to screen only a few types of transactions and to accumulate knowledge in this special activity within the organization. For example banks could, and frequently do, establish affiliated companies dealing exclusively with financing innovations.

risky, not uncertain states of nature can be incorporated ex ante. Vice versa frequently occurring standard transactions under risk need limited screening and monitoring, and learning effects are reduced to a minimum.

The market based way of financing implies the least developed governance capabilities as continuous supervision is difficult when buyers and sellers in the market are anonymous and dealing on a once and for all basis. One argument for that possibilities of exploiting the other part opportunistically are weak in the market way of financing (Neave, 1991, p.40) is because the other part is often not identified. As explained in chapter 3 opportunistic behaviour thus requires incentive and enforcement systems of a more complex character than in a pure market and this is why agency theory is mainly concerned with intermediaries. However, there is still room for cheating in this system. For example, a firm could, theoretically, make an emission and afterwards act independently of shareholders interests. The standardized way of trading and the small amount of screening and monitoring possibly make the market way of financing superior in terms of costs. Calculable, homogeneous and simple forms of transactions are thus channeled through this market.[4]

In contrast, financing by intermediaries or internal financing provides greater capabilities for learning and ex post adjustment of the incomplete contracts resulting from uncertainty. Problems with adverse selection and moral hazards stemming from asymmetric information can better be alleviated by an intermediary or internally in an organization as both initial screening procedures and subsequent monitoring and reporting requirements are more thorough than in the corresponding market governance mechanism. In principle differences between the intermediary way and the internal way of financing are smaller than those markets and intermediaries. However, there is a difference, mostly a matter of degree,

---

4 One could add that in theory small transactions should be channeled through the market as well because the per unit costs of governance by way of intermediares would exceed those of a market without the administrative set up for screening and monitoring. However, in practice small transactions are rarely traded on a market basis (unless it is part of a number of small transactions pooled to a securitization by an intermediare).

between capabilities for continuously monitoring[5]. Another difference is that opportunistical behaviour is less likely to occur and presumably is less costly when it does. Finally, internal financing rules out any legal problems connected to ex post adjustment.

In summation, intermediaries or internal financing are the most relevant mechanisms of financing when investing in innovations because they are better capable of dealing with uncertainty. Banks may be superior to markets in promoting economic development and growth. This may be particularly true in the early stages of development of both economies and firms before reputations have been established and adequate incentives exist to bring borrowers' and lenders' interests into line. In the longer term intermediaries may be less central to the development of firms. But in the early stages of the growth of firms and economies an efficient banking system may be an essential requirement for expansion. During these periods, securities markets are unlikely to be effective substitutes. The problem with internal financing is, of course, that it is not always available. Consequently I shall concentrate on financial intermediaries in this exposition, but I shall return to the analysis above at the end of this chapter. Now I shall show what the general roles of financial institutions are. This provides a basis for discussing risk taking by financial institutions in section 3.

6.2.2. The role of financial institutions

Most theories on financing are developed for the pure market case, most often under the assumption of a perfectly working market. If financial markets did function perfectly, there would be no need for financial intermediaries; borrowers would obtain there finance directly from depositors.

---

5 To modify this point one could claim that, depending on the organization and size of the firm, in some cases it would be more efficient to make an external agency or financial intermediare supervise a project. The original idea behind venture capital was among other things that firms buy "intelligent capital", i.e. they get additional competence from venture capital firms who continously participated in supervision of the project. Consultants would be non-existent if this was not the case.

"Banks, like other middlemen, have always been something of an embarrassment for mainstream neoclassical economics. Intellects nursed on Walrasian cream would be much more comfortable with an auction-type market in which ultimate savers supplied capital directly to ultimate investors." (Friedman, 1991, p.298)

However, the medium of exchange in financial markets is of a special character. To be more precise, money is exchanged for a promise of a return in the future and this implies some fundamental differences between auction markets and financial markets. As earlier explained such a promise is contingent on some advents, the likelihood of which are difficult for individual lenders to estimate.

Recent theories of financial intermediation have stressed problems related to incomplete markets and informational asymmetries discussed in chapter 3 as the causes of intermediation.[6] The argument is that asymmetric information increases decentralized - or even insider - trading. This leads to increased needs for risk diversification and consequently larger transaction costs. Therefore an efficient market is difficult to establish, and financial institutions occur to mitigate information problems.[7]

The argument rests on the (realistic) assumption, that some of the information gathered when conducting the transfer function is private to banks. This also applies to the information collected in connection with ex ante screening of projects and the ex post monitoring of the outcome of projects. Private information arises both due to scale economies (and initial costs of establishing the screening and monitoring capacity) in these functions and because the bank possesses information on the particular customer, if it is a long-term relationship. The importance of private information is further enhanced if the needs of the customer are very complex or if the project to be screened is very complex. Therefore, the

---

6 Important, early references include Leland & Pyle (1977) and Diamond (1984).

7 The asymmetric information can be reduced in several ways. A close relationship between the borrower and the lender has already been mentioned, but also signalling is a means. This signalling could take place by the management or owner's investment in the project, dividend politics, or by paying an independent institution to judge the firm (accountants, credit rating agencies etc.). There are, however, problems in judging the quality of this information.

relationship between the customer and the bank is what makes banking special (Diamond, 1984).

Essentially the above argument is that market imperfections may be mitigated by specialized financial institutions, which have economies in scale in transactions, information gathering and in portfolio management. For example the individual (principal) lender will most likely put his money in an investment fund rather than invest directly in order to take advantage of his analytical capacity and to diversify the aggregate portfolio on several borrowers. This diversification is rarely possible for an individual due to substantial transaction costs and costs of screening and monitoring. What lenders do then is to notice how the management of different investment funds perform, and subsequently to invest in the one with the expected best development of the portfolio.

Related to diversification, another function of financial institutions can be added. Financial institutions provide insurance services to both lenders and borrowers. Banks developed from a safekeeping function, but now also include various kinds of risk diversification mechanisms. Special institutions, the insurance companies, have now developed to serve this particular function.[8]

Furthermore, financial institutions have a transfer and an agglomeration function. The latter is simply to overcome problems with the size of deposits compared to demands for capital by collecting the small deposits and channelling them into larger pools of loans. The former concerns different preferences between borrowers and lenders especially with regard to time profile. For example entrepreneurs borrowing for an innovation project could not live with an early redrawal of funds, if depositors for some reason or another pulled out in an early stage of the project. Banks can help overcoming these problems and transfer short term deposits to long term investments. To attract deposits the financial institution offers financial advice, accounting, security, admission to loans and interest rates.

---

8 Actually the merchants in the Mediterenian started to organize the insurance principle systematically 1000 years ago. On the average one out of every seven ships was plundered. Therefore seven merchants made a profit sharing deal and collectively paid for the plundered cargo.

From a social point of view the ability to distinguish between good and bad projects is important to the aggregate use of resources in the economy, to the direction of technology and to the evolutionary viability of the economy. Competence to screen projects is important to financial institutions because they are themselves subject to a selection pressure[9]. Competition ensures to that those institutions showing little screening efficiency are eventually eliminated. This selection pressure is consequently important if continuously bad screening is to be avoided.

The mere action of banks towards firms is in itself an information transfer. Individuals are not able to obtain all the information the bank has, and the public takes a credit judgement by the bank seriously. Thus, banks function as a kind of social accountants by classifying firms through their screening procedure (Stiglitz & Weiss, 1988). This classification is reflected in the interest rate policy, in issuing guaranties to selected firms, and in the content of contracts.

Both debt and equity financing faces the problem of screening cheaters, who deliberately or unintendedly exaggerate the expected outcome of the project, but the relationship between the firm and the financial institution, which is normal through loan financing, helps identifying "charlatans".

> "While the selection problem arises in both credit and equity markets, the scope that equity contracts provide for charlatans makes these contracts extremely attractive to them, and makes the selection problem central there". (Greenwald & Stiglitz, 1990, p.10)

One of the reasons, is that there is often a volatile and diverse population of owners of equities.[10] Another is problems of one-way communication,

---

9 Criteria for screening is likely to differ between the two viewpoints. If seen for the economy as a whole it may be disereable to let some technological prosperous innovation projects pass screening procedure even if not directly profitable measured in market terms. On the other hand, commercial success is the dominant criteria in private financial institutions, although deviations from this criteria occur.

10 If this is the case another problem arises: there may in general be conflicting interests between managers and shareholders (as has been discussed intensely in the literature), but in this case it is a problem to identify what the interests of the shareholders are in the first place. In addition, attempts to improve management is a public good - that is, some efforts

but I shall return to this issue later.[11] Now the basis is established for discussing some aspects of taking a risk by financial institutions.

6.3. Determinants of risk willingness in banks

In chapter 5 some of the most important requirements for innovation financing were listed in the perspective of the single innovation project. Whether these requirements are met or not is of course not only dependent upon the attitude of the lender but also on the general conditions for the lender. I shall now turn to those underlying factors determining the risk willingness of the lender[12]. In particular I shall point to seven determinants.

Firstly, the past performance of the bank is important to how willingly banks go into risky lending arrangements. The overall profitability of the bank, and especially the amount of losses on loans to industry are taken into account before further investments. The development of the projects, which the bank is already financing, will also influence incentives to risky behaviour.[13]

Secondly, the mere composition of the outstanding loan portfolio has an impact upon possibilities to meet the innovation financing requirements above. In principle, banks try to borrow long and lend short in order to minimize liquidity fluctuations, and a too short termed portfolio may restrict a bank from long term innovation financing.

---

by a fraction of the shareholders will benefit all shareholders.

11 The logical consequense of this, is that selection is a relatively important function of financial institutions and markets in financial systems with emphasis on equity financing compared to financial systems where credit financing is the predominant way of financing investments (Dosi, 1990) (Christensen, 1992). This point is explained in chapter 7.

12 Willingness to take a risk is not something easily defined and determined. Whether or not banks are risk avers is nevertheless often discussed. For example, one evaluation of the Report to The Wilson Committee stated that "deciding on commercial viability involves taking risks, which institutions are not good at; indeed their obligations to their own customers or members make them cautious and rulebound." (Ray and Hutchison, 1984, p.137).

13 The ability of third world countries to pay back loans to U.S. banks may for example influence loan decisions and collateral requirements in these banks in the domestic market.

Thirdly, macroeconomic fluctuations have an impact. For example increased profitability in the corporate sector increases possibilities for self financing, decreasing dependency on the banks. Moreover, increased profitability may lead to better possibilities for collateral, and in combination with general prosperous outlooks for industry, this will be an incentive for banks to take risks. Another example on the impact of macroeconomic fluctuations is an investment boom in industry. This may increase demands for loans as may a rapid technological development. Reactions in banks are difficult to determine a priori without close examination of the circumstances surrounding an investment boom or rapid technological change. In a generally optimistic business climate banks are likely to be more prone to finance risky investments than if investments are mostly for restructuring a crisis ridden business.

Fourthly, structural change within the financial sector will affect willingness to take risks. Increased competition between banks may force banks into more risky loans, but competition from other financial institutions, may also have this effect.[14] On the other hand, the competition pressure may get so severe that banks cut expenses by reducing personnel who should otherwise contribute to the knowledge base of screening and monitor innovations. The development in revenue of alternative investments is another factor affecting incentives to finance innovations.

Fifthly, the regulatory framework affects risk willingness in several ways. One is credit rationing from the central bank (which can take various forms such as loan limits, oral warnings to the banking sector etc.), which is in turn often a consequence of government monetary policy. Another is the specific regulations of the banking sector such as requirements for solidity, aimed at increasing the overall stability of the financial sector and protecting investors. A third is the regulation of what is defined as banking, i.e. the regulations determining the division of labour between financial institutions. An important example is the degree of involvement of bank ownership of industry.[15] Finally, requirements for introduction on the stock exchange can

---

14 In the present trends of increased internationalization of financial markets, one could add a competition pressure from foreign financial institutions.

15 This aspect is dealt with in further detail in chapter 7 and 8.

be mentioned as a regulation indirectly affecting the behaviour of banks towards innovation financing.

Connected to the regulatory framework the nature of loan contracts affects behaviour as previously mentioned. Thus, the relation between the downside risk and the potential upside gain, is important to risk willingness. In most countries there is a limit to how high an interest rate can be, even if it is a very risky project. The amount of money lost on a failed project usually corresponds to gains from several successful projects, if banks are only allowed to take a limited risk premium. Consequently, debt financing is sometimes combined with some kind of profit sharing, but the precise potential revenues of the project are always compared to the risk of loosing all the money lent. The first part of the argument - that a limited possibility of taking risk premia may hamper innovation financing - is most likely not very strong at all. Even substantially increased risk premia would not prevent banks from rejecting an applicant if they have reasons to believe that his project is a very risky investment. The other part of the argument, however, provides a stronger argument for hampering innovation financing.

The seventh determinant of risk willingness in banks concerns the time horizon banks employ on investments. Time horizons determine risk willingness but at the same time are themselves determined by risk willingness. This is an important topic and in subsequent chapters I shall frequently refer to time horizons in investments. Therefore, I shall elaborate upon the topic, broaden it a bit, and give it its own subsection.

6.4. Time horizons in financial institutions versus those in technical innovations -a temporal mismatch?

Innovations are evaluated mainly using financial criteria in a private business. But it is of utmost importance when this is done, or in other words in what time perspective financial criteria are used for evaluation. Since the innovation process is often separated physically from the financing of that process there is no guarantee that the surroundings (read sources of external finance or other departments internally in the firm) have the same perception of what a reasonable time perspective in innovations is.

Previously I mentioned the differences in time perspective between ordinary investments and innovations. There seems to be a difference in time perspective between different financial institutions, as well as one, between the same kind of financial institutions in different countries. The debate on this difference has been intense, and especially the fear of "short-termism" in the anglo-saxon countries has been put forward as a major obstacle to industrial development in these countries[16]. This discussion has been going on for some time. Thus, Dean (1974, p.12) pointed to exactly the issues still debated almost twenty years later:

> "Why is management's view so short sighted? It is because most U.S. industrial corporations are automatons, whose strings are manipulated by financial minds to perform the current-profit/stock-price dance before institutional stock owners, directed in turn by financial minds. It is because the omnipotence of financial analysts judging the value of a company's stock (and often by long-term-insensitive indicators) has brought to the top of many major U.S. corporations men with the narrow, specialized training of the accountant. It is because the money game now dominates our industry. It is because boards of directors have become minions of the stock market. It is because our business schools have taught that profit is all. It is because profit has been read as short term profit (i.e. this year's profit)."

But why are there differences in time perspectives between financial institutions and between financial institutions in different countries? There is a wide range of determinants of lenders time perspective some of them are more or less inherent characteristic of innovation processes compared to ordinary investments while others are more institutional or cultural bound and therefore may explain cross-country differences.

As mentioned in chapter 5, the duration and costs of developing a product are highly uncertain and usually under-estimated. Likewise is the introduction on the market concerning the reactions of customers.

---

16 The general view is, that short-termism is most pronounced in the U.K. and the U.S, whereas German and Japanese shareholders act more as investors, rather than traders in shares. See the discussion in The Economist, May 5, 1990.

Development costs set an objective amount of receipts which is necessary for compensating for expenses. But as explained in chapter 5 the time the product is sellable has generally decreased in recent years due to rapid technological and social changes. This makes it even more difficult to predict future long-term commercial perspectives of a product which may cause lenders to desist from long-term projects. If they are expecting a return in a short term, or are reluctant to finance extra development costs this may pose problems on innovation projects.

Not only the uncertainty in long term innovation projects may cause managers and markets to emphasize the short-term performance, but also the costs of capital and the acceptable returns on investments. Ellsworth(1985) has compared these in the U.S. Japan and Germany. A lower acceptable return on investments and lower costs of capital in Germany and Japan allow firms in these countries to undertake investments with a time horizon, that U.S. managers would find unacceptable. This applies especially for innovation projects and investments in penetrating new markets (op.cit. p.177).

In innovation projects time horizons are thought usually more important than costs of capital (cost of capital and time horizons are of course interrelated to some extent). In addition to the arguments in chapter three against the importance of interest rates pure calculations would show this.

International deviations in costs of capital and time perspectives are in turn to a large extent explained by the relations between the corporate and financial sector in the countries. In Germany and Japan ties with banks are much stronger than in the U.S., and there is a heavy reliance on debt financing rather than equity. This has important implications: Banks in these countries are more prone to support firms in financial distress (Hoshi et.al., 1990); banks have an incentive to support the long-term growth of firms and banks influence decisions in firms to ensure compatibility of corporate goals.

For the time horizon this is important in several ways. The equity holdings of banks are rarely traded, and managers are more oriented toward the growth of the firm rather than the short-term profit performance. The large degree of loans in financing the corporate sector makes the banks interested in expanding the business of the firm, thereby increasing the demand for the services and loans of the bank, rather than increase the prices on stocks to get a capital gain. Therefore there is less pressure towards increasing short term stock exchange performance. The degree of loyalty (and overlapping ownership) between the bank and the customer also has an impact. If banks have a long term relationship with the firm, possibilities for gathering information and monitoring the firm increases, and the negative sides of debt financing (increased sensitivity to liquidity fluctuations) is off-set. Consequently the cost of capital is reduced and investment projects with a longer time horizon become possible.

Differences also arise in the information exchange between lenders and borrowers, according to the time perspectives and institutional set up of financial systems. If lenders trade their shares in a fluctuating manner, they are more concerned with diversifying investments and risks than with obtaining information on how the firm is doing in the long run, and how they may be able to influence decisions. This information is, of course, relatively more expensive the more the portfolio is diversified, and emphasis tends to be on the short term value of assets and possibilities of arbitrage, instead of long-term growth and technological development (Tylecote and Demirag, 1991). The consequence for technology financing is a pressure on projects to show results in a period of time that may be inexpedient to innovation.

Thus, there are differences in which pay-back periods firms and banks employ. These are dependent on the expectations on the development of competing technologies and cost of capital. This is only the micro level of aggregation. At the national level, differences in pay-back periods also exists (Silverberg, 1990). These are rooted in the historical, cultural and social characteristics of the society (Tylecote and Demirag, 1991), and tend to limit the importance of the size of interest rates.

Finally, the incentive structure of management differs. Ellsworth (1985, p.182) mentions that U.S. managers are held accountable and rewarded for the development in their companies' short-term profitability, and therefore are reluctant to undertake long term projects, that may disturb short-term gains.

One could go on by asking why different relationships between financial institutions and industry exists. I shall return to that subject in chapter 7. At this stage I shall only mention that choice of governance structure explained at the outset of this chapter may have important implications for possibilities of hostile take-overs which in turn affects time horizons in investment strategies. If take-overs are a large part of allocation in the market for corporate control and firms are largely equity financed there is probably a larger incentive for sticking to short-sighted investment strategies (Hall, 1991).

In addition, Dean and Tylecote & Demirag are right in pointing to the importance of historical and cultural factors. Veblen (1919) emphasized these factors as well, as was described in chapter 2. Dean (1974, p.13) refers to an investigation on a number of major innovations from year of conception to first realization. On the average the duration of innovations was 19 years ranging from 6 to 32 years. The inherent logic of The City and other parts of the financial institutions is not geared to time perspectives of that length.

6.5. Various degrees of active bank behaviour

The degree of risk aversion in banks is, however, not only dependent upon the above discussed determinants. Even if it may be objectively able and willing to take a risk in a particular situation a bank may not wish to take the risk because it is incompatible with the general strategical considerations in the bank. In different institutional environments and in different epochs of time, there will be various degrees of how active banks are in financing innovations and in how deeply it is involved in the industry sphere.

Following Dahmén (1988c) and partly following the routine-innovative dichotomy previously discussed behaviour of banks is below grouped into three different degrees and modes of bank conduct in the industry sphere. Even though a bank should adopt one particular kind of behaviour as its main strategy, there is no reason to believe that different activities could not co-exist. A conscious selection of strategically important firms as clients and partners may be important for a bank and in industrial change within one sector, but a bank may choose another strategy towards financing firms in another sector.

One class of bank activities is their function as intermediaries in a rather passive way. Banks serve as a link between credit-worthy borrowers and the credit market, and investment decisions - as well as other issues about the management of the client firms - are not interfered with by the bank. The selection of credit acceptance is highly routinized and in principle anonymous or even one-time relations.

Another kind of bank behaviour is in situations in which banks discriminate between clients based on a selection of firms who have developed stable relations to the bank over time. In some cases the bank or its affiliated companies are among the owners of the firms and bank representatives may join the board of a client firm but usually as observers and monitors. Though some kind of mutual business advantages is expected firms may have more than one bank connection. Usually the bank does not use a firms' dependency on the bank to control the client firm or to take strategic actions.

The third classification I want to make, is that in which banks have a decisive control over important industrial firms, and actually use this potential power to influence industrial change. The means of control are various from direct minority or majority ownership to informal "gentlemen agreements". There are of course differences in the needs for bank action depending on the current trends in business. Both a highly positive trend and a crisis might lead to action by the bank either through giving credit to prospective firms/industries or through a measure of restructuring firms of industries in crises.

There are of course some institutional boundaries for bank behaviour. Regulations impose a limit not only on who is permitted to do banking in what regions, but also on how banking business is to be performed. Even though many countries are deregulating their financial systems there are still national rules on what a bank may do and not do. In addition, there are limits to what extent it can do the businesses permitted. One important legislation in relation to the present subject is the regulation controlling banks owning shares and providing venture capital to businesses. In Denmark banks are allowed to own shares in a firm up to a limit; Germany and Japan allows extensive bank ownership of industry; the well-known Glass-Steagall Act in the U.S. divides commercial and investment banks, and in Sweden commercial banks were prohibited from owning shares in 1933. In addition governments - or rather national banks - regulate banking by way of ceilings on loans, cash requirements, solidity, interest rate ceilings etc.

Theoretical exercises on the behaviour of financial institutions in general and banks in particular, are important to the coming chapters as well as in themselves. In the next section I shall extend the theoretical elaborations by modelling risk taking by banks.

6.6. Modelling risk taking with the borrower and the lender

6.6.1. Introduction

In this section I shall show how risk taking may be modelled. I shall start out with a keynesian inspired model which incorporates uncertainty and the views of both lender and borrower simultaneously. However, two major points of criticism are levied against it and this motivates alternative suggestions. I shall consequently develop another model and last consider how to pursue further modelling, which is closer to how the innovation process takes place.

6.6.2. A model of borrowers and lenders risk

This model is inspired by work of Hyman Minsky (1975, 1989, 1990). I have adjusted the model to illustrate investments in innovations rather than ordinary investments, but the basic features of the model remain largely the same. A firm in this exposition decides to invest in an innovation project. It has expectations, denoted Qie, to gross profits after taxes, payments on debt and dividends, in the coming period corresponding to what the expected internal financing capacity of that firm will be in the subsequent period where the investment is undertaken. As previously discussed the supply price of capital assets in innovation projects are highly uncertain, and consequently this is also an expected figure, denoted P^{ie}. The possible investments to finance internally is then expected to be $I^{ie} = Q^{ie}_{t-1}/P^{ie}$.

Let us consider a situation where the firm decides to invest more than I^{ie}, and consequently has to apply for external finance.

The estimation of Q^{ie} is a subjective judgement, which is not necessarily the same by the lender and the borrower. Actually, the borrower will most likely tend to estimate the risks lower than the lender. The risk estimated by the borrower is denoted (r_1). The risks of the borrower is determined by the confidence in the estimation of net returns, which in turn depends on the expected costs of the innovation and the demand for the product.
The lenders' judgement (r) of the borrower will be $r = r_1 + ar1$, with $0<a<1$. As discussed in chapter 4 there is a variety of determinants of risks, but let us just mention the borrowers' estimation of the technical and market uncertainty, denoted (r_1) and the judgement of the borrowers ability and willingness to fulfill the contract (r_2). Other determinants are denoted (r_n), the aggregate risk premium Σr, and transaction costs t. Then $\Sigma r = (r_1 + ar_1) + r_2 + r_n + t$.

In the illustration below the x-axis is the level of investments (in money terms). The y-axis is two-dimensional: the expected costs of the investments (P^{ie})[17], and the demand price for loans (PL) (which among other things depend on Q^{ie}). Q^{ie} is included in order to show the share of the investment necessary to finance externally.

The demand price for loans (PL) will thus depend on the entrepreneurs capitalization of expected net cash flows, using a capitalization factor $1/(1+e)$, where e is an internal interest rate. As long as the demand price is higher than expected costs on the investment, the entrepreneur is willing to undertake the project. This price will decrease with increased debt-equity ratio, because the required repayments on debt are certain, while the cash-

---

17 This is for simplicity drawn horizontal, which means that the expectations of the investor are assumed constant, and the level of investment is assumed not to affect the supply price of the investment good.

flow is uncertain (Minsky, 1975, p.108). The entrepreneur will hedge against increased risk of default by lowering PL with increased d/e ratio.

The lender will, on the other hand, take an extra risk premium as the debt-equity ratio increases. Thus, the lenders risk increases with the investment level above what is internally financed.

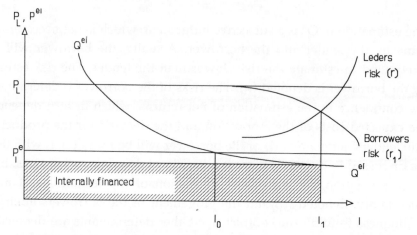

The intersection of the demand and supply curves for loans (r_1 and r) determines what scale of investment is possible. Various slopes of the curves could be applied, e.g. as a consequence of changing expectations to sales, changing judgments of the borrower etc., and there will be a different level of investment for each shape of curve.

This model is said to capture important aspects of the innovation financing process. However, two major points of criticism invalidate this picture. Firstly, as with the models discussed in chapter 3 the time perspective is under-emphasized. The model describes a one-time contracting situation. Therefore, it is unable to take into account lenders' strategical considerations and reputation effects. Secondly, the model is only valid in a very narrow sense. The implicit assumptions are that of a capital market based financial system, where prices are clearing supply and demand for credit. As previously discussed, this is a limited part of how external financing for investments is taking place. Another exposition is called for.

6.6.3. An alternative model for bank behaviour

In this section I shall discuss the behaviour of banks - or more broadly financial institutions - towards financing innovations in terms of a model which incorporates some of the points of behaviour developed in chapter 4, takes strategical considerations by banks into account, and is valid for more than one period. The method used in accomplishing this will be through setting up two extreme cases of stylized behaviour. One is an entrepreneurial type of bank, which meets many of the requirements discussed in section 6.5, while the other is for a more cautious bank, which in Schumpeterian terms is more prone to finance circular flow investments. Subsequently I shall discuss how an hypothetical average bank (AB), chooses its mix of these behaviours over time.

Let us take a closer look at these two types, starting out with the pro-innovation type of bank, denoted IB for innovative bank. The scope of business for this bank includes innovations, but not necessarily within established, known technologies. The bank also engages in projects exploring new areas of use for known technologies or completely new technologies. Thus the bank not only learns retrospectively or by establishing routines, it also learns by experimenting. It is also a financial innovator, as it invents and introduces new financial products and services. Projects are screened by judging the potentials of the investment project and the technology in terms of creating new markets or prolonging existing markets. In general the time perspective and pay-back periods are long. The bank will experience many failed projects, but a few successful projects will provide a substantial financial backing for the failures. There is usually an element of profit sharing in the investment. Often the strategy of the bank is to restructure and actively participate in industrial, structural change.

The routine bank (RB), on the other hand, is financing known technologies in well established technological trajectories, and its investment behaviour is highly routinized. Past, successful behaviour is transferred to new situations, and the learning takes place through evaluating relatively rigid routines. These routines will tend to be self-reinforcing as long as the expected outcome is approximately corresponding to the real. The screening of projects takes place on the basis of past performance of the firm plus the available security. The income from projects is a stable flow of relatively small amounts on short term projects.

The behaviour of the average bank (A^{ab}) is a mix of these two extremes. In the process of financing innovation projects, the bank learns and adjust the behaviour accordingly. Once again I must emphasize the theoretical, simplified character of this discussion. There is no reason why a bank should choose one specific mix of behaviour instead of simultaneously using different kinds of behaviour towards different - or even similar - investment projects. However, if we for a moment consider an average case, then the mix may be chosen as illustrated formally in equation (1) below.

(1) $A_t^{ab} = \sigma_t A^{ib} + (1 - \sigma_t) A_t^{rb}$

where $1 > \sigma > 0$, denoting the weight the banks put on the behaviour of the innovative bank. This weight is in turn determined by

(2) $\sigma_t = f(\alpha A_{t-1}^{ib} / \alpha A_{t-1}^{rb})$

(where $1 > f > 0$)

(3) $\alpha_t^{ib} = f(\hat{u}_i - u_i)_{t-1}$

(4) $\alpha_t^{rb} = f(\hat{u}_t - u_t)_{t-1}$

with α denoting an index for the ex post performance of the mix of behaviour. α is thus determined by the indexes $(\hat{u}_i - u_i)_t$ and $(\hat{u}_r - u_r)_t$ which describe the difference between the performance of the actually pursued purely innovative and routinized policy respectively, compared to the potential performance of the two groups had they financed all the projects they were offered. In other words, $\hat{u}_i$ is the performance of the actual persued innovative policy. u_i is the performance of the potential innovative policy. $\hat{u}_r$ is the performance of the actual routinized policy, and u_r is the performance of the potential routinized policy.[18] This demands an assumption , that the bank is following the projects they rejected which are financed elsewhere, and it is necessary that the bank can distinguish between the two types of behaviour. These assumptions are, however, not unrealistic.

In the subsequent period a change in behaviour will be

$$(5) \quad \Delta A_{t+1} = \gamma \sigma_{t+1} \Delta A_{ib}^{i} + (1 - \sigma_{t+1}) \Delta A_{t}^{rb}$$

,where γ is an adjustment variable regulating the speed at which the bank learns from the past performance α if the bank considers past information to be valuable at all. γ is a key variable, which can change over time and is dependent on a number of factors discussed in section 6.3.

By the end of each period[19] - in practice continuously - the bank evaluates the performance of innovative and routinized behaviour and adjusts the future behaviour accordingly. Banks are bounded rational in this model. Moreover, they employ "irrational" considerations (which are of course very rational, but not in a strictly economic sense) listed in the schematic model below, in addition to the surroundings guiding behaviour.[20]

---

18 A common method would be to relate the performance to the average performance of the banking sector. However, in this model there is less than perfect information. In other words the average performance is not known to the banks; hence they use this kind of evaluaton method.

19 In many dynamic models the subscript t is never defined. It is a sign denoting time but it is rarely considered what periods are and if they themselves are constant or vary over time. This deficiency is particular pronounced in theoretical stylized models. In predictive models meant for testing a given set of data the organisation of the data most often on a yearly basis, determines what t covers. Two kinds of periods are relevant in this kind of model. One is the duration of a single financing arrangement. Experience from each project could be incorporated after its termination. Another is the duration of an accounting period - usually a year. Experience is then drawn from the development of the aggregate port folio of firms.

20 The bank in this model is bounded rational and forms its expectations partly in an adaptive way partly by whim, or perhaps could it be called animal spirit. The adjustment variable γ regulates the relative importance of the formation of expectations. The bank is not only bounded rational in the usual sense. As previously discussed there are some institutional, regulatory boundaries for the bank.

Figure 6.2.: Determinants of bank behaviour

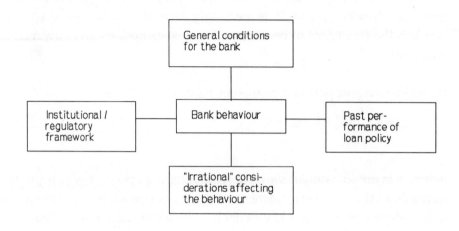

One such irrational consideration concerns the time perspective. For example it may be that in order to maintain a customer, the bank is behaving irrational in the short term, hoping to gain in the longer run. Another not strictly economic rational behaviour could be a preference to support regional, local industry, e.g. by rescuing firms in crises, even though it is not profitable in the long run. A third could be that banks want to establish or maintain a certain image. Finally, it has been suggested, that some banks tend to have a "herding" behaviour, i.e. small banks are adopting the behaviour of larger banks in order to benefit from the larger screening and monitoring capacity of these banks and to feel more secure about lending decisions.[21]

One kind of behaviour may be more appropriate towards one kind of investments than others. In general, the more radical the technical innovation, the more risk willing, innovative behaviour is necessary. This is of course a very pro-innovator statement. As discussed in chapter 5 there is usually a higher risk connected to these investments. Therefore, it is only natural that investors are more cautious to go into these projects. In any case it will take a high degree of knowledge and competence to evaluate the risk and immaterial investments usually involved in such ventures.

---

21 See Jain & Gupta (1987) and Torell & Dohner (1987)

Furthermore, the degree of discretionary screening and monitoring is likely to affect learning effects and consequently possibilities of adjusting or building routinized behaviour.

6.6.4. Extending the model - an evolutionary theory on the behaviour of financial institutions towards financing innovations

The simple, stylized model above incorporates many of the previously discussed requirements to a model describing the innovation process. It intends to establish procedures for decisions to finance in a process perspective; it considers transformation through feed-back from one state of routines to another; agents are bounded rational and imperfect decision makers; and some kind of path-dependency is included in that successful past behaviour is self-reinforcing. All in all it includes some of the properties of what could be termed an evolutionary model.

An evolutionary approach to innovation studies has emerged[22] during the past decade[23]. Analytical focus and method in this approach is useful for studying the evolution of new technology. However, the process of financing innovations may also be analysed using that framework. It is not the purpose of this book to formalize an evolutionary model of financing innovations[24] but I shall mention a few basic propertes of such a model.

With analogies to biology, it is essential in evolutionary models to explain transmission-, variation-, and selection mechanisms. In the economics of technological change this would imply explaining transmission of behavioural rules, changes in such conventions, and specifying the selection mechanisms such as competition and the capital market. Features of evolutionary modelling of financing innovation would, cf. chapter 4, include

---

22 Actually "reemerged" ought to be the term because evolutionary thought was used quite early in the history of economic theory. See for instance Marshall (1898), Schumpeter (1912/1934) and the austrians. Alchian (1950) is another, more recent example. In 1898 Veblen wrote an article entitled "Why is economics not an evolutionary science?".

23 A seminal contribution is Nelson & Winther, which in turn owes a lot to Alchian (1950), Simon (1976) and Cyert & March (1963).

24 Silverberg (1988) formalizes evolutionary models in line with Nelson & Winther (1982). Schuette (1980) includes financial rules and capital market in his evolutionary model of industry growth.

a specification of behavioural rules as well as the environment in which the firm and the financier operates.

To be more precise the latter involves a competition intensive, uncertain, and information-poor environment (in evolutionary modelling a specification of information is important). It was explained in chapter 4 what the uncertainties were with respect to the firm and in this chapter uncertainty was further specified with the financier as the primary point of departure. Decision rules with respect to innovation in the firm were discussed in chapter 5 and corresponding rules for banks are dealt with here in chapter 6. The information deficiencies were dealt with in chapter 3 and 4 and the institutional environment, which is also of great importance to uncertainty is dealt with in chapter 7 and 8. The previous discussions on the uncertainty in the process of innovation financing has been linked to how firms and financiers react to this environment.

What they do in evolutionary models - and in the model above - is to use routinized decision rules to guide behaviour. For example, firms establish investment rules depending among other things on the initial capital structure in the firm, retained earnings, and the nature of external financing. These rules are adjusted according to changes in the competitive environment and according to results of the rules in previous periods. On the other hand financiers establish lending routines, and parameters in these routines may include capital structure in the applicant firm, collateral, solvency, estimated uncertainty, and retained earnings.

For both the firm and the financier their long-running competitiveness is determined by the appropriability of decision rules to the selection environment. Firms are selected by industrial competition as well as by financial institutions (when firms need external capital). These selection mechanisms enhance some decision rules relative to others. Thus, compatibility of decision rules in firms and financiers may be essential for firms in the possibility of obtaining external finance. The interplay between these decision rules in financial institutions is also subject to selection. The rules in financial institutions may change in response to experience of whether the screening procedure selects a satisfactory ratio of succesful projects to failures.

In an evolutionary theory the variation mechanism in the industry and financial sphere is, respectively technical innovations and financial innovations. These "mutations", to use the biological analogy, act as progressive factors in the evolution of the industry and the financial sector. Thus, the evolution of a financial system may be driven by the effect on standardized financial routines of financial innovation that facilitate more efficient operating procedures. Financial systems capable of absorbing and developing such innovations may be more viable in the long run relative to other systems. The particular "mutation" is thus contributing to what area of business the financial system is good at serving compared to other areas.

To sum up, the overall structure of such an evolutionary theory of innovations with special attention paid to the financing of innovations is suggested in figure 6.3.

Figure 6.3. Linkages in an evolutionary model of financing innovations

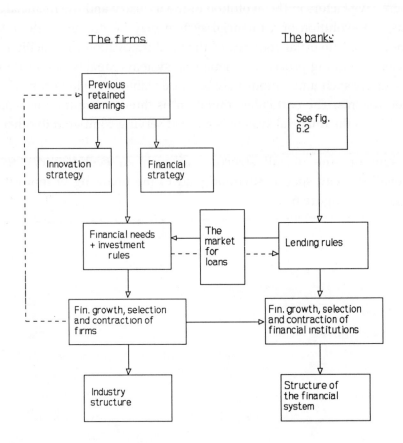

In the first chapter it was pointed out that the behaviour of financial agents is important to the system level as well as the micro level. Figure 6.3. illuminates this statement in that decision rules in financial institutions and markets are decisive for firms wishing to innovate. Furthermore, it confirms the importance of bank-industry interplay emphasized earlier. Financial needs and investment rules are adapted to external financing conditions (i.e. rules in financial institutions) but a mutual influence is shown in the figure. The growth and contraction of firms will have a spill-over effect on the performance of financial institutions and -markets, and this will in turn make financial agents adjust decision rules.[25]In addition, although weak, a direct influence (shown as a dotted line between financial needs/investment rules and lending rules in financial institutions) is likely to occur because, for reasons discussed in section 4.5.2., articulation of financial needs of firms may have an effect on how lending procedures look in the future.

Extensions and specifications of this model may render fruitful analytical tools in the analysis of the process of innovation financing. There are, of course, limits to how far you can get with stylized, highly theoretical models showing human decisions in uncertain situations. Such decisions are highly influenced by the context in which they are taken. In particular, institutions may be guidelines for behaviour in uncertain situations. I shall now leave the theoretical perspectives in favour of a more concrete, institutional point of view.

6.7. The ability of specific financial institutions to support investments in new technology

6.7.1. Introductory reservations

I shall now turn to an analysis of different kinds of financial institutions in relation to the above (chapter 5) discussed requirements for innovation financing. Again I shall take the "archetype approach", and speak of typical institutions in spite of international differences, or even differences within nations. This reservation is a strong one because defining an average bank involves aggregation of banks, which may be very unlike each other.

The institutions are not isolated. The role and behaviour of an institution depends on the existence of the other institutions and the specific division of labour developed in the concrete socio-economic context. This interdependence poses another problem for the present "archetype approach". In addition, one could ask if it is financial instruments that matter rather than institutions. It is difficult to keep the discussion of instru-

---

25 As discussed in the previous section and illustrated in figure 6.2. decision rules are determined by a number of factors other than past performance.

ments strictly apart from institutions, but the starting point here is financial institutions, but not just any institution. Those treated here are chosen on their relevance to innovation financing, and the criteria for evaluating them are derived from the discussion on requirements for innovation financing in section 5.5.

There is obviously a danger of making a too static analysis of financial institutions. Some financial institutions are appropriate for financing innovation at one stage of development, while others are better suited for entering at another stage. Moreover, institutions may change character and behaviour over time. Consequently one of the points to keep in mind is the time perspective of the innovation financing process, discussed in section 5.3. In addition, perhaps the ability of changing the institutional setting rather than having an established, inflexible range of institutions, is the most important merit of a financial system supporting technological investments in a rapidly changing industrial and financial world.

The way to approach this comparison of requirements for innovation financing and features of financial institutions is to, firstly, give a short description of the institutions chosen and the criteria used for evaluating them[26]; a schematic illustration of the relation between these institutions and requirements for innovation financing follows, and finally a more thorough discussion of the pros and cons of these institutions ends this section.

6.7.2. Selected institutions and innovation financing requirements

Although the group *"banks"* actually ought to be divided into several subgroups covering universal banks, investment banks and commercial banks, the broad concept of banks is used and related to innovation financing. Several different kinds of institutional investors now enter corporate finance, but *pension funds* are chosen as representatives of these

---

26 The analysis could be simplified if divided into the three governance types dealt with at the beginning of the chapter. However, in order to get closer to the differences between financial intermediation and thus, be better equipped for giving policy recommendations, financial intermediares are specified and financing in hierachies largely neglected.

(which also include insurance companies)[27]. *Venture capital institutions* are chosen because of their direct orientation towards innovation financing, but again there are many different kinds of venture capital institutions. In addition, they are not easily separated from the other institutions, because they are often owned by banks, government or pension funds or part of their funding comes from these sources.[28] *Government institutions* are often an important source of financing in early stage, and there is a considerable debate on the way government supports technological development. Again there is a variety of institutions, but they are all included under the general heading government institutions. Finally I evaluate *the stock market* as a source of finance for innovation. In principle, this corresponds to the market way of financing in the triad of section 6.1, although some semi-debt instruments like junk bonds may be subject to the market way of financing but not belong to the stock market.

The innovation financing requirements have already been discussed in section 5.5. They are, of course, also interdependent but I have chosen to separate them into:

- time horizon

- screening effectiveness, which among other things is the ability to judge market- and technical uncertainty

---

27 With some important exceptions the role of institutional investors in innovation financing is mainly indirect in that they often finance more specialized institutions like venture capital firms.

28 An EVCA survey from 1990 lists that the volume of venture capital funds in Europe comes from[%]:

Private individuals	3.7
Corporate investors	5.1
Government agencies	2.7
Banks	39.3
Pension funds	16.1
Insurance	15.2
Universities	0.4
Other	6.7
Reinvested venture profits	10.7

- closeness between borrower and lender. The distance in question relates to cultural, economic, organizational and geographical distance. This variable is very much intermingled with some of the other categories, and has a lot to do with information processing and -transmission.

- flexibility, understood as the ability to adapt to changing conditions in production, and in the financial sector, or the ability to utilise or invent new financial innovations.

- the advising capacity of the institution. This is taken into account, because additional competence rather than solely finance is sometimes what firms need, when implementing an idea.

- accumulation of knowledge, which is the ability of financial institutions to store generated knowledge about the financing process and the industry in general.

- monitoring effectiveness, which is closely related to the closeness and the accumulation of knowledge, but it is also an important factor in itself.

6.7.3. An overwiev of the pros and cons of different kinds of financial institutions in relation to innovation financing requirements

This schematic overview of how the institutions relate to requirements for innovation financing, should be interpreted with some caution. In the table below a + stands for a pro-innovation financing concern, a % indicates that the institution is not well suited for meeting this aspect of the requirements, and a 0 is neutral. Adding the +,% and 0's and thus concluding which institutions should be built to induce investments in new technology, would not make sense for several reasons. First, the different aspects quoted are not all equally important and their relevance is likely to vary with the specific project in question. Secondly, the institutions may be suited to support the same project at different stages, i.e. they often supplement rather than provide alternatives to each other. Thirdly, the financial system serves other purposes than innovation financing, and so do the institutions. Therefore, recommendations would only apply to the innovation financing aspect of the financial system, while there are a variety of other tasks for the system.

Nevertheless, the analysis has ultimately been done in order to provide a basis for evaluating different set-ups of financial systems in relation to innovation financing. Below are some hints on which institutions are better or worse in this respect.

Requirements Institutions	Time horizon	Screen efficiency	Close- ness	Flexibi- lity	Advice efficiency	Accum. of knowledge	Monetoring efficiency
Banks	0	0	+	0	+	0	0
Government institutions	+	+	+/%	%	+	+	%
Vent. cap. institutions	+/%	+	+	0	+	+	+
Pension funds	+	%	0	0	%	0	0
Stock market	%	0	%	+	%	%	%

From this overview *banks* may seem to be largely neutral in what advantages and disadvantages they have. Time horizons differ a lot between banks and between projects. It is hardly fair to say that they are particularly short-sighted or employ a long-term time horizon. On the other hand, banks are concerned with their liquidity. Consequently they generally try to borrow long-term and lend short-term and this may lead to a short time horizon.

Screening capacity usually does not match specialized government agencies or venture capital firms but later stage financing is usually made entirely by using financial criteria.[29] Venture financing is, to the extent they do it, often made by affiliates specialized in that field.

---

29   In an empirical investigation of credit judgement capabilities in Swedish banks Edenius & Bäckstrand (1989, p.136) found that even banks themselves see government agencies as superiour in credit judgement. A typical statement from the interviews was that: "Even if we in the banks have a considerable more business-like way of judging financial risks then the government agencies have, we must admit, they possess better competence for judging the technical perspectives in a project. In addition, they make considerable more thorough evaluation of market potentials etc. Such things we are in fact, generally, not able to handle. Furthermore, we cannot afford investigating infinetely."

Relationships to borrowers differ substantially. In some countries there is a tradition for very strong relationships while other banks are not close to their customers to the same degree.

Flexibility is set as neutral although recent liberalizations may induce a further flexibility. It shows in expansion of areas of business and penetration of foreign markets. However, some rigidities are likely to persist depending on the organization and size of the bank in question.

The advising capacity of banks is likely to differ according to what stage the firm is in. Economic management of a company already set up and running is presumably the area where banks are best at advising whereas technology management is difficult for a bank to assess.

If banks spend resources on accumulation of skills in screening it is possible to accumulate experience from previous contracts. On the other hand, turbulence in the banking sector has made personnel enter and leave the sector and shift between banks. In this way people with valuable knowledge and skills may leave the banks.

Monitoring capacity is of course also dependent on the amount of resources spend on it. Banks sometimes have supervisors on the board of firms but usually banks finance by way of debt and this leaves them with limited resources to take actions against inexpedient developments in the project.

To sum up, banks are perhaps too diverse to put in a scheme like this. There is scope for both + and % in each category but actual practices level out differences in behaviour.

Government institutions are likewise difficult to treat too schematically. They often finance by grants or subsidised loans and often they do not expect a net return because social welfare criteria are part of the motivation for giving grants in the first place. Consequently they are often patient lenders and time perspectives are fixed at the outset.

Both market uncertainty and (especially) technical uncertainty is often reduced substantially during the initial screening procedure where entrepreneurs are assisted in carrying out a thorough investigation of the assumptions in the business plan. Resources are often devoted to a thorough screening compared to, for example those done in banks (see note 29).

Closeness with borrowers is set at both + and %. The reason is that it differs substantially according to what kind of firm is in question. Contact with a new start-up firm is usually intense and both parties learn from the experience of that firm. If a large firm is subsidised for example because of a crisis threatening to set many people out of work the contact is not very close and persistent.

Flexibility of government institutions is likely to be small. Procedures for granting credit or subsidies is not only routinized but often strictly procedural or legislatively bound.

Extensive infrastructure is often provided for both education of actual and potential entrepreneurs and advice to start-up businesses. The precise way this infrastructure is set up differs between countries and is subject to intense political debate. In general it is most often efficient although firms are reluctant to use it or ignorant about its existence.

Knowledge generated through interaction with borrowers is easily accumulated in government institutions because they are often specialized in branches or technologies, they have resources for thorough screening and mobility of personnel is low compared to the private, financial sector.

The close contact in the first stages of a firm enables government institutions to monitor entrepreneurs closely. However, when it comes to later stages government agencies tend to be passive in their follow-up of lending.

Government institutions generally perform well in early stage financing whereas established businesses find other sources in later stages.

Placing + or % for *venture capital* firms is somewhat tricky because there is a difference in how the idea and practice of the original venture capital industry was and the practice today. Thus, in the first category both options are placed reflecting that the original venture capital firms invested in new firms or start-ups and stayed with them until introduction to the stock exchange. However, nowadays venture capital firms tend to be short-sighted and finance later stage restructuring and buy-outs instead of early stage financing. The original idea has been taken as a basis here.

Often venture capital firms specialize internally and careful procedures are used to reduce initial uncertainty. Screening capacity is largely enhanced by the fact that personnel in venture capital firms in some cases have an industrial background.

Likewise interaction with partner firms is intense. Venture capital firms have an equity stake in their portfolio firms and are actively involved in the management of these firms.

An equity stake in a firm may induce some rigidities because it is often created at a stage where no secondary market exists if venture firms wish to exit. On the other hand they are not regulated to the same extent as many other financial institutions and may therefore have the flexibility to change strategy.

Additional competence is supplied by venture capital firms and to some extent buying "intelligent capital" also relates to technical knowledge.

Both possibilities for accumulation of knowledge and monitoring are large because venture capital firms are organized for learning in their interaction with partner firms.

To sum-up, an analysis based upon the original idea behind venture capitalism would lead to a + being placed in most of the blanks which is not that strange as they where created for this specific purpose, however, actual practice has disturbed this picture.

It is the strategy of *pension funds* to protect their members interests which are to have a certain and high pension. To pursue this goal they invest in a diverse portfolio of well known, later stage firms. Their time horizon is long because claims by their members are easily calculated.

It follows that initial screening of start-ups is rarely done. Well established firms are of course also screened but mainly financial criteria are used and this is often routinized and therefore does not produce large learning effects concerning judgement of innovation projects.

The involvement of pension funds in firms is usually limited due to a limited capacity and necessity for such involvement. Occasionally a member of the board represents a pension fund or the pension fund force a replacement of management if the firm is in crises.

In most countries pension funds are heavily regulated especially with regard to how much they are allowed to invest in a single firm and how large a share of the total fund can be invested in stocks. This may reduce the possibilities of responding to external changes. On the other hand, investments are mainly in firms listed on the stock exchange thus making fast exits possible.

The monitoring function is often undertaken at an arms-length basis without any interference as long as the project is proceeding well. Competence for direct management is rarely present, although there are exceptions to this generalization.

The volatility of *the stock market* makes time horizons short as explained in section 6.4. This may be hostile to innovations but on the other hand the stock market provides firms with equity capital which is often lacked by innovative firms. Requirements for being listed on the stock exchange are often too high for small and medium sized firms which may be innovative and therefore the stock market is not a financing option for these firms.

Screening is done carefully and there are agencies which deal exclusively with rating investment opportunities. However, possibilities are limited for a thorough screening as the information firms are obliged to provide is determined by legislation and further information is difficult to obtain when potential buyers and the firm are not interacting directly. This is why

175

Greenwald & Stiglitz (1990) claim that there is considerable room for charlatans in the stock market (cf. quotation above). Furthermore, screening is often done in relation to past performance and expectations to the development of the price on the shares in the short term rather than to the strategy, competence and capabilities of the firm.

The arms-length relation between the borrower and the lender excludes possibilities for adding competence to the borrower. Discontent with the development of the firm - or rather the price of its shares - often leads to exit. This fast exit possibility makes the stock market very flexible in that shifts of ownership and restructurings are easy. Whether this is hostile to innovation or not is a different question which is difficult to answer a priori and in general. The performance of the stock market compared to financial institutions can be evaluated by different criteria. If we look upon the ability to support the various borrower-lender interplays described in chapter 5, it is weak in this system for several reasons. First, communication is mainly one-way leaving the borrower without any opportunities of convincing (many and anonymous) lenders about the merits of his project.

Second, the volatility of the stock market implies that funds move from one asset to another, which limits the possibility to build up codes and channels of communication. Furthermore, the risk assessment might be determined not by the future, long-term potentials of the firm, but rather by the psychologically determined peculiarities of the stock market.[30]

Third, interactive learning processes are hampered by the fact that the valuation of the firm's assets is not made in connection with a single project but in relation to the performance of the company as a whole. In principle, it is possible to get access to funds for financing a dubious project, as long as the company is doing well in other fields. In companies with several different products and projects, the single project will have a kind of anonymity when raising funds from the capital market.

_____

30 Keynes (1936, p.160) elaborated on this point, and he suggested, that buying an asset should be made permanent, so that the valuation of the asset would be tied to the performance of the firm and not to the expectation at the future performance of the stock market. Less radical concern is reflected in the debate on capital gains taxation in the U.S.

A diverse population of owners makes it difficult to accumulate knowledge as the monitoring effectiveness is also small. Exept for shareholders meetings and accounts monitoring is limited and coordinated actions of shareholders are difficult.

6.7.4. Evaluating costs and benefits of different kinds of institutions - a summation

Looking down the plus and minus table may give the impression that government agencies and venture capital institutions are the only ones performing well in relation to innovation requirements. The stock market, on the other hand, is about to close down if the minuses are to be taken seriously. However, as mentioned above, each institution performs different tasks in the financial system and they differ in when to finance innovation projects. Thus, they are complementary in their roles in the financial system.

The specific mix of institutions and markets is of course not created according to what is appropriate for innovation financing only. As pointed to in the subsequent chapters this mix is a result of the historical development of the national industry - financial system interplay as well as the degree and mode of intervention of the government.

In chapter 4 and 5 the degree of uncertainty at different stages of the innovation process was discussed and it was pointed out that information reducing uncertainty is a necessary prerequisite for innovation financing. Uncertainty can not be eliminated though only reduced but this reduction is more or less necessary according to how developed the project is. The above features of different financial institutions with respect to innovation financing requirements reflect abilities to provide or process such information. In early stages when uncertainty is substantial, government agencies and venture capital firms are effective due to their screening and advicing capabilities, and their use of cumulated knowledge. In later stages when uncertainty has been reduced and screening may be done more or less automatically banks and pension funds may be an additional source of financing because of their close contact with the borrower. Finally, when the firm has proven to be potentially expanding, needs restructuring, or needs additional equity, the stock market may be an appropriate source of funding.

6.8. Summing up and conclusions

In this chapter focus has been on the financing side, that is in our terminology, the lender. It was argued that financial intermediares are better suited for financing innovations than markets, their main advantage beeing the ability to reduce future uncertainty by learning from past experience. Important elements of the behaviour of the lender have been identified, as well as the existence and role of financial institutions in the first place. It was found that one constraint in relation to financing innovations concerns the competence in screening and monitoring the projects. This constraint is mitigated if financial institutions and borrowers enter close relationships the effect being that both parties learn from the interaction to the benefit of future, similar situations. This fact is rarely incorporated in theories which describe the process of financing investments. Although these elements, and the determinants of risk willingness of lenders, are crucial in understanding the process of innovation the systemic perspective is still an element, which is underemphasized in the above.

The behaviour of financial institutions towards financing innovations is governed by a variety of determinants which stem both from the situation and strategy of the institution, and from the environment, like the macroeconomic setting, the technological development, the level and character of competition, the financial system, etc. Different financial institutions are more or less well-suited for supporting innovations. The ability of the system to develop in order to preserve and stimulate links between borrowers and lenders and diffuse generated knowledge is a substantial characteristic of a national financial system able to support technical innovations. The ability of the financial system to meet financial requirements and develop/take advantage from productive learning processes depends on the flexibility and specialization of the financial institutions. These differences and the bounds on behaviour indicate the necessity of a further investigation of specific institutional set-ups of financial systems which is the topic for the next chapter.

I have pointed to determinants of risk aversion and the establishment of standard operating procedures within financial institutions as responses to the fundamental uncertainty in investment projects and especially in innovation projects. In an era of stable, predictable technological change this may be an appropriate way of risk assessment. However, these procedures may create problems if they are maintained when technology is changing rapidly and the life cycle of products and processes become shorter. When the size and diversity of loan applications increase bankers face a situation of inadequate operating procedures compared to the needs for credit.[31] Innovation projects rarely fit a schedule-like set of rules to allocate credit and select among projects, because of the generic diversity in the sample of innovation projects put forward to a potential lender.

As discussed in section 6.5. bankers (or financial institutions in general) may have a strategy of more or less active involvement in industrial and technological change, and they may be more or less oriented towards the entrepreneurial behaviour as opposed to the routinized behaviour. According to Cox (1986, p. 4-5) financial institutions may cope with the problem of an increasingly risky lending environment by adopting one of three strategies.[32]

The first is a laissez-faire internationalist role where financial institutions act in the interest of shareholders profits in the short term. Short term loans and investments in areas which has proven safe in the past will be preferred. The financial institutions favour ability to operate on the inter-

---

31 Diversity in innovation projects, in financial institutions and in behaviour of individuals, firms and institutions, is a prerequisite for learning processes. How should financial institutions learn about innovation projects and develop financial innovations if the projects were all alike? And how should organizational flexibility develop without diversity in behaviour, not to talk about the flexibility and division of labour in the financial system towards financing innovation projects in different stages. So even though a certain degree of social and cultural coherence between the borrower and the lender is important to the development of stability in borrower-lender relations, the diversity in modes of behaviour between the lender and the entrepreneur, is at the same time inducing dynamics.

32 This is, however, not only a question of strategy. It is even not only a question of pursuing microeconomic goals in financial institutions as opposed to national economic goals. The mere structure of the financial system is a key variable to take into account, in addition to the decision in the financial institutions, when giving a proper picture of the process of financing innovations.

national financial markets in order to be able to switch investments to paper transactions internationally. They tend to dislike using resources on too much involvement in industry.

The second approach is one in which financial institutions try to cope with asessment of new perspectives in technology. They then decide to develop close relationships with their customers in order to learn about the viability of industry. Rather than safe investments this strategy implies taking greater risks and lending on a medium or long term basis. In addition, it is more oriented towards the needs of the national industry as opposed to the international orientation.

The third strategy mentioned by Cox is a cooperative variant. Financial institutions do take national economic goals into consideration but they are still risk avers. Therefore, long term, risky investments are often supported by government through guarantees and/or subsidised interest rates. Another way to support is to establish special institutions for this purpose.[33]

The three categories mentioned above corresponds in some degree to theoretical ways of describing the institutional set-up of financial systems commonly used in the literature.[34] In the next chapter I shall elaborate more on these categories the purpose being to develop an analytical framework for understanding the institutional set-up of financial systems.

---

33 If financial institutions fail to provide long term capital to industry a fourth variant may appear - that of nationalisation or creation of a state investment bank (op. cit. p. 6). There are however other strategies for the state to assist the financing of innovation.

34 This applies to e.g. for Zysman (1983) and Rybzinsky (1984).

Chapter 7: The role of the institutional set up of financial systems

7.1. Introduction

Having discussed the financial requirements of the innovation process in chapter 5 and the decisions to finance this process in chapter 6, I shall now continue the analysis at a higher level of aggregation. This chapter focuses upon actual financial systems using a comparison of 6 major western economies as an illustration. The intention is to show that the institutional set up of financial systems does have an impact on possibilities for financing innovations. More specifically it is suggested that credit based financial systems with frequent intermediation in some important aspects may be superior when it comes to innovation financing.

This was already indicated in chapter 6. Some of the explanations of institutions provided in that chapter are used in this chapter in the analysis of the impact on innovation financing of the specific mix and functioning of financial institutions.

This environment for innovation financing is by no means stationary. Financial systems of today are in flux and consequently this chapter and the next take a dynamic view of the interdependency between development at the macro level and financing processes at the micro level.

Previous research in this area is limited, as mentioned in chapter 2, but is beginning to appear. However, the studies done in this field are, for the most part, limited in scope in that they tend to disregard the dynamic forces inducing changes in the systems. These forces are vital for a full understanding of how the development of financial systems affects the process of financing innovations. Furthermore, such studies are often hampered by a lack of comparable statistics.

An analysis of financial systems requires some type of analytical framework. Therefore, in the first section I shall develop a typology for financial systems and some predictions on how actual financial systems should look and whether they are exactly as indicated by the typology. Secondly, I take a look at the financial systems in some of the most important economies in the western world. The purpose is twofold. One is to test the usefulness of the analytical framework. Another is to indicate the background for the subsequent chapter in that the comparison may help understanding implications of recent changes in financial systems. Before a brief summing-up I will discuss plausible explanations as to why financial systems differ in the manner shown.

7.2. The institutional set-up of financial systems - an analytical framework

This section develops an analytical framework by presenting some archetypes of financial systems. These archetypes are inspired by established conceptions of how to group financial systems.[1] In the next section they are compared with data for actual financial systems.

Financial systems are here grouped according to two criteria. One is the relative importance of savings and of different financial markets and financial institutions in the agglomeration transformation to investments. Another is the role of governments in this process and in the regulation of the financial markets as such. Three distinct categories of financial systems emerge from applying these criteria[2]:

a) a market oriented system, where funds are allocated through a developed, competitive capital market with little goverment influence
b) a credit based system with financial institutions - mainly banks - transferring savings to investments and with heavy government control and regulation and

---

1 See e.g. Rybzinsky (1984,1985), Zysman (1983), Hu (1984)

2 Cf. Zysman (1983). Actually a fourth category is, theoretically, possible using these two criteria. That category is a market oriented system with heavy government influence. Perhaps one should think that this is a contradiction of terms. But government could be active in regulating the system in a manner that ensured the workings of market mechanisms. In fact the U.S banking system is heavily regulated but nevertheless market mechanisms are dominant. However, influence is here taken as active participation in the market and therefore the market oriented system is only one category in the following.

c) a credit based system dominated by private, financial institutions with little government intervention.

This short description demands some further explanations.

7.2.2. Archetypes of financial systems

7.2.2.1. The capital market oriented system

In the capital market oriented system a relatively large part of the transformation of savings to investment takes place through a competitive capital market. Variations in prices of funds are an important mechanism of capital allocation whereas institutions in credit based systems use credit rationing to a larger extent.

Institutions and financial intermediaries are highly specialized, but so numerous that prices are determined by market forces. Firms are supplied with long term equity capital by the developed capital market, and banks provide short-term capital or link firms with potential funds. In this type of system the lender's influence on the borrower is quite anonymous. As there is an elaborate secondary market it is easy for the investor to buy and sell bonds or assets, and these kinds of investments do not require a close and long term relationship with the borrower.

The role of government is to act as a marginal stabilizer and to control aggregates like money supply and inflation instead of actively to support allocation of credit (Zysman, 1986, p.13). The U.S. and the U.K. have been said to be examples of capital market based financial systems.

7.2.2.2. Credit based system influenced by government

In this system, long term capital is provided mainly through loan markets where some prices are controlled by government. Government discriminates between institutions for allocating funds in order to influence the flow of capital to areas with high priority. The relative importance of the capital market is small.

183

Due to the relatively small importance of complementary markets, owners do not engage in buying and selling of stocks as frequently as in the capital market based system. If something goes wrong lenders stay with the borrower and try to influence them by taking part in the management, introducing restrictions on loans etc.[3] But this kind of intervention is even more important at the aggregate level - i.e. the government "voice" in relation to financial institutions. An important - but often overlooked -aspect of this kind of system, is that the institutional set up resulting from the regulation of the financial markets needs to be generally accepted. Without this confidence in the institutions and their performance, the stability and efficiency of the institutions is likely to be small.

Even though France and Japan differ in many respects - also compared to the groups indicated above - it is possible to characterize them as credit based financial systems influenced by government. Although liberalized in recent years technological and industrial development is still heavily influenced by government in both countries, and one of the means of influence is the control of the financial system.

7.2.2.3. Credit based institutional system

This system is different in that financial institutions influence prices independently of government. Government does not intervene in the market to any large extent except for pursuing open market operations and establishing general rules. Intermediaries are the dominating allocating mechanism and they may also even be the gateway to other forms of finance. The stock market is of little importance, and loans or stocks are not easily accessible to the company. The German and to a lesser degree the Swedish financial systems are examples of this type of system [4].

---

3 In the A. Hirschman-terminology (1970) this is the distinction between influence through "voice" or "exit".

4 Deviations in the Swedish system were historically a somewhat larger degree of stock and bond financing. However, this is not the case to a large degree today even though large Swedish firms raise a considerable amount of capital on domestic and foreign capital markets.

7.2.3. Predictions of characteristics of financial systems

The better possibilities for obtaining loans through intermediaries or government in the two credit based systems indicate a lower degree of self financing of firms in this type of system. Likewise we would expect firms in countries with these kinds of financial systems to rely relatively more upon debt than equity in their choice of sources of external capital. The expected higher degree of debt relative to equity in these systems provides an incentive for lenders to monitor lenders and we expect a closer relationship between firms and banks in this system. The degree of concentration is also expected to be higher in this system because of the less developed market for exchange of control - the stock market[5].

This has implications for the type of owners in the two systems. Whereas the entrepreneur, and more active ownership, is likely in credit based systems, we would expect a higher degree of "punters" - that is traders in shares with the purpose of maximizing portfolios only - in the capital market based system. Due to the developed market for corporate control and the low debt-equity ratios takeovers are likely to be more frequent in this system as well as is "exit" behaviour rather than voice. Finally we would expect the countries with the highest degree of intermediation to have the highest cost of capital because intermediation is costly.

The table below summarizes our expectations of the characteristics of the different types of financial systems. The first of these is the role of banks[6], which is used for classification and therefore should not be taken as a stylized fact. Obviously this crude classification does not reveal all interesting international differences, and it ought to be taken with some reservations. In spite of the variations within the categories, there are however some stylized facts, which manifest themselves, when actual financial systems are compared.

---

5 In several credit based systems the stock market is even restricted in this sense, in that there is a division of stocks into A and B, with A-stocks being the only ones to give you access to voting. A-stocks are rarely traded in some countries.

6 Banks are here used as representatives for financial institutions in general.

Table 7.1: Stylized facts of financial systems.

Type of system	Capital market based	Credit based government	Credit based institutions
Role of banks in external financing	Small	Large	Very large
Degree of selffinancing	High	Low	Low
Debt/equity ratio	Low	High	High
Concentration of credit + ownership	Low	High	Low
Cost of capital	Low	High	Very high
Ties between industry and finance	Weak, anonymous, standardized	Strong, known, non-standardized	Strong, known, non-standardized
Way of influence	Exit	Voice	Voice

Let us now take a look upon how these expectations are fulfilled.

7.3. Comparing financial systems

Cross-country comparisons of financial systems involve immense methodological problems and statistical inadequacies[7]. Maybe this is why there has hitherto only been limited attempts to make cross-country studies.[8] This section compares characteristics of financial systems relevant for the classification and predictions above.

Attention should be directed toward the mainly quantitative character of this comparison. In reality the organization of the financial systems is equally important. For example segmentation of the financial system and bank specialization affect the functioning of the system, as may differences in how much banks are oriented towards financing industry, special kinds of industry, or even special technologies. However, not only is the banking

---

7 As discussed in Mayer (1990). Also Berglöf (1991, p.108,177f.) discusses figures for the relevance of this grouping and points to the methodological problems that indeed are substantial in this cross-country statistical exercise.

8 Noteworthy exceptions are Carrington and Edwards (1979), Zysman (1983), Rybzinsky (1984,1985), Goldsmith (1985), Cox (1986) and Mayer (1988,1990).

sector quantitatively larger in bank oriented financial systems, it is also geared more to corporate finance than in the capital market oriented systems (Berglöf, 1988, p.59). Thus, not all of the characteristics are easily quantified. The relationship between borrowers and lenders is one example. To cope with this problem I shall later deal with this aspect by discussing some concrete illustrations.

7.3.1. Classification - the relative importance of bank credits in external financing of firms

A credit based - or "bank oriented" - financial system would typically have a large degree of bank credits in relation to other types of external capital to firms. In table 7.2 bank credits to non-financial firms in recent years are calculated as a percentage of total liabilities, and the proportion of short term and long term credit is separated.

Table 7.2: The relative importance of bank credits in financing industry.

(short and long term bank credits[9] as a percentage of total liabilities)

	U.S.	UK[10]	Germany	France	Japan	Sweden
1981	6.1		N.A.	27.5	37.1	
1982	7.1	16.7		28.5	36.8	24.9
1983	7.3	15.8		27.1	36.2	24.2
1984	8.1	16.6		28.1	34.5	23.3
1985	8.4	15.4		26.1	34.4	21.9
1986	9.0	11.2		25.1	34.4	21.0
1987	8.6	9.5		22.9	31.9	19.9
1988	8.7	11.5		21.4	30.1	23.4
1989	9.0	13.8		20.3	27.8	23.3

Source: Calculated from OECD, Financial Statistics, part III, 1991.

---

9 Taken as group 5.2.2. "loans from financial institutions" plus 6.2.3. "owed to financial institutions".

10 Figures for the UK, France and Japan are for industry only.

187

Recent data on the size of bank loans relative to other kinds of debt supports the pattern outlined in the a priori classification of financial systems. The credit based financial systems can, according to the tables above, be identified together with capital market based systems (U.K. and U.S.). Thus 21.4 and 30.1 % of liabilities in French and Japanese firms are bank credits in 1988, while the figures for the two capital market based countries, the U.S. and the U.K., are 8.7 and 11.5 % respectively. The development of the share of bank credits in external finance shows a rather stable pattern, but if national are to be deduced, it is that the importance of banks has increased in the U.K. financial system in the past few years, while it has decreased in France and Japan.

The statistics allow us to divide bank credits into short term and long term. The picture is not unambiguous, but the one trend that is possible to identify is that the U.S. banks lend long term in an increasing proportion. The same goes for France, but the increase is not as fast as in the U.S. Furthermore, at first glance it seems as if Japanese banks do not lend long term to a large extent especially compared to U.S. banks, which is in contrast to what would be expected.[11]

Table 7.3: The share of long term bank credits to total bank credits.

	US	UK	Germany	France	Japan	Sweden
1981	39.8		N.A.	52.2	37.3	
1982	40.7	21.2		51.6	36.6	76.5
1983	46.7	13.4		54.7	37.0	77.8
1984	48.4	11.5		57.4	33.9	74.9
1985	53.9	14.3		59.0	33.9	71.9
1986	56.5	44.5		61.7	35.5	73.4
1987	65.7	44.1		61.8	36.7	64.9
1988	70.6	47.4		66.0	37.6	72.8
1989	75.3	50.2		59.8	37.6	70.4

Source: OECD, Financial Statistics, part III.

---

11 One explanation may be that firms and banks have close relationships in Japan. As previously pointout a close, long-term relationship may well consist of a series of short-term contracts.

To conclude directly from these figures that this and that country is suffering from "short-termism", would not be fair because there may be institutions other than banks which traditionally provide firms with long term finance in some countries while banks would be the natural option in other countries. Furthermore the initial value -or basis - tells us how large a share long term bank credits are of total liabilities. Table 7.4 (which is in fact a combination of table 7.3 and 7.2) shows these figures.

Table 7.4: The share of long term bank credits to total liabilities

	U.S.	UK[12]	Germany	France	Japan	Sweden
1981	2.4	NA	NA	14.4	14.8	NA
1982	2.9	3.5		14.7	13.5	19.0
1983	3.4	2.1		14.8	13.4	18.8
1984	3.9	1.9		16.1	11.7	17.5
1985	4.5	2.2		15.4	11.7	15.7
1986	5.1	5.0		15.5	12.2	15.4
1987	5.7	4.2		14.2	12.7	12.9
1988	6.1	5.5		14.1	11.3	17.0
1989	6.8	6.9		12.1	10.5	16.4

From these figures a different picture emerges which is more in line with expectations. The share of long term bank credits to total liabilities in non-financial firms is generally smaller in the Anglo-Saxon countries than in the countries with a credit based financial system.

7.3.2. Sources of corporate finance

Certainly self financing is the most common form of investment and innovation financing, but there are large differences between countries in the degree of self financing. Even within external finance there are differences across countries in the way firms finance investments. In table 7.5 the sources of finance are shown.

---

12 Figures for the UK, France and Japan are for industry only.

Table 7.5: Unweighted average net financing of non-financial enterprises 1970-85[13] [14].

Country	U.S.	U.K.	Germany	France	Japan
Retentions	85.9	102.4	70.9	61.4	57.9
Capital transfers	.0	4.1	8.6	2.0	.0
Short term securities	.4	1.7	-.1	-.1	N.A.
Loans	24.4	7.6	12.1	37.3	50.4
Trade credit	-1.4	-1.1	-2.1	-.6	11.2
Bonds	11.6	-1.1	-1.0	1.6	2.1
Shares	1.1	-3.3	.6	6.3	4.6
Other	-16.9	3.2	10.9	-1.4	-3.8
Statistical adjustment	-5.1	-13.4	.0	-6.4	N.A.
Total	100.0	100.1	99.9	100.1	100.0

Source: OECD Financial Statistics and Mayer(1990) p.310.

From these figures[15] a number of conclusions can be derived. First, the main source of financing is -not surprisingly - retensions. Mayer (1990, p.318) shows, that this is the case also if we look specifically at small and medium sized firms, although these firms are considerably more reliant on external finance than large firms. Second, the countries classified as capital market based financial systems, the U.K. and the U.S., do have the expected higher ratio of self financing to external finance. Third, the figures confirm that the term "capital market based system" ought to be used in a cautious manner. Rather than a dominance of capital market the net financing figures show that all the countries in the sample are bank oriented to a greater or lesser extent, if the relative share of external capital supply determines how the system is classified. However, this rather controversial conclusion would

13 Net financing is shown as a proportion of capital expenditures and stock building. Gross financing is a proportion of total sources.

14 A number of statistical reservations are not mentioned here. See Mayer (1990, p.310).

15 Using Gross financing figures reveals roughly the same pattern as these figures show.

probably be modified if the figures were divided into short term and long term capital supply. Fourth, another controversial conclusion is that German banking is not as dominant as maintained. Loans do not account for a large proportion of external financing compared to the other countries. Also this conclusion has to be modified, because German banks are extensively involved in other sources of external finance to firms. In addition, there are large variabilities in the figures for small and large firms (Edwards & Fischer, 1991). Fifth, the securities market is of very limited importance in the period of observation. Only the U.S. bond market is of any significance.

The rather long span of years used for this important table, and the end year of 1985 motivates a closer look at more recent data in relation to some of the other predicted stylized facts of financial systems.

7.3.3. The capital structure of firms in different financial systems

The developments in debt-equity ratios for the countries discussed are shown below. We expect to find higher d/e-ratios in countries classified as credit based financial systems. The main argument for this is related to the close relationships between lenders and borrowers in these countries. Financial institutions allow firms a higher d/e-ratio because monitoring of the firms is easier (and more necessary). Another argument is the difficult access to funds on the capital markets for some firms. Net debt-equity ratios show that these predictions are valid. D/e-ratios in the U.S. and U.K. are significantly lower than the average. The development of the ratios indicates a tendency towards convergence of the financial systems, as the ratios of U.S. firms increased from a low level and those of France and Japan decreased from a higher level.

191

Table 7.6: Capital structure in firms - net

debt/equity net: net liabilities/equity

	US	UK	Ger-many	France	Japan	Sweden
1979	0.49		1.65	1.95		
1980	0.47		1.62	2.14		
1981	0.47		1.78	2.33	3.52	
1982	0.47	1.13	1.71	2.60	3.27	2.01
1983	0.50	1.10	1.64	2.56	3.16	1.88
1984	0.55	1.19	1.57	2.47	3.02	1.60
1985	0.61	1.04	1.53	2.35	2.78	1.88
1986	0.67	1.04	1.45	2.02	2.58	1.89
1987	0.71	1.03	1.50	1.80	2.41	1.75
1988	0.76	1.03	1.51	1.67	2.33	1.75
1989	0.82	1.14	1.53	1.45	2.22	1.98
1990	0.79	1.10	1.61			

Source: Calculated from OECD, Financial Statistics part III.

But how should this stylized fact of national financial systems be explained? Why should lenders in bank oriented financial systems accept a high degree of debt, and why is this preferable to firms? Colin Mayer (1990, p.318-325) reviews five groups of theories, which may give an answer to these questions.

The first of these is the famous, and often cited Modigliani-Miller proposition of capital structure irrelevance, that is, firms choose their proportion of debt to equity independently of decisions on investments and cost of capital. The stability over time of the stylized facts described above, is an indication of the opposite, and the indifference proposition must be rejected as an explanation of cross-country differences.

Second, a transaction cost explanation has been provided. Due to transaction costs in obtaining external finance, firms will prefer retentions to external finance and direct financing instruments instead of financial intermediation in external financing. Mayer argues that the most developed and efficient financial systems - generally regarded as the U.S. and the U.K. - following this theory, would have the highest external finance proportion in the balance sheets of firms, but this is not the case. On the contrary, these countries have the lowest degree of external finance. On the other hand, as I have noted above, there has been an increase in the use of direct financing instruments in general, and this may indicate, that transaction costs do have some importance. This theory alone does not, however, provide an adequate explanation.

One of the main explanations - at least one of the most used - relates to differences in taxation across countries. Mayer investigates this issue by ranking tax incentives to different forms of finance compared to actual financing proportions. This comparison shows poor relationships, and other explanations are called for.

The fourth class of theories are those in chapter 3 which have been called information and economics theories. The arguments rest on comparing different incentives for issuing equity or debt in incomplete markets. Thus, these theories mainly focus on the demand for capital and disregard the ex post consequences of contracting. One argument in these theories does have some appeal, and fits with the observations above. The higher d/e-ratios are explained by closer relationships between financial institutions and firms in some countries. These relationships may reduce asymmetries in information, and provide both an incentive and a possibility to monitor firms more closely. Firms are therefore allowed higher d/e-ratios, and they tend to develop close links to financial institutions. In section 7.3.5 I shall discuss this argument in more detail.

Finally, the fifth class of theories relevant for explaining the d/e-ratios, are those known as control theories. According to these theories firms choose their capital structure depending upon when it is optimal for control to be transferred from entrepreneur to creditor, and the external financing is determined by the relative productivity of creditors and entrepreneurs in particular states of nature (ibid.,p.323). These theories are seen by the author as supportive of the empirical observable facts of financial systems.

To sum up, one has to turn to control theories and the information and economics literature in order to explain cross-country differences in capital structure of firms.

In addition to the relationships between borrowers and lenders, it is important to take into account the concentration of credit and ownership structure in firms when explaining differences in capital structure. Variations in ownership structure provide different incentives to choose debt or equity. The monitoring function may also be different dependent on the ownership structure as may the mode and degree of intervention in case of financial distress and risk of default. Thus, capital structure is a reflection of some of the institutional properties of financial systems and the, just mentioned, ownership structure which I shall now treat briefly.

7.3.4. The ownership structure and concentration

In countries with developed capital markets and extensive stock market trading we would expect extensive risk spreading due to more diversified ownership compared to the bank oriented countries. Historically a larger extent of household savings has been utilized through buying stocks for smaller amounts in the U.S., and the degree of concentration of ownership has been very low, and continues to be so. This is evident from the table below, which shows the diverse ownership and the development to a still further diversion.

Table 7.7: Ownership concentration in the U.S.

(The number of shareowners in the 200 largest non-financial enterprises in the U.S.)

Number of owners[16]	1929 Firms	1929 Share	1974 Firms	1974 Share
- 4999	41	24.9	1	0.5
5000 -19999	53	32.1	8	4.0
20000 -49999	39	23.6	52	26.0
50000 -99999	22	13.3	69	34.5
100000 199999	7	4.3	43	21.5
200000 499999	3	1.8	21	10.5
500000 999999	-	-	4	2.0
1000000 -	-	-	2	1.0
unknown and others	35	-	-	-
total	200	100.0	200	100.0

Source: Herman, Edward S. (1981): "Corporate Control, Corporate Power", CUP.

Private placements are much more common in the U.S. In recent years ownership by the household sector has been still more diversified in all countries, but the proportion of shares owned by financial institutions increased. Another common trend is that ownership concentrations are increasing in bank oriented countries (Berglöf, 1988, p.104).

Berglöf (1991, p.126) compares the concentration of ownership in the U.S. with similar concentrations in the other countries in this study. The results show that ownership of both debt and equity in firms is generally more concentrated in bank oriented countries. Moreover, holdings of institutional investors are large in the U.S. and the U.K. but much less likely to be control oriented. Shareholdings of banks in bank oriented countries are thus more important both for the firm and as a share of bank portfolios.

As a result, there is a difference in the way ownership is carried out in the two types of systems. Risk is more diversified in capital market oriented

---

16 The least number of owners in 1929 was 1 and the highest 469801. The similar figures for 1974 was 6477 and 2.229615.

financial systems, and the incentives to be "active" owners rather than "punters" are smaller in these systems. The ownership structure in the U.S. and U.K. does not provide the same information exchange, and neither perhaps the same incentive structure as in credit based financial systems. The entrepreneurial type of owners with strong incentives to collect information, monitor the firm and accept long time horizons, are more common in bank oriented financial systems.

The many anonymous and disengaged shareowners in the U.S. have provoked a debate of "the punters of capitalism" (The Economist, May 5th, 1990). The problem is that the old-style entrepreneur is disappearing, and being replaced by diverse shareholders who take little interest in the development of the firm, except for the short term prices of their shares. This kind of passive ownership reflects the conflict in logic of, respectively, the financial and the industrial world.[17] A well functioning market for management eventually becomes important for this system in order to distribute skilled management to the firms (Pelikan, 1991).

One of the situations where this difference shows is in cases of financial distress. In firms with very diversified ownership a coordination of shareholder influence is very difficult compared to intervention by a single bank or a small group of investors. The incentives of a bank who has engaged itself heavily in a firm are similar to those of the firm itself as opposed to those present if owners invest a part of their portfolio with the sole aim of moving it somewhere else if the results (understood as the development of prices on shares) are unsatisfactory. In the Hirschman (1970) terminology owners tend to "voice" in bank oriented financial systems, whereas "exit" is more usual in capital market oriented systems. Consequently time horizons tend to be shorter in capital market oriented systems as discussed in section 6.4.

---

17 The discussion is by no means new. Adam Smith(1776) also treated the subject and wrote "The directors...being the managers of other peoples money than of their own, it cannot be well expected that they should watch over it with the same anxious vigilance with which the partners in a private co-partnery frequently watch over their own". Recently Thurow (1992) discussed the issue.

7.3.5. The cost of capital

One would expect the countries with the lowest level of financial intermediation to have the lowest cost of capital, provided intermediation is costly. In addition the small debt proportion in the firms should make external finance cheaper. Apparently it is the other way around. In table 7 countries with an extensive net of financial institutions, like Japan, are at the low end of costs, as opposed to countries with direct financing, like the U.S. and the U.K.

Table 7.8: Cost of Capital in different countries.

Research and development project with 10 year payoff lag.
[Returns requested].

Year	1984	1985	1986	1987	1988
Country					
US	20.3	20.2	16.8	18.2	20.3
Japan	7.7	9.2	9.4	8.4	8.7
Germany	14.6	13.9	13.2	14.4	14.8
UK	24.4	25.4	18.9	20.6	23.7

(Source: Federal Reserve Bank of New York: Explaining international differences in the cost of capital, Quarterly Review, summer 1989)

According to this table, capital for investment in a British R&D project with a ten year pay-off period had to provide a return nearly three times as high as the same project in Japan. Let us save an explanation for later because it is possible to explain this apparant paradox if we take a closer look at the institutional set up of the financial systems and the way their institutions work.

7.3.6. The relationships between financial institutions and firms

It is extremely difficult to give a quantitative illustration of this area, but with the discussions above as a basis, plausible deductions can be derived. These are largely in line with the general discussion in chapter 5 and 6 and therefore I shall point to some concrete illustrations from the countries studied in this chapter.

In *Japan* the financial system supports technological development through government influence but compared to the case of France the government influence is more coordinative and indirect. Of course, the finance-industry relationship in Japan cannot be properly described without mentioning MITI (Ministry of International Trade and Industry). MITI has had a powerful coordinative role in the postwar period sustained by its influence on price and quantity of credit, and in this regard the creation of financial institutions was a major step towards a coherent industrial policy, using the financial system as a means of allocation.

Loans from government were important, but more important was interest rate control, not so much because it reduced the cost of capital for firms but because it limited destructive competition and stabilized the business atmosphere for financial intermediaries. Thus, industrial growth was encouraged by developing the banking system and the indirect way of financing (as opposed to a capital market based financing), which made loans easily accessible for small firms with large growth potentials (Suzuki, 1990, p. 22f).

Today 123 government bodies implement long term economic goals such as financing risk intensive or unprofitable industries; rescuing and restructuring old industries and developing new key industries (Mullinuex, 1987,p.74). In general, the financial system is very segmented and different institutions are highly specialized, both concerning the terms of lending, size of companies, and sector. For instance, ten different government agencies finance small and medium sized enterprises in special industries, where a general, social benefit can be expected.

Obviously, the wide range of specialized financial institutions, the overall guidance and social acceptance of MITI, the personal and economic coherence between finance and industry, implies a high degree of interaction between financial institutions and industry. Indeed, this interaction is an important part of the Japanese success story.[18]

In *France* the indicative planning procedure has traditionally assured national goals for production in key industries, and heavy government influence on credit allocation is an important method of fulfilling the national plan. Projects like TGV, Ariane, Airbus and the nuclear program are examples of major, state initiated, programs of technological by advanced production (Zysman, 1986, p.38). Government has special institutions for this credit allocation and, in addition some of the largest banks have been nationalized. As the Ministry of Finance has significant influence on the capital market, the level and structure of interest rates are also influenced by government.

Due to the relatively small importance and difficult access to the capital market, companies have to turn to banks or special lending institutions. A high priority for the industry or the particular project is an advantage. If the project does not gain direct financial aid or credit from the government then terms of credit in private banks will probably be favorable provided the government gives its quality mark. Lately, the banking sector has been deregulated, and steps has been taken to improve the supply of venture capital (Derian, 1990, p.6-7).

As in Japan, the *U.S.* financial market is rather segmented. In the 1980s deregulation in the U.S. has led to concentration of capital in national commercial and investment banking institutions, making it still more difficult for small, local firms to get their projects financed. This is due to national banks' lack of experience with industrial banking and their specialization in short term lending (Cox, 1986,p.38). In general, long term lending is scarce, and legislation prohibits commercial banks from going into investment banking.
However, some U.S. government agencies have been established to support lending for special purposes or to small businesses but in general, they are

---

18 Another paradox can be seen here. In spite of these apparent advantages, the Japanese financial market has recently been extensively deregulated and internationalized, and firms increasingly rely on direct finance. At the same time, the deregulation of the U.S. financial market has switched into a reregulation trend (Mishkin,1990). I shall return to this apparent paradox in the next section.

not directly involved with the borrower. Instead, they give loan guarantees or they lend to special institutions, which relend the capital. In the military sector, however, government funding of R&D is substantial.

The lack of borrower-lender interaction limits the development of stable, long-term relationships. One exception to this general picture is the story of venture capital development in the U.S., which illustrates that the development of financial institutions for financing technological change is a mutual learning process leading to accumulation of skills (Bullock, 1983).

Let us now return to the unexpected relation between low costs of capital and high level of financial intermediation. The main explanation of this financial cost-intermediation paradox is in the role these institutions play in mitigating informational constraints. The favouring of selected firms or branches, and the associated accumulation of knowledge and monitoring skills within institutions reduces uncertainty and monitoring costs, and enable firms to borrow relatively cheaply.

In recent studies, Hoshi, Kashyap and Scarfstein (1989, 1990) compared the performance of Japanese firms with close relationships to a bank with firms loosening these relationships during the deregulation of the Japanese financial market. They found that investments in firms, who kept their relations to the bank (Keiretzu), where less constrained by liquidity than in the other group of firms. Rate of investments and turn-over in the former groups were higher and the costs of financial distress were reduced through the close relationship. The authors relate their findings to the U.S. case and point out that U.S. firms have an incentive to avoid a heavy debt burden. This is because they have diversified owners and lack an institutional set-up to limit problems with financial distress.

Similarly, the close relationship between financial institutions and industrial firms has been said to be an important explanation of the strong performance of the *German* industry. Historically, the German tradition of strong banking influence in the process of industrialization goes back to the middle of 19th century.[19] In 1852 The Darmstader appeared as the first industrial bank and 20 years later, the three major banks in Germany - Deutsche Bank, Commerzbank and Dresdner Bank - were set up with the purpose of supporting industrial development in coalmining and heavy capital goods (Cox, 1986, p.27). Later they developed to performing commercial banking as well.

In the German financial system of today, commercial banks - or rather "universal" banks - are important in credit allocation. Through their privileged access to capital market banks they are intermediaries to other forms of financial capital than loans. According to Cable (1985) bank representation on company boards reduces informational asymmetries and monitoring costs. However, Edwards and Fischer (1991) argue that the aggregate figures for external finance do not show a dominance of banks and the large firms (who primarily have supervisory boards) are primarily internally financed. Banks, and government grants, are important in financing small and medium sized firms. In addition, even though the proxy vote system enables the three large banks in Germany to control a large part of the votes, the actual assessment of the management is not particularly close.

7.3.7. Methods of influence

Takeover frequency is predicted to be larger in capital market oriented countries whereas credit based systems facilitate informal arrangements of restructuring firms in crises or resolving conflicts of interest between shareholders and management. The reason for this is that diffused creditor structures and legislative restrictions on the degree of creditors involvement in firms in capital market oriented systems hamper informal solutions. In credit based systems where concentration of ownership is larger and interaction with firms closer negotiated solutions are more likely. This has to do not only with structure of ownership but also with the lock-in effect financiers face when entering a market without elaborate exit possibilities.

---

19 The Prussian economic historian F. List argued in 1841 for a national, active role of financial institutions in the process of industrialization, and Prussian bankers recognized the need for a well functioning financial system.

In this case creditors are induced to "voice" for changes rather than pay the high costs of exit.

Franks & Mayer (1990) prove a significant difference between frequencies of acquisitions in the U.K. compared to France and Germany. For example, cross-border takeovers in 1988 were as listed in table 7.9 which also show acquisition activity defined as the purchase of majority stakes and full takeovers.

Table 7.9. Cross-border takeovers and acquisitions in France, The U.K. and Germany 1988.

	UK	France	Germany
Cross-border takeovers	767	372	180
Acquisitions	937	537	534

(Source: Franks & Mayer, 1990, p.198-199)

On the one hand a low frequency of takeovers may hamper innovations because new owners, new capital, and new management may restructure firms towards more innovative strategies and - possibilities. On the other hand, frequent shifts in ownership and management may prevent firms from committing themselves to customers, financial institutions and partners on a long term basis. The effect is inability to built up reputation in firms and a short time horizon in both the financial markets and in the decision making of management of firms.

Furthermore, not only the frequency but in particular the nature of takeovers differ. In credit based systems hostile takeovers do not occur as frequently as in capital market based financial systems. Hostile takeovers may imply that the latter effect on innovation is most pronounced.

7.4. Stylized or real facts of financial systems?

Comparisons of the predicted and actual characteristics of financial systems show both a relatively good coherence and some deviations from expectations. In particular, the term "capital market based" financial systems is perhaps somewhat exaggerated. Truly, the securities market is more important in the countries that have been placed in this group but one could argue, that all the countries in this study are more or less bank oriented, as bank loans are the main source of external finance in all countries.

The most important deviations from expected archetypes of financial systems are that German banks do not provide firms with as large a share of their funding as anticipated and to some extent that loans in U.S. banks are long term to a larger degree than expected.

In spite of these deviations the general impression is that the analytical framework is helpful in structuring analysis of financial systems. Furthermore, new trends in the development of financial systems are better understood if viewed in the light of the institutional set-up. For our purposes it is also useful for understanding the environment of innovation financing. In addition, the development shows a tendency towards convergence of the systems, and this apparent blurring of lines between the archetypes, may reflect an increasing internationalization and is perhaps an indication of a breakdown of previously accepted archetypes.

Some improvements in the framework could be pointed to in light of theoretical developments in previous chapters. One such improvement would be to consider if the framework could be differentiated to take into account different sizes of firms. Even though financial systems have features and institutions that are important to the overall viability of industry, the sectoral structure of the national industry, the distribution of firms of different size and characteristics may also be relevant. For some firms only parts of the financial system are relevant in their financing. For example, the stock market is unaccessable for small, innovative firms in early stages although important to the evolution of the whole industry. If the framework incorporated financial institutions of importance to these firms it would be a step forward.

Another improvement - at least for the present purpose - would be to take the starting point in the features of the innovation process previously discussed. With such a point of departure the analytical framework would to a larger degree consider information processing and -transmitting as a means of reducing uncertainty. Furthermore, it would clarify which parts of financial systems are relevant to the financing of the firm during its life cycle. Thus, it would make the framework more geared to deal with dynamic processes rather than static describtions.

A third improvement would be to include a richer variety of financial institutions relevant for innovation financing. Although banks are quantitatively important as documented in table 7.4. it may well be that other institutions are qualitatively more important to innovation financing. For example, some financial institutions may be more efficient at judging intangible investments than others and capacity may be greater in others.

Fourth, and finally, although this is a typology of financial systems it would be relevant for innovation financing if the analytical framework (if not included) at least considered factors other than financial institutions. The education system, advicing infrastructure, tax rules, savings rates etc. may be very important for possibilities and needs in innovation financing.

7.5. Discussion

Above an explanation of how national financial systems differ and the interdependency of some of their features is indicated. These interdependencies are not enough to explain *why* differencies occur in the first place. I shall point to some plausible explanations.

7.5.1. Explanations to why financial systems differ

Differences between financial systems today may be explained by factors related to especially the quantitative character of the society of which the financial system is a part but also to the nature of the financial system itself.

One is the internal innovative viability of the financial system. The inherent dynamics of the system may affect the flexibility of the system and consequently the need for financial institutions and instruments[20]. However, search for new combinations within finance is not random.

---

20 Dahmén (1961, 1990) shows how innovations in the Swedish credit system had substantial effects on the ability of the financial system to support industrial development.

Private financial institutions are primarily governed by what is expected to be profitable when searching for new options. This raises the question of what it is profitable to search for. How can these areas of business differ across nations?

Nations may differ in the degree and quality of information that firms and financial institutions exchange. Likewise they may have different possibilities for monitoring firms and the degree of intangible investments in industry may differ. This will affect the information production function in financial institutions, or in other words how much financial institutions are willing to pay for improving their competence for gathering and processing information. The structure of the financial system may also be important in that the amount of diversification of financial institutions effects how sharp the division of labour between financial institutions is.

Nations may also differ in how necessary the agglomeration function is in the financial system. If capital is already concentrated and accessable in an amount sufficient for industrial investments then the financial system may not need a large degree of intermediation. Thus, the national distibution of incomes, concentration of capital other than income such as taxes, pensions etc. effects to how necessary institutions for agglomeration are.

National financial systems may also differ in their servicing of industry because the structures of industry differ across nations. The industrial structure may differ with regard to the organization of production, the type of products most commonly produced, and the size of projects to be undertaken. The effect on the financial system of the latter is illustrated above by the railroad investments in the U.S. and the French government induced projects. The former features may affect financial systems if for instance the national industry is dominated by new branches or new products. These sectors of the economy are likely to have many new firms with an overaverage need for external capital. The financial system may respond to such structural characteristics either by gearing financial institutions to finance early stage industries or, as explained in chapter 4 to fall back on a convention and imply standard operating procedures thereby hampering innovations.

In chapter 4 the importance of the nation state was discussed. The openness of the economy also effects the structure of the financial system. In recent years extensively internationalization and coordinated deregulation has been on the agenda of changes in financial systems. Even though some would argue that the nation state is increasingly unimportant due to these trends there are still national differences. The propagation of trends in financial systems in other countries differ according to how open the economy is for such changes.

New financial structures and new financial instruments may be created as response to macroeconomic changes. For example, in the beginning of the 1970s increasing oil prices, fluctuating interest rates, break down of Bretton Woods and high inflation rates induced a large variety of new financial instruments meant for hedging against the increased general uncertainty in society.

Similarly, countries with a large budget deficit may develop together with extensive bond market provided the deficit is bond financed. This is the case in Denmark where also increased bond financed housing building since 1958 contributed to an expanding bond market. Today mortgage credit and mortgage institutions are still an important feature of the Danish financial system and development of mortgage bonds contributed to a developed and well-functioning bond market.

The degree of corporatist tradition is also important to the financial systems. This has implications for the need for interventionist policies and consequently for whether credit based financial systems are of the one or the other type outlined above. For example, the bargained corporatism in Germany and Sweden is important in how the state-industry-bank relationship develops. If successful a bargained corporatism may leave the implementation of agreed policies to industrial and financial institutions. Success depends to a large extent on trust. In chapter 4 and in this chapter it was pointed out that stability of institutions depends on whether the agents accept the role of institutions established. A short digression to a historical comparison between the development of financial systems in

Norway and Sweden may illustrate that informal institutions play a crucial role in industrial and technological development.[21]

Comparing the development of Swedish and Norwegian banking systems reveals interesting differences. Both systems developed in the middle of the 19th century. In Norway several attempts were made to establish a central investment bank with the purpose of allocating idle capital to industrial investments, instead of letting the Wallenbergbanks finance industrialization. But the attempts all failed. A main reason for this was that it takes a general acceptance of a bank as a coordinator of a process of adaptation and technological and industrial change, if it is to be effective. It appeared in Norway that neither the public and political authorities nor the business sector had the confidence in the bank as a national coordinating power. This lack of legitimacy stopped the development of a central investment bank.

The central point of this case is that it illustrates the importance that informal institutions have played in the explanation of the present system. This shows that the scope and methods for analyzing these financial systems should not be limited to static description of financial institutions. The interaction with industrial development and the importance of informal institutions must be taken into account. As it is the transformation process which is interesting in this subject, quantity methods for analyzing the financial and industrial development separately, are likely to be inadequate.

7.5.2. Regulation and intervention

A second important explanation is that the regulation and legislation differ between nations. These differences have important implications for the possibilities of banks exercising control, for division of labour between financial institutions, for their industrial investments, and for their concentration, capital- and reserve requirements.

In general the capital market oriented financial systems, notably the U.S., impose the most extensive restrictions on banking. The Japanese banking

---

21 The example draws mainly on a study carried out by the economic historian Francis Sejersted (1988).

sector is also heavily regulated - probably even more regulated than the U.K. banks. The U.K. have a number of restrictions on the market for corporate control. In the banking sector many rules are not written laws but rather "gentleman agreements" although there is still not as many regulations as in the U.S. (Berglöf, 1991, p.131). It may sound a bit paradoxical that market oriented systems have such extensive regulations but it reflects that a well-functioning "pure" market requires the establishing of well-defined rules of the game.

More specifically in spite of recent deregulation Japanese and U.S. banks are more regulated in the following ways[22]: Banks in both countries face restrictions on their branching. In the U.S. these restrictions are geographical while the Japanese Ministry of Finance tightly controls branching by banks in Japan. In both countries, but especially in Japan, banking is highly segmented. Prohibition of corporate security underwriting is another restriction in these two countries. Diversification to for instance insurance activities is, thirdly, not allowed or limited. Fourth, banks are restricted on the amount of equity they are allowed to hold in nonfinancial firms (Frankel & Montgomery, 1991, p.278).

Related to regulation the degree and direction of government intervention is also a determinant of how financial systems look. Thus, Cox (1986, p.14-15) argues that truly, as Zysman (1983) pointed out, governments have to recognize that the structure of financial systems is a constraint on implementation of policies. The scope of possible policies is limited by the existing institutional set-up of financial systems and policies that are not compatible with this set-up are likely to render disfunctional political conflicts and failure of industrial policy.

This allow us to some extent to understand the relative economic successes of post war Japan, Sweden, France and West Germany. As Cox mentions

> "These countries have fashioned policies which have not challenged the structure of the financial system. Other countries -Britain in

---

22 Frankel & Montgomery (1991, p.274-277) provides a valuable compilation of banking law features in U.K., U.S., Japan and Germany. Franks & Mayer (1990, p.205f.) investigates regulation of corporate restructuring.

particular - have attempted to implement industrial policies without the requisite financial structure of controls to facilitate a positive state role, and this has led to disfunctional and economically wasteful political conflict." (ibid., p.14)

Zysman and Cox do not agree on a fundamental causality in this regard. Whereas Zysman argues that for instance France and Japan have state-led economies due to their credit based, government influenced financial systems, Cox reverses the argument. In his view the credit based, government influenced financial systems in Japan and France are results of a deliberate choice to have state-led economies. The U.S. and the U.K. have capital market systems because they choose not to be state-led economies.

In my view the truth is somewhere in between these arguments. The financial system should not be viewed as an immutable, constraining entity. Governments have scope for changing financial systems and adjust financial institutions to industrial policy rather than adjusting policies to the structures of financial systems. But, on the other hand, such a change does not take place over night. Financial systems have grown in importance relative to the rest of the economy in most of the western economies. In addition, financial systems have become more interrelated than hitherto was the case. Both these facts give a certain inertia in changing financial systems.

Furthermore, this inertia is enhanced by a financial system lock-in effect. This effect has to do with the development of competence and division of labour within financial institutions as discussed in chapter 6. If a certain kind of transaction frequently occurres in one type of system competences and economies of scale in undertaking this transaction will improve further, enhancing competitiveness in that particular business. Implementing policies that requires new kinds of transactions may be costly because it takes time to built competence in undertaking these transactions efficiently.

7.5.3. Historical explanations of the evolution of financial systems

My third point is that history matters. More specifically some of the present features of financial systems like the degree of interaction between borrowers and lenders are rooted in the historical development of the mutual influence between industry and the financial system.

The process of shaping financial systems and selecting institutions is not always easy to display, and the need for historical studies of institutional development is not widely recognized. Particularly, it is often overlooked, that sometimes the important factors are not only what exists and what did happen, but in particular what did *not* happen. In addition, the importance of informal institutions must be taken into account when explaining the present systems. Legislation is, in other words, not the only factor shaping financial systems. The development of financial institutions is also rooted in the culture, history, and interaction with industrial development in the nations. After World War II, the U.S. occupying authorities, altered the Japanese legislation along U.S. lines and prohibited the "zaibatsus". If legislation was the only important thing in developing of financial systems, the Japanese system ought to look like the system in the U.S., and "keiretsus" would not be present. As shown above this is not the case. Keiretsus are important in exerting influence on industrial firms and financial institutions in Japan own about one-fifth of shares on the Tokyo stock exchange. Another example is the regulation of ownership of industrial firms by banks. This is prohibited in both Sweden and the U.S. but there are large differences in both how the financial systems look and in how banks act with respect to ownership of industry. Legislation and regulation form legal frames for the workings of financial systems. But it is neccessary to complement the explanation with a description of how these frames are filled in.

It is beyond the scope of this study to treat the history of e.g. bank-industry relationships in the six countries because a full explanation would require a detailed historical analysis of the development of financial systems[23]. Instead I shall use the development of these relationships in Sweden as an example illustrating how past relationships may influence the functioning of financial systems.

---

23 Mowery (1992) analyzes the development of bank-industry relationships 1900-1950 in 5 of the countries also the subject in this study. Cox et.al. (1986) add Italy to their study of bank-industry-state relations in the afterwar period. In Sweden a number of studies have focused upon bank-industry relationships historically, especially within The Banking Project at Uppsala University. Per H. Hansen (1991) investigates these relationships in Denmark.

7.5.3.1. Development of bank-industry relationships in Sweden

In the beginning of the 19th century the need for external capital in Sweden was limited. Rich people were also the entrepreneurs, and suppliers of credit in addition to merchant houses. In the middle of the century the needs for credit increased. The banking system gradually developed, and banks became more effective intermediaries than the merchant houses. One major innovation in the credit system was that the banks became cash-holders for the public (in Keynes' words a convention was established reducing hoarding substantially). This - together with new means of payment and services and no government regulation of the level of interest rates -made the process of credit creation much less dependent upon the general propensity to save in society, and banks were able to cover financial needs in new industries to a much larger degree.

An European development in the banking systems (other than the Scottish) had an influence on the development in Sweden. The German universal banks, and their participation in the rapid German industrialization was known and admired in many parts of Europe, including influential groups in Sweden (Lindgren, 1990, p.267). Swedish commercial banks gradually developed into a kind of universal bank. This was brought about by an increased engagement in long term industry financing as a response to the large needs for capital in the industrial breakthrough by the turn of the century. There was a radical shift in technology and restructuring of production towards brand new areas of production without possibilities for self financing and security.

As the industrialization brought with it new requirements for external capital, new means of payments and loans were developed. Together these innovations in the credit system provided the financial basis for exploring new trajectories in industrialization. The new situation was met by qualitative changes in the credit system. Bank owned holding companies were a major innovation, risks increased in bank lending and there were less strict economical criteria for lending. In addition to these changes the quantity of credit increased. The widening of the business area for the banks became an especially important factor in financing industry and for development of close contacts with firms (Dahmén, 1961).

But these new methods in the banking sector and new possibilities in the industrial sector for rapid technological development demanded closer contact between bank and entrepreneur. Banks had to participate in organization and strategic development in the industries and had to require a feeling for the financial needs in industry in order to be able to innovate effectively (Dahmén op.cit. p. 449). Later, during the mid-war crises, the Swedish banks participated in the restructuring of industry, so that Swedish industry was fairly strong by the end of the crises. This function of the bank - as an institution operating at a meso level coordinating micro activities and macro goals - is an important factor in the explanation of the relatively fast industrialization in Sweden.

Legislative boundaries for bank ownership in industry were easily avoided. The banks controlled holding and investment companies which bought shares in firms, and these various bank mutations formed - together with the commercial banks - a financial group, that could offer the same product as the universal banks in Germany. In this period banks were very active in taking part in the restructuring of industry and in establishing close contacts to industry.

> "Leading managers of the larger banks organized themselves into consortia or syndicates, eagerly looking for opportunities to engage in share underwriting and structural reorganization operations.....Thus more permanent banking groups were established, offering a complete program of investment banking to industry, and close contacts developed between the larger commercial banks and their industrial clients." (Lindgren, 1990, p.268)

During and after WWI a lot of investment companies popped up. Some were connected directly to a bank, others were financed by bank loans with shares as collateral. After a deflationary crises in 1920-21 many of these companies went bankrupt and banks suddenly owned large amounts of shares in Swedish industry, which of course reinforced the above mentioned ties between finance and industry (Lindgren, 1990, p.269). After legislative changes prohibiting bank ownership of shares, these relationships did not vanish, and the control of the shares was kept because they were transferred to affiliated investment companies.

The character of relationships between banks and industrial firms

As discussed in the theoretical part, there is an interdependent evolution of financial and technical innovations. The classical example of financial innovations as a response to industrial development is the diffusion of the railroad in the U.S. The large railroad companies were unable to raise the immense amounts of capital needed, and this induced a series of innovations in the financial system. The development of the Wall Street stock exchange and of specialized Merchant banks were particularly important innovations (Santarelli, 1987, p.43).

The emphasis below is on the reverse causality - the importance of financial innovations and credit on industrial development. In particular I shall specify what the relations between firms and bank actually are and compare these with the theoretical suggestions above. The method is to focus on the performance of Stockholms Enskilda Bank.[24] This bank was established in 1856 and controlled by the Wallenberg family. The reason for choosing Stockholms Enskilda Bank (SEB) is that the special credit information department established in 1900, has kept detailed informations on all contacts with clients and credit decisions. This provides us with material for interpreting actual bank-firm relations.

Classification

According to Lindgren (1990, p.272) lending was concentrated on a low number of clients, who may be grouped into three. One group is the independent clients. Although these firms were not owned by the Wallenberg group - or if they were only with a small minority - they were from time to time dependent on additional credit from the SEB, and the bank supplemented its creditor functions by "voice" pressure or appointing observers to the board of managers. Another group is the firms where the SEB had a large influence through minority ownership and representation on the management board. Finally a third group of companies is controlled and owned by the Wallenberg group, and is more or less a part of - rather

---

24 There has been several case studies on SEB. Foremost both the studies by Olle Gasslander (1962) and Lindgren (1987) ought to be mentioned. This section draws heavily upon Lindgren (1990).

than a client of - the Wallenberg group. These companies include finance, holding and investment companies. From a bank-firm relationship point of view, this group is not that interesting. The description below consequentely concentrates on the two former groups.

The character of relations to independent clients

In this group of firms the relationships to large firms and small firms were different. In large firm the relationships were very stable over time, and due to an extensive network of managers of large firms and banks, it was costly to leave this relationship. The top persons in the large firms were recruited to the Board of directors in SEB, and often became socially connected to the Wallenberg group through friendship or family. The contractual relationships were often oral and implicit. Most businesses were however written down, but often without any stipulations of time limits or sanctions.

The small firms were usually more independent in management, but were considered important as a future market for the bank. On the other hand small firms were interested in the connection to SEB, because of the protection it gave in times of crises. Implicitly, it was expected that the bank would support the firm and use its network to other firms to make them prefer buying from this client firm. On the other hand SEB expected the firm to give extensive informations in times of crises, and preferable that SEB should be the only bank connection (Lindgren, 1990, p.274-75).

The character of relationships to part-owned clients

SEB performed a more active ownership to this group of clients. The firms had to accept observers on the board or accountants appointed by SEB, and sometimes SEB took part in both strategical decisions and daily routine operations (ibid.,p.276). In other companies the engagement was much smaller, and these were primarily companies where SEB did not have a majority or dominating minority interest.

Due to the lack of sanctions in the contracts SEB were not able to exercise influence in minority owned companies compared to the companies where the ownership permitted it to coordinate activities.

Summary and conclusions

In summary, one can say that in the terminology of section 6.3 the banks moved towards a still more active and controlling function. The Swedish financial system developed into a bank oriented system, with close relationships and even overlappings between firms and banks. The concentration of both industries after the mergers in 1910's and the three large banks SEB, Svenska Handelsbanken and Skandinaviske Banken, enabled the Wallenbergs and other influential men to coordinate industrial activities and restructuring crises ridden industries and branches. In this strong integration and coordination, the information- and competence dependent barriers to financing innovations were eliminated or reduced substantially. The cost is a high degree of concentration of industry as well as limited government possibilities for coordination.

Even though legislation was not like that in Germany, the situation is comparable with the German banking system. If the Swedish development blocks are to be compared with something internationally, then the Japanese "keiretsus" could approximate. The strong links between firms, suppliers, users and financial institutions - often through non-written contracts - in "keiretsus", correspond in some ways to the hierachical coordination in Swedish development blocks.

Together historical studies of the development of bank-industry relationships can reveal patterns of corporate and financial system evolution which is helpful in understanding the present day structures of financial systems.

7.5.4. A short summary

To summarize, explanations as to why financial systems differ are primarily devided into three blocks of interrelated factors. One is that the past is important in shaping financial systems in several respects as examplyfied by the story of bank-industry relationship in Sweden. Second, a number of features of both the internal functioning of the financial system and surroundings have an impact. Finally, the past and present regulation of the financial system and government intervention is important to how it eventually looks. A satisfactory explanation of national differencies of financial systems thus requires an integrated approach covering several aspects. In a dynamic perspective it is necessary to take into account how the features of financial systems are developing. In the subsequent chapter I shall deal with the development of the environment in which processes of financing innovations take place.

Chapter 8. The impact on innovation financing of current trends in the development of financial systems

8.1. Introduction

The previous chapters have mainly focused on past and present features of innovation financing and financial systems. This chapter is concerned with future perspectives. In the chapter above the environment for processes of financing innovations has been said to be in flux. This is confirmed by the discussion in this chapter. But this chapter goes one step further in that it specifies in what way this environment is turbulent. The primary aim is to answer the question: Are conditions for innovation financing improving or deteriorating as a consequence of the current trends in financial markets?

An unambiguous answer to this question is at best difficult to give. The trends are interdependent but different trends may result in different effects on conditions for innovation financing. The same trend may even have dual opposite effects on these conditions. The answer is further complicated if size of firm, innovation stage, kind of technology and national differencies are introduced. A careful, detailed analysis of the possible impacts of trends on financial markets seems necessary if a complete answer is to be given. This is a formidable task which is beyond the scope of this book. Nevertheless, below an attempt has been made to capture the essence of trends, relevant from previous discussions on how possibilities of innovation financing have changed and will continue to do so in the future. The discussion uses the framework developed in chapter 7 to evaluate whether the trends are likely to have a positive or negative effect on innovation financing. Furthermore, this framework is useful for making generalisations in order to avoid a too detailed description of developments in the six countries in chapter 7.

A first prerequisite for giving an answer to the question above is to identify what are the most important trends in financial markets. Deregulation, internationalization and integration are some of the catchwords used when describing the recent development of financial systems. Others are despecialization, financial innovations, reregulation and securitization. But what is the actual content of these concepts, how are they interrelated, what consequences do they have, and just how important are they?

The first section (8.2) deals with the content of the trends whereas section 8.3 dicusses some of the links between the trends. In section 8.4 I focus explicitly on implications for innovation financing.

8.2. Current trends in international financing markets

8.2.1. Regulation

In the current debate the term deregulation is often used in a too general manner. In many articles and books the deregulation trend is considered a global, homogeneous trend going on in all western countries. The fact is that the degree and mode of regulation differs across nations. In addition, it is essential to take into account the structural characteristics of the national financial systems as well as national attitudes towards regulation, the general state of the economy and the demand for financial services, when explaining these differences. In other words deregulation ought to be considered in its socio-economic context.

The deregulation trend could be explained in a sequence of general phases - which are not easily separated and to some extent going on simultaneously. Given an incentive to deregulate (I shall return to the reasons for deregulation later), the first deregulation phase leads, secondly, to a competition intensive, phase. Due to higher aggregate risk of instability and potential conflicts of interest between financial institutions entering new spheres of business, there will be an increased need for regulation, and a reregulation trend may occur. Fourth and finally, the convergence phase will be predominant, in which integration of financial markets urging regulation to take legislative and institutional structures in other countries into account occurs (Llewellyn, 1990, p.36)[1].

---

[1] As far as I can see, this is part of the background of how deregulation is proceeding on in the EEC. Deregulation may be regarded as a prestage to future harmonisation of regulatory conditions in EEC countries. This is no linear process as trends in regulation may shift from regulation intense politics to laissez-faire.

The first, natural question is what is regulated and why? Despite national differences in deregulation there has generally been a tendency to omit regulations on interest rates. Another target for deregulation has been the extensive liberalization of exchange rate control, further intensified by the EEC countries working towards an internal market - based on the principle of free movements of labour and capital - and subsequently a monetary union. Other initiatives are the dismantling of barriers for establishment of foreign banks, removing restrictions and fees on loans, providing incentives for new financial innovations and information on new financial products and services, inducing wider fields of working for the same financial institutions and preventing tendencies to concentration (OECD, 1989, p.13).

The reasons for deregulation do of course also vary but in general regulation aims at controlling the degree and extent of competition, the extent of the fields of action of financial institutions and the regulation of incentives and moral hazards within the financial sector (Llewellyn, 1990). In addition, the overall stability of the financial system and the protection of investor and consumer interests is an important reason for regulating. More specifically, the present deregulation trend has been motivated by a wish to increase the effectiveness of financial markets[2]. Regulation is often avoided through financial innovations, or financial services are moved to countries with less burdensome regulations. This trend is enforced by inter-nationalization and is one motivation for convergence of regulative efforts between nations (Courchene, 1989).

> "...when regulation is based upon home country principles, and all other countries must recognize the authority of partner-country regulators, the competitive implications of different regulatory arrangements will inevitably force a convergence of regulation within the EC." (Llewellyn, 1990, p.39).

In addition, there are of course political motivations - both in terms of domestic monetary policy, the integration process and the ideological reasons for free competition.

---

[2] There is however no evidence showing that deregulation increases effectiveness of financial markets, and skepticism has been expressed against this argument. In addititon, "effectiveness" is rarely defined in the literature.

"Policy action in this direction has essentially been guided by the conviction that the allocation of financial resources through markets for negotiable instruments is in many respects superior to institutional allocation, in particular as regards cost efficiency." (OECD, 1989, p.20)

In the EEC-countries specifically, a number of measures have been used to deregulate the financial sector. Deregulation has removed or relaxed restrictions on credit ceilings, minimum bond investment requirements, the scope of business, controls on interest rates and taxes on financial activities (Mayer and Kneeshaw, 1988, p.138). Moreover, mortgage institutions, savings institutions and the postal system have been permitted to undertake banking businesses, and banks to engage in mortgage lending, pensions and especially insurance. All countries (except Germany) have had, or still have, some form of legislation regulating the amount of equity stakes financial institutions are allowed to hold in nonfinancial companies, but in a number of countries these restrictions have now been relaxed. There are however still a number of restrictions left, rooted in the national, structural characteristics of the financial systems:

"This worldwide move towards greater financial deregulation and liberalization is an ongoing process. There are still a number of restrictions, often rooted in historical country differences in financial system structures which affect the nature and degree of competition in national financial services markets and pose problems for the international financial integration process." (OECD, 1989, p.20)

Simultaneously the deregulation process is accompanied by a reregulation. Exposure of national financial institutions to more competition, conflict of interest between institutions in new areas of activity and increased fragility of financial institutions and -systems, as well as consumer and investor protection, has motivated authorities to tighten regulation in some areas and expand the extent of regulation to more institutions (Østrup, 1989, p.355f.).

In the U.S. for instance, the wider range of business for financial institutions and increased competition has led to banking crises and moral hazards among the commercial banks, but the savings- and loans institutions have also had problems, as they entered risky businesses too ill-equipped (Mishkin, 1990, p.21). The results have been more regulation on banks and savings- and loan institutions, and there is still a debate on restrictions on program trading and issuing of junk bonds. Essentially there is a worry about the general stability of the financial system in a too deregulated market (ibid., p.23).

Financial regulation is less complicated when the regulation has simple objectives, if there is a weak competition pressure, if the financial system is segmented with specialized financial institutions, if only national considerations are relevant, and if the regulating authorities is generally accepted. These conditions are to a large extent not present in the financial systems of the 1990s, and this is likely to lead to great challenges for regulation in the future (Llewellyn, 1990, p.38).

> "It can, indeed, be expected that international financial market activity will increasingly gravitate to those financial centers which are not only characterized by a high degree of functional efficiency but in which market operators and market practices are well regulated and supervised." (OECD, 1989, p.23)

8.2.2. Competition, despecialization and diversification

Increased competition is one of the natural consequences following internationalization, deregulation, despecialization and diversification.[3] Competition pressure has increased inside financial subsectors, between subsectors, between the banking sector and the capital market, and internationally. It shows up in more flexible and differentiated interest rates, more financial options, administratively set interest rates being more market oriented, more integration of financial markets between countries, more financial innovations, and more securitization (Llewellyn, 1990, p.34).

One example of diversification of activities is that pension funds invest more intensively in industry, and further deregulation in this area is about to come. This will inevitably lead to increased competition.

---

[3] OECD (1989b) has performed a detailed study on competition in banking. Therefore the following discussion will include general considerations only.

One major factor behind increased competition has been the diversification and despecialization of financial institutions, which in turn has been facilitated by the extensive deregulation described above. There have, however, been national variations in the speed and intensity of this process, depending upon the institutional set-up of the financial systems, the historical and legal framework, and the tradition of regulatory changes (OECD, 1989, p.17). Nations with very segmented financial markets have been the most rapid in diversification and despecialization.

Another factor behind intensified competition has been links to internationalization and financial innovations. The new information technology provides possibilities for on-line information on all prices and markets and around the clock trading on different stock exchanges throughout the world. It is likely that this in itself will give further pressure to deregulation and liberalization of financial markets.

8.2.3. Financial innovations[4]

The propagation, just previously mentioned indicates that there are some leads and lags in development of new financial services. Some countries are more innovative with respect to financial products and markets, whereas others are primarily imitating. In addition to entry of foreign banks, the lack of legal protection of new instruments increases the international propagation of these, and limits the advantages of being a leader (Artus and de Boissieu, 1988, p.102).

The way new financial instruments are introduced is rather different. In Anglo-Saxon countries private, decentralized innovation by financial institutions such as banks and firms is the main route, whereas other financial systems also introduce new instruments through the public sector (Artus and de Boissieu, 1988, p.107).

---

[4] Viñals and Berges (1988, p.181) provides an overview of the content of financial innovations and discusses how important they have been for financing firms. An overview of the new financial instruments in Denmark is contained in Østrup (1989, p.31).

But why are financial innovations created in the first place? One explanation is of course the search for profits and the competition between financial institutions. Another is possibilities from new information technologies, and a third the changing market conditions. As already mentioned, the latter involves, in general, the greater overall uncertainty in financial systems following the break down of Bretton Woods, fluctuations in interest and inflation rates and rising oil prices of the beginning of the 1970s. This stimulates incentives, or rather put on pressure, to invent interest rate risk transferring instruments like futures, options, swaps etc. (the risk redistribution does, of course, not reduce the initial uncertainty in the single investment project).

A very influential theory on financial innovation emphasizes constraints in explaining the development of new financial products (Silber, 1975,1983). One such constraint is the regulations placed upon banks, other financial institutions, and firms. If regulation is too burdensome for financial organizations a way of avoiding it will be developed. This induces further regulation, and in turn other financial innovations. Regulation, risk management and competition is thus seen as main determinants of financial innovations. This applies especially to the Anglo-Saxon countries. In other financial systems catching-up, budget deficits and financial needs of special categories of firms are also important determinants. This theory is, however, not adequate. In fact, regulations can be an advantage to financial institutions and promote innovations in the financial systems. Furthermore, taking it literally, it would predict that the pace of financial innovations would slow down during the deregulation of the 1980s, which is obviously not the case.

8.2.4. Securitization and disintermediation

In recent years a tendency has been that financial institutions pool credits to marketable claims, and financial institutions themselves obtain their finance from issuing e.g. bonds. Another way of direct financing is the financing of large firms. Some of these firms in the U.S. have better credit ratings than the banks, so why borrow from an organization with a rating worse than your own? Instead internal banks or financial departments in firms have been established and bond issues have increased. The distinction between "financial sector" and "industrial sector", is indeed not clear from this development.

This disintermediation is though perhaps limited in importance, because some of the institutions which buy the bonds issued by firms are bank-affiliated mutual funds (Artus and de Boissieu, 1988, p.115). In addition, banks have entered the securitization market by issuing them and serve as links to different forms of securities. Thus, bank income increasingly changes in proportion from interest rates towards fees (Courchene, 1989, p.15). This is though not likely to compensate for lost profits from disintermediation, and the cost of credit for firms has probably decreased.

Increased budget deficits in many countries has been one of the most important factors explaining increased securitization. The deficits have forced governments to borrow large amounts from the public in a market form.[5] Another driving force is financial innovations in the 1970s.[6]

The securitization trend is strongest in the capital market based financial systems, and it does have some effects in terms of less information and monitoring, financial instability, and more cautious investment decisions (Østrup, 1989, p.445).

8.2.5. Internationalization

In addition to the integration mentioned above there are other signs of increased internationalization of financial markets. Listing and investing on

---

[5] This development is especially pronounced in Sweden and Japan.

[6] At the beginning of 1987 it was believed that U.S. financial markets would expand extensively at the expense of financial institutions. However, after the stock market crash in October the securitization process was slowed down (Minsky, 1990, p.69). Even so the process towards market orientation continues: "It is common wisdom among observers of U.S. banking that relationship banking is becoming less common and is being replaced by market-based transactions using explicit, standardized contracts. Advances in technology have abetted this process by reducing the cost to market participants of computing the values of complex financial instruments." (Frankel & Montgomery, 1991, p.286).

stock exchanges abroad has increased, loans to foreigners have increased (table 4.3), and foreign bank entry has increased (table 4.4).[7]

Table 8.1: Cross-Border Bank Credit to Nonbank by Residence of Borrower

Year	United States	Japan	Den-mark	France	Germa-ny	Sweden	United Kingdom
1981	48.5	12.7	11.0	10.3	39.8	8.5	13.3
1982	57.2	9.7	11.9	14.4	41.4	10.0	13.6
1983	58.4	11.4	12.4	16.5	40.8	10.4	15.9
1984	68.7	8.6	10.3	17.2	35.2	7.0	14.0
1985	94.1	10.4	15.6	19.7	43.3	9.3	16.9
1986	120.2	16.5	18.7	19.9	49.7	10.2	24.8
1987	146.0	52.3	25.0	21.8	66.5	12.1	29.6
1988	185.9	69.7	25.9	19.6	65.1	10.4	34.7
1989	207.5	101.2	25.9	21.5	68.4	12.9	42.0
1990	270.3	160.7	33.5	29.2	83.9	19.2	56.7
1991	297.1	207.6	31.8	31.8	93.0	21.5	63.7

Source: IMF, International Financial Statistics Yearbook.

The units are billion dollars.

Taking table 8.1. as a measurement of internationalization, the figures show a gradually increased internationalization in the U.S. and the U.K. This also applies to Germany, and for the last few years, there has been an extremely rapid increase in Japan. In Denmark the internationalization of borrowing continued until 1987, and has stayed at a stable, but very high level compared to the size of the economy.

---

[7] Oxelheim (1990) provides an empirical based analysis of the process of international financial integration using Sweden as an example. The globalisation of international financial markets began in the mid 1970s when the U.S. and Germany removed capital controls. A few years later the U.K. and Japan took similar measures and most other OECD countries have gradually through the 1980s removed or eased exchange controls.

Table 8.2: Foreign banks in selected countries

Year	1986	1987
Denmark	5	7 (1988)
UK	300	347
France	131	151
Germany	148	137
Japan	64	
U.S.	469	

Source: Østrup (1989, p.349) and Grilli, V. (1989, p.308)

Earlier regulation and financial intermediation was largely national in character due to entry barriers, restrictions on flows of capital and domestic regulation. Now the development of information technology, political changes, financial innovations, strategic considerations of banks and changes in the needs of customers, has made finance international (Llewellyn, 1990, p.38). Some of the other reasons behind this process are increase in international trade, the possibility of avoiding regulations and reducing tax payment, a wish to distribute risk, and the possibilities of a better feeling for the market (Østrup, 1989, p.58f.).

The mobility of financial services across borders does of course limit the possibilities of an independent, national policy towards the financial markets. Entry of foreign banks e.g., has increased propagation of financial innovations, as financial services already tested in other markets may be introduced through foreign banks (OECD, 1989, p.19). Improved information systems have facilitated identification of the cheapest source of finance. But price is not necessarily the only criteria for the choice of bank connections. Important non-price criteria may be geography, personal relationships, advising capacity and other services of the bank, together with its technical expertice and experience.

8.2.6. Political and financial integration - the EEC-perspective

One of the trends in the financial sector today is the integration - here treated as the financial integration of most of the European countries. The intentions of the Rome-act from 1957 were to establish free movements for persons, services and capital between member nations. In the financial sector this means free establishment and exchange of financial services between member nations, and establishment of a common set of regulations. In order to achieve this goal a number of measures have been used, including the above discussed deregulation. The most succesful liberalization has been in the areas of bank services and investment funds. Most nations have at some point of time had a form of Glass-Steagal Act regulating the bank ownership of industry, but in the EEC only one country (Belgium) (in the OECD also Sweden and the U.S.) prohibition of bank ownership of shares remains. The EEC countries have agreed upon working towards a directive which limits total bank involvement in industry to 60% of the equity of the bank, and up to 15% of its equity in a single firm (Svenska Bankföreningen, 1991, p.12).

The deregulation process in the EEC has been relatively uncomplicated due to the political interests connected to other aspects of the EEC, and the limited national influence on a still more international financial market. In addition, financial institutions which move to countries with less regulation may impose problems e.g. for national tax rules and this motivates nations to harmonize national regulations. The question remains what will be the effect of the efforts in the EEC in terms of economic efficiency and servicing industry? To give a complete answer to this question is a formidable task, but a few general hints are given here and some further comments are added later.

First of all there are some limits to integration independently of deregulation. Entry costs (building up reputation, knowledge about tax system, legislation and customers) are substantial for banks in foreign markets - especially small markets like the Danish. Confidence in foreign banks is likely to be smaller, and there may be informational barriers in monitoring and judging borrowers. Second, the structural characteristics of the national industry may be a barrier for foreign banks in that a relatively large number of small and medium sized firms (as in Denmark) mean high costs on monitoring and credit judgement compared to the volume of lending. Asymmetries in information is likely to be higher and many firms may compare prices and services on an international basis through their own financial department or bank (Østrup, 1989, p.329).

In theory the positive effects of financial integration would be: increased allocative efficiency; distribution of risk and thereby more stability in the financial system; competition pressure to reduce costs in financial institutions and to develop and diffuse financial innovations, with cheaper and more possibilities for obtaining finance for industry as a consequence. But according to some observers (Østrup, 1989, p.351) (Strange, 1986) these effects are not likely to result from the financial integration of the EEC. The arguments are that in spite of the deregulation process there are large differences in regulations, and the historical tradition for regulation and the institutional development in the nations are likely to be a more important determinant of competition than objective comparative advantages. The possibilities of avoiding regulation may increase financial instability as may the high and homogeneous informational level because it creates a large propagation throughout the system of exogenous chocks and program trading. On the other hand one positive effect may come from a larger market. In such a market possiblilities for specialization of financial institutions may increase.

8.3. Interdependencies of changes in the international financial markets

It has been indicated in the discussion above that financial markets today are turbulent and the processes of change within them are intermingled and interdependendent in a very complex manner. These links between trends in the international financial sphere are illustrated below and the effects of some of the most important on the present issue are subsequently discussed.

Figure 8.1: Interdependencies of financial processes.

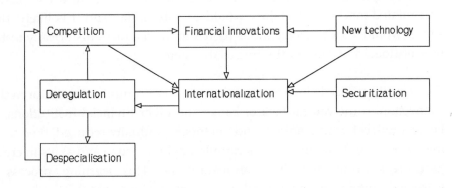

The connection between deregulation, despecialization and competition is one such link. A deregulated financial sector has changed the division of labour between financial institutions. Regulations on what business financial institutions are allowed to take part in have relaxed and this has had a direct effect on competition. An indirect effect is that diversification and subsequent despecialization is likely to change. The degree of competition is not necessarily likely to change but the character of competition might move towards competing on a wide range of different financial products.

High competition pressure has led to mergers in the financial sector -both between domestic banks, and banks and insurance companies together with cross-border mergers or cooperations between banks. One could perhaps add a concentration phase to the development of regulation described earlier in this chapter. The competitive environment and the internationalization force financial institutions to prepare for even tougher competition and less regulation by searching for ways of exploiting and developing economies of scale.

Policies in the EEC countries differ widely in how active governments are in the process. Some take part in restructuring the financial systems by inducing and protecting financial innovations, while others let financial innovations and institutions develop in response to demand and technological development. This is to say, that there are of course national differences in the relevance and intensity of the links shown in the figure above. Likewise the links are not, in time, certain. Thinking over what an unlimited deregulation process would lead to, the answer is not necessarily increased internationalization as indicated in the figure. In a completely deregulated market uncertainty would be substantial, and it is likely, that agents would stick to conventions rooted in the national, historically tested way of doing business in the financial system.

The securitization/disintermediation process is a complicating factor in this connection. If the central task of banks and other financial institutions, as being a link between creditors and debtors is gradually reduced, then there may be a limited possibility of accumulating knowledge and skills in credit judgement within the financial institutions. This learning process is extremely important, but weaker and more impersonal ties between borrowers and lenders can limit the intensity of the learning process. In addition the despecialization of financial institutions hampers the accumulation of knowledge, because learning requires some kind of institutionalization to be useful for the future. Diversification is thus not unproblematic even if legislative restrictions are removed. A level of competence to compete in other areas of specialization than the one you were previously participating in is required. The competence in credit judgement and reduction of asymmetries in information between the borrower and the lender is especially important.

Furthermore, another aspect of trends in financial markets has an impact on innovation financing. In many countries the welfare state expanded in the postwar era with many public and private funds as a result (for example, pension funds, social insurance funds, etc.). These funds manage large amounts of money and maximize portfolios by buying and selling bonds and shares. However, the growth of the "Managed Money Capitalism" (Minsky, 1990, p.69) is likely to be hostile to innovations if management of the funds are reluctant to take a long-term perspective and if they are too risk averse. Thus, Minsky (1990, p.72) claims that

"Whereas venture capital funds may do the job for smaller innovative efforts, when the capital needs of advanced technology require financial investments that, in effect, bet a highly leveraged company, the investment decision is likely to be passed over. One paradox that

230

emerges from the growth of managed money capitalism is that the financing of truly innovative technologies and products may become a state responsibility. Capitalism may require intervention to remain technologically dynamic in an era of managed money capitalism."

8.4. Perspectives and conclusions with special reference to innovation financing

With the background of the trends discussed above I shall consider likely implications for innovation financing. In particular I shall discuss if the described development affects the types of financial system as classified in chapter 7. In that chapter it was pointed out that financial systems differ with respect to generation of borrewer-lender relationships. Thus, the present discussion will also have this perspective. A first question to ask is whether these changes are compatible with industry needs, or if they are a more or less independent development in the global financial system with no connection to industrial and technological change in specific nations. In addition, it is plausible that different nations have specific developments and that they also have their own speed of technical and industrial change. Can the global process of deregulation, integration and homogeneity be adjusted to cope with such country specific needs?

This is of course a very difficult and complex question to answer, but in general I believe there is not so much reason for optimism. As discussed in chapter 6 and 7 the advantages of the capital market based system are not the generation of lender-borrower relations, and provision of long term capital. However, many credit based financial systems are moving towards this kind of system and the current trends in international financial markets are indicating the same trend in systemic change. If this change towards more market orientation is too fast some countries may face severe problems.

The reason for these problems is that the present national financial systems have been built in close interaction with industrial development and government policy measures through many years, and institutions for coping with specific, national problems have gradually developed. A radical change in financial systems during a short period of time, calls for an adequate institutional framework to be built in the same period, if the advantages of the specifics of national systems are to be upheld. Thus, the stability of the financial system, the ability to reduce asymmetric information through close relationships between firms and banks, the accumulation of knowledge in specialized financial institutions, a long time horizon in investments and ability to handle financial crises in firms without hostile take-overs, may be merits of some of the old national systems worth keeping for the price of homogeneity, integration, and increased competition. But they will not be kept, if the old institutions are torn down without replacement.

In the words of Colin Mayer (1988, p.1183):

> "The distinctive feature of successful financial systems is their close involvement in industry. A primary characteristic of a market based system is an arm's length relation between investor and firm. There are well documented exceptions, but the basic requirement of a market, that investors be treated equally, acts against the close involvement of any one party. ... The fundamental challenge that faces any institution or government that can affect the practice of finance is to encourage the emergence of closer relationships and to direct the wealth of talent that has now been concentrated in British financial institutions into direct participation in corporate activities. In the process, the apparent attractions of intensifying competition in financial markets may have to be resisted. The benefits of competition may only be attained at the expense of longer term economic prosperity."

Therefore, extensive, careless deregulation is not the road to follow if financial systems are still to serve the needs of national industry and finance innovations. Harmonization of legislation and type of system is likely to have inexpedient effects on financing innovations even if it may be sound for other purposes.

> "In the first place financial markets need a certain degree of regulation and supervision. Financial innovation has proceeded extremely fast in the last ten years. This process was supported by

the belief that full deregulation in the financial market was possible and desirable. That opinion has now changed. In countries where the process was fastest, it is recognized that a legal framework and a certain amount of supervision are indispensable. To try and organize supervision - which is a highly legal and technical matter - at the world level would, of course, be totally unrealistic." (Bieber et.al., 1988, p.286)

Rather it is the reduction of uncertainty in industrial investments and the encouragement of special, national financial innovations, which are suited to the national financial system and the character of industrial and technological development in the nation, that should be a political priority. Having said this, it must be recognized that the effects of the trends in financial markets are not only negative in the sense that they dismantle borrower-lender relationship. In fact the opposite effect may result from the same trend. To take one example, deregulation may really have negative effects on the financing of corporate investments, but deregulation may also be an advantage. It depends on the specific type of regulation and the specific area which is regulated. As already mentioned regulations exist on how much financial institutions are allowed to be involved in industrial firms. Experience from Germany with universal banking and heavy involvement of banks in non-financial enterprises are of course not completely paritive, but nevertheless indicate that borrower-lender relationships are enhanced which in turn may facilitate innovation financing. Pension funds and other institutional investors are also regulated in the same way and are critizised for being as short termed in their investment policy, especially when there are exit possibilities. Deregulation in this area may be a step forward with respect to innovation financing[8]. Alternatively with the words above quoted by Minsky in mind, the opposite solution is likely; a heavy government intervention is likely to result from "managed money capitalism".

---

[8] It could be argued that it is not - and should not be - the purpose of pension funds to expose themselves, and consequently its' members to risks. Rather it is the purpose of a pension fund to ensure a high and certain future pension for its' members. On the other hand, if financing problems prevents the development of a viable industry there is a risk of balance of payments - and government budget deficits. If pensions are large compared to the average development of income it is likely that measures are taken to reduce the real value of pensions anyway.

Similar arguments could be put forward on the other trends of financial markets. But the crux of the matter is that developments of financial markets and financial systems should ensure the compatibility of the development of industrial and technical change. One possible method of dealing with this problem and reduce that of asymmetric information, is to encourage more specialized, national financial institutions (Kolesar, 1990, p.255)[9]. If these for example lend to one sector of industry it is plausible that they will have better ability to provide a qualitatively improved advising, screening and monitoring of potential borrowers inside that sector.

> "Thus, specialized institutions are likely to "choose" more competently, to develop specialized knowledge, to foster relatively more "learning" than selection and to favour the development and reproduction of relatively stable and concentrated industrial structures." (Dosi & Orsenigo, 1988b, p.32)

Regulation and national considerations impinge upon integration and internationalization. In addition to advocating market segmentation and warning against a too extensive despecialization there are limits to integration, which need to be recognized as long as the nation state exists. In reality, the internationalization process does have its own boundaries besides the political ones. For example, despite entry of foreign banks, national banking systems are persistent as two observers point out below.

> "However, the reality is that national financial markets remain separated from each other, do continue alongside international markets, and do continue to matter...national institutions have primary access to national savings because the retail banking networks in place are difficult to push aside.....Global banking remains, for the most part, wholesale banking." (Zysman, 1990, p.27)

> "A second reason is that national barriers still exist....The fact is that there are still national barriers to capital mobility, and even more

---

[9] The OECD (1989) has also advocated increased specialization of financial institutions to support small and medium sized, innovative firms. On the other hand the pros of specialization may not add up to the cons, which could be said to be lower flexibility. If the financial institutions is engaged in a lot of different areas the possibilities of switching between areas of business, is likely to be larger.

obstacles to the supply and organization of financial services. It is quite difficult for financial institutions to establish themselves and provide a full range of financial services in countries other than their home country." (Bieber et.al., 1990,p.287)

Reasons for these national barriers have been mentioned above. Additionally, confidence in national banks will usually be relatively higher when norms, language, regulation etc. are national. In other words, the access to first order savings is important to competition between domestic and international banks, and the national level of savings and degree of intermediation will have an impact on the conditions for competition between national and foreign banks. Furthermore, liberalization and deregulation does not necessarily mean that competition increases so that prices are equalized. For example, it is stated that

"Even without formal controls and trade barriers, in fact, financial markets may remain segmented and geographically separated. Because of the high degree of concentration in the industry, these markets may be, in practice, noncontestable." (Grilly, 1989, p.317)

Competition between banks on the market for large firms is likely to increase because these firms are increasingly quality minded and value a broad, flexible range of financial products within the same bank. However, the competition for small and medium sized firms will probably remain local, culturally determined and here foreign banks are not competitive.

To sum up, this chapter has discussed impacts on innovation financing of the development of the environment in which the processes of financing innovation takes place. The discussion brought forward another dimension to the previously discussed difference in logics between the industrial and financial world. It seems particularly that the development of the financial sector and the industrial sector is taking place independently to a large extent, and increasingly so, in spite of increased internationalization and in spite of the fact that some especially large firms have become important actors on the financial scene. Complexity in technology, increased immaterial investments, shorter product life cycles, greater uncertainty, and larger market entry barriers are some of the trends in production. Increased needs for advice and information exchange which may be better handled in institutions rather than markets is a result of these trends. However, generally taken, the trends in the financial sector do not seem to encourage institutional financing of corporate investments and they do not seem to encourage considerations of specific development of national industry.

8.5. Summary - the impact of trends in financial markets

Summing up the net impact on possibilities for innovation financing of current trends in financial markets is likely to be negative, especially for the countries with credit based financial systems. The arguments leading to this conclusion are first, that the trends are going in the direction of dismantling the traditionally stronger ties between lenders and borrows in these countries. For several reasons discussed earlier these relationships are important to innovation financing. Second, the development is likely to impose further short-termism which has been mentioned as hostile to innovation.

Third, an increased market orientation requires that the institutional set-up of the financial systems are geared to spread information previously exchanged decentralized through close relationships between borrowers and lenders. Monitoring mechanisms must also be developed. However, it takes time to develop such institutions and legislation and this may not be done in time to match the speed of change within financial markets. The consequence may be that the propensity of finance innovation projects which require relatively much information exchange, may diminish.On the other hand, the market orientation may have some benefits with respect to flexibility, allocative efficiency, and possibilities for restructurings through ownership transfer.

Thus, this chapter has provided us with a tentative answer to the question posed in the introduction: Are conditions for innovation financing improving or diminishing as a consequence of the current trends in financial markets? In addition, it explained in more detail how the stage for the processes described in earlier chapters is likely to develop. It was pointed out that in spite of increased internationalization, deregulation and convergence of financial systems, national differences are likely to persist.

Chapter 9. The ability of the financial system in Denmark to finance innovations

9.1. Introduction

The analysis has so far been progressing from the abstract, theoretical considerations towards the concrete, real world illustrations of financial systems. With this chapter a step further in that direction is taken as we shall now take a closer look at the Danish system of financing investments in new technology. I shall emphasize, that I do not intend to give a detailed description of the financial system in Denmark. Recently this has been done by Østrup (1989, 1992). Therefore, the focus is on the specific features of the financial systems relevant for financing innovations.[1][2]

In chapter 5 requirements for financial institutions supporting the innovation process efficiently were developed with the firm as the starting point. In chapter 6 the point of departure was reversed. That chapter shifted focus to the financier side. This and the subsequent chapter are split into two in roughly the same way. This chapter analyzes innovation financing in DK from the demand side whereas chapter 10 takes the supply side approach. With this subdivision I hope to capture some of the problems related to focusing solely on one of the sides.

In chapter 7 an analytical framework for analyzing financial systems was developed. Using that framework on the Danish financial system shows that

---

1 This leads to a problem of defining what is "relevant". Firms do not differentiate where capital comes from, but what it is used for. If financial conditions are made better in one part of the firm, other parts may have more financial resources for technological development. Furthermore, institutional changes are often interdependent, that is, what seem to be isolated changes may have large impacts on innovation financing. Therefore, I shall also treat institutions, which are not of direct relevance for technology financing.

2 One could of course ask if technological development in Denmark differs substantially from the picture described in chapter 4 and 5, and consequently if it is a different innovation process that needs to be financed. The answer to that question is, in short, that the general characteristics in chapter 4 and 5 also apply reasonable well to the Danish case. Therefore, I shall desist from describing how innovations take place in Denmark. Studies of the nature of the innovation process in Denmark are contained in DYS (1991), Gjerding et al.(1991), Kristensen (1992), Edquist & Lundvall (1992).

it is a bank oriented, or "credit based institutional", financial system. Consequently, there is not much point in a detailed analysis of the stock market as a source of finance for technology investments. Markets have a minor role to play compared to intermediaries and hierarchies. Instead attention is directed towards the institutions channeling finance to these investments. It would be natural to analyse banks in more detail when dealing with a bank oriented financial system. This is done in a separate subsequent chapter. Therefore, banks are almost absent in the present chapter.

Key questions to answer in this chapter are the following: a) What is the magnitude of the financial barriers to innovation in the Danish financial system? b) What is the character of these barriers? c) From what sources do Danish firms finance innovations, and are they adequate for that purpose? and finally d) how does the Danish system of financing innovations fit into the theory developed above?

The outline of the chapter is as follows. First, I shall give a brief discussion of the relative importance of different sources of corporate finance in Denmark. The purpose of this is to give a general impression of the structure and set up of the financial system in Denmark with respect to innovation financing.

Secondly, I shall briefly discuss possible origins of financial barriers to innovations in Denmark. In addition it is important to specify the content of financial barriers if policy steps aimed at overcoming financial barriers are to be effective.

Thirdly, I shall include in the analysis aspects of the financial system in Denmark which are either directly supportive at innovations or indirectly of great impact. More specifically, I discuss possible impacts for innovation financing from public support, the development of mortgage institutions and the bond market, and the role of institutional investors - in particular the pension funds. bank financing is not treated in that section because it is the sole subject of chapter 10.

238

Then, in section 9.5., Venture capital firms are dealt with in some detail because of their direct orientation towards financing innovations.

The final section concludes and summarizes the chapter briefly by relating the discussions to the theory in the previous chapters.

9.2. Corporate finance in Denmark

How do Danish firms finance investments and how important is the financial system in Denmark to technological development in the country? Precise answers to these questions - especially the latter - are at best difficult to give. The sources of external financing for industry may give an impression of how the Danish financial system relevant for corporate financing looks. The latter question may be approached by taking a look at how large a part of R&D expenditures is externally financed.

Both measures are, however, not perfect as explained below.

If we first turn to external finance, the table below shows some important sources of obtaining finance for industry in Denmark.

Table 9.1: Private sources of external finance for industry in Denmark 1985-1990

	Banks	Pension funds	Insurance comp.	Mortgage inst.	15 fin. companies	Stock emmission	Total
1985	34.8	8.6	16.6	28.2	5.1	6.7	100 (54.9)
1986	32.9	7.4	15.2	27.9	5.8	10.8	100 (72.8)
1987	37.5	8.6	13.7	28.8	7.5	4.0	100 (74.7)
1988	32.8	11.5	17.0	26.2	7.1	5.4	100 (74.5)
1989	34.3	13.8	22.4	12.2	5.8	11.5	100 (92.9)
1990	35.9	16.1	28.0	7.3	6.3	6.3	100 (96.6)

[Percentages] numbers in brackets are absolute numbers in billion dkr

Source: The national bank of Denmark, Quarterly and annual reports 1991 and 1992).

As pointed out the figure are for lending to industry in general and not for investments in new technology. They are not even divided into investment purposes and other purposes. In addition, the figures do not give a totally correct picture of corporate financing in Denmark because figures for insurance companies and pension funds are not for industry only. If they were, and if investment in buildings were excluded, banks would be even more dominant in lending to industry than indicated in the table. Another conclusion is that the stock exchange supplies industrial firms in Denmark with a small fraction of their external financing. A third point derived from the figures is that market shares between the groups of institutions are relatively stable to the changes in other OECD countries. Bank lending has particularly decreased in the OECD as a whole but this is not shown unequivocally in Denmark.

The figures do, of course, not tell us how investments in innovations are financed, and they say nothing about the share of external financing.

R&D financing can approximate only one aspect of innovation financing,[3] but the table below may nevertheless give a feeling for how much is externally financed.

Table 9.2.:   The share of externally financed R&D in industry

	1985	1987	1989
External financing in industry	7.7	9.0	9.6
-- in total manufacturing	12.8	16.0	16.7

Source: Undervisningsministeriet (1990, p.8).

The table shows that around 1/10 of R&D in industry is externally financed whereas the corresponding figure for total manufacturing is 1/6. Both have increased in the period of observation.

---

3 A survey of innovation activity in Danish industrial firms (Kristensen, 1992) showed that 50% of expenditures for innovations were listed by the firms as R&D expenditures. However, there were large differences between branches and the figures were probably characterized in this way because firms usually only report R&D expenditures.

A low rate of external finance to internal finance could perhaps indicate lesser needs for a well functioning financial system and special institutions for corporate finance. However, the very absence of special credit institutions could equally be an incentive for or even make it necessary for firms to try to finance their investments internally. It is probably impossible to come to a firm conclusion on this.

9.3. Financial barriers to innovation - impact and content

9.3.1. The importance of finance in the innovation process

It goes without saying that a quantitative measure of exactly how important finance is to the process of innovation is not possible, just as a measurement of the importance of innovations to the whole economy is difficult. Except for the intuitive deduction, that any process cannot finance itself, but needs outside finance until proceeds from sales has begun, the two logical ways to illustrate the importance of finance seen from the firms point of view are a) make the firms list a priority of different prerequisites for innovation and b) make the firms give their view of the character and magnitude of the financial barriers to innovation

A ranking, as described, has been carried out in a study of barriers to innovation done by The Commission of the European Communities. A number of surveys in the member countries were put together and compared. One of the main conclusions was that

> "Incidentally, all the national reports on Barriers to Innovation lay stress on the difficulties of financing innovative enterprises, particularly the smallest of them." (ibid.,p.206)

The background for this conclusion was that a ranking of different barriers to innovation showed the following results (ibid.,p.173):

Table 9.3.:   The most important difficulties, in decreasing order of significance.

1st rank   Effect of education and training upon employment in enterprises

1st rank   (equal importance to education and training) Effect of action by banks upon the financing of innovation

3rd rank   Effect of action by venture capital companies upon the financing of innovation

4th rank   Norms and standards - product controls - effect upon the manufacture of new products

Both the first and the third most important factor hampering innovation in the community were financial constraints. A few Danish studies have recently also used this method. As a part of a Nordic Innovation study Kristensen (1991) asked a sample of industrial firms what the factors were promoting and hampering innovations respectively. Among options for answering was "too large a uncertainty compared to potential profits". Of course most of the respondents listed that category as a hinderence to innovation. But "lack of risk capital" was seen as the second most important factor and "lack of government support" was also listed as an (out of 13) important factor hampering innovation.

Jakobsen (1992, p.25) interviewed 54 entrepreneurs who received government grants for start-up. The main problem in a start-up was seen as raising the necessary capital (56%).[4] [5]

The results at the studies indicate the significance of finance to the innovation process, but financial constraints can be many things. To be a little more specific about the character of the financial barriers, I shall below point out what they are in the Danish financial system.

A number of early studies from the firms point of view showed what the problems actually were when innovations needed external financing. To my knowledge there has not yet been any survey on the financing side. Even today, 10 years later, the problems are roughly the same. Thus, Håndværksrådet (1983) found that the start-up of firms was often financed in an inexpedient way because of lack of knowledge about possibilities of

---

4 The main source of finance other than equity was banks (55%) and government support was the second most important source (47%).

5 A similar conclusion was reached by Sørensen (1990, p.29) in an earlier evaluation of the same support programme.

finance and lack of external advice. Furthermore, it was found that more than one out of every three firms experienced problems with getting external finance, and this was due to large demands for security and absence of risk willingness by the financiers.

T.Bak-Jensen (1982) showed that firms - especially small firms - are generally unable to recognize and deal with financial problems as well as being unable to raise capital in the first place. Investments in small firms are often large compared to their ability to give collateral and in particular immaterial investments involves financing problems. Banks usually use accounts and budgets as criteria for screening projects without knowing much about the project, and there was a lack of channels for contact between investors and firms. Risk capital was generally found to be scarce.

Mønsted (1985) claims that an important barrier is the way the system of advising is set up compared to the needs of small, innovative firms. The reason this system is that important is because of a lack of competence in these firms. Högberg (1981) found that access to capital was a crucial prerequisite for the innovation process in 48% of the interviewed firms.

These early reports are still valid with respect to the financial barriers to innovation, and similar conclusions have been reached in all such studies for the past decade. More recent reports confirms this pattern. For example, Håndværksrådet produced a small questionnaire in 1991 among some of its members of small, manufacturing firms in industry. It showed that 40.5 % of respondents answered yes to the question "Has the firm experienced increasing difficulties in obtaining loans from banks during the past year?"

Nelleman a/s (1990) found that almost 2/3 of interviewed innovators met problems with financing and this was the most serious barrier to development of new, product innovating firms.

Industriministeriet (1991) points out some of the same problems, but emphasizes, correctly, that the barriers vary according to what phase the idea/firm is in. Consequently in order to be somewhat more specific on the barriers to financing innovations I shall discuss them in line with the theory in chapter 5. In that chapter three important issues were discussed; the importance of firm size, various problems for the firm during the financial life cycle of a product, and financial requirements of different innovation strategies. From these discussions requirements for financial institutions were derived. Below I shall see how the two first issues present themselves in the Danish case.

9.3.2. Firm size and possibilities for financing innovations

Financial barriers to innovation may be influenced by, or consist of, firm specific factors, such as age of the firm and firm size. It is likely that small and medium sized firms are more constrained regarding external finance, and likewise new firms will presumably be regarded as more risky investments than older, established firms. This is a problem of special relevance to the Danish case, due to the particular Danish industrial structure with relatively many small and medium sized enterprises compared to larger firms. In the Danish innovation survey mentioned above (Kristensen, 1991) a marked difference was found between large/medium sized firms and small firms, when they where asked whether lack of risk capital and lack of public economic support had hampered innovation[6].

Table 9.4: **Barriers to innovation. Lack of risk capital as a barrier against innovations [%]**

	Denmark [N=194]	Finland	Sweden	Norway
Size of firm				
Small	47.7	31.7 (65.4)[7]	66.7	25.6
Medium	18.2	32.5	14.0	33.6
Large	16.1	32.8	5.6	27.0
All	35.9	35.1	22.4	28.8

Source: "Innovation activities in the Nordic countries", Nordic Industrial Fund, Information no.3/1991.

---

6 In Denmark 29.8% of small firms, 12.3% of medium sized firms, and 4.7% of large firms listed lack of public economic support as a factor hampering innovations.

7 Small, R&D-intensive firms.

In the debate about financial barriers to innovation it has been claimed, that there is plenty of idle capital to be invested. On the other hand, entrepreneurs maintain that many projects are unable to raise external capital. There is some truth in both points of views. A definition of a good project for an investor is one that produces a pay off on a satisfactory level, but this is an ex post definition. Investments in new technology, on the other hand, are characterized by the difficulty in predicting the ex post pay off. At the time of the investment decision investors have little possibilities of knowing the actual, future proceeds from sales as well as the costs and time for developing the product. The additional uncertainty in innovation projects is a major reason for financial barriers for innovation.

The two points of view will therefore persist no matter how many investigations are made on the issue. However, in the debate some agreements can be seen on whether problems exist or not. It is recognized both by firms/policy makers and financiers that small firms in particular face financing problems. It is, though, not clear if the problems stem from an insufficient aggregate amounts of idle risk capital, from an inefficient allocation of the risk capital, or from special problems related to the interface between financier and applicant.

But why should a SME be a less attractive investment to borrowers than a big company? From the point of view of the financier the small company has important disadvantages, as discussed in chapter 5. In that chapter a number of small firm disadvantages were pointed out. Thus, it was claimed that, among other things, small firms have a volatile development, higher risk of default, lack of competence, lack of reputation, and require higher interest rates together with the fact that collateral cannot protect innovations legally, and the firms often insist on preserving independence. Apparently these disadvantages also apply to the Danish case. From the discussion below specific problems in the various stages in the development of firm, financial barriers related to the size of a firm are demonstrated.

9.3.3. Early stage and provision of seed capital in Denmark

In the first phase of a typical project[8] the main problem for the firm is to provide as much documentation of the merits of the project as possible. Various types of investigations on technical feasibility and market perspectives can show the firms' expectations of possibilities for patenting, development and production costs, size of potential market, degrees of competition, profitability, present organization and competencies, and needs for expansion and additional resources.

In the case in which the project is undertaken by a small, new firm, a group, or a single person, it is likely that a need for additional competence will be required in order to make a realistic project plan. Therefore, the advisory system is important to the project, and the competence of the advisors and the communication between advisor and entrepreneur is important as well. Advisors are often expensive and reluctant to take the risk associated with an uncertain project. External advisors and other middlemen such as lawyers and accountants are likely to be very important to innovation projects. The role they have is not only to be advisors but also to be a link between the entrepreneur/firm and both other external advisors, potential customers and potential financial sources. It is likely that more could be done in terms of improving the competence of these middlemen and to improve the interaction between firm and bank. For example, Swedish regional Development Funds assist entrepreneurs with the business plan and make a bank follow the process of conducting this plan. Then the Fund invests part of the necessary capital and the bank also has an incentive to invest because it followed the business plan. The point is that a closer interaction between the firm, advisors and credit judgement in banks is induced (DTI, 1990, p.28).

The advising system has been analyzed and criticized as being insufficient. One reason is the before-mentioned communication problem and

---

8 In fact the stages described in chapter 5, which are used here, could be added to by including and dividing the pre-stage of the early stage into, for example, a phase when the idea is conceived; one containing conceptualization; one containing preparing for entering early stage and thus actual development of business plan. This prestage has only recently been given any attention in terms of government support - often in the form of locally organized courses for educating entrepreneurs.

competence mis-match. Another reason is the set-up of the advisory system compared to the problems, that firms are actually facing. The advisory system in banks is more oriented towards finding security than stimulating potential developments of the firm (Mønsted, 1985, p.52). In addition, the advisory system is set up in a sectoral manner whereas the problems that small firms are facing are integrated and the firms are non-specialized compared to large firms. This is a main reason for communication difficulties between the advisory system and small firms (ibid., p.224, 252 and 269). B. Hollingsworth (1988) supports the critique of the advisory system.

Investors are rarely involved directly in this stage. Usually the project plan is financed by personal loans or savings; often also by bank loans in the form of cash credit with security in real estate, or other personal security, (often amounting to 2-300%)(Håndværksrådet, 1983). Banks rarely have the necessary competence and resources to evaluate project plans in the very early stage (DTI, 1990, p.13). Consequently entrepreneurs are often dependent on expensive external advice for which they have to take private loans from their bank.

In addition to external factors the entrepreneurs may also hamper realization of project plans (DTI, 1990, p.13). Often they are reluctant to take professional, external advice, and they are reluctant to cooperate and share influence with investor.

Government programmes support the preparation business plans and on a very general level there is a tax premium on savings for start-up purposes, but the definition of start-up does not include expenses for project planning. The other main initiatives in Denmark aimed at helping out entrepreneurs at this stage include[9] The Technology Council's establishment programme, The scholarship programme for entrepreneurs and The Technology Council's product development programme.

---

9 A large variety of support programmes make it difficult for small firms to assess their actual possibilities. According to one report there were 52 different possibilities for industrial support administrated by 21 different authorities in Denmark in 1988 (Forum For Industriel Udvikling 1988, p.60).

In Denmark the technological service centers and the technology council support firms at this stage with financial and consultative aid. In addition there is a programme of supporting networks including financial backing for industrial R&D cooperation between firms or between firms and technological service centers.

9.3.4. Start-up and supply of capital and competence

The most important tasks for a new firm in the start-up phase is to raise funds to bring the business plan into effect, and to add the necessary competence to carry the project through. Danish surveys have shown that small firms do not have the necessary fund raising ingenuity.[10] This applies to for the knowledge of financing possibilities, the personal ability to convince a potential lender and the competence for filling out applications for government support programs, business plans and information to potential investors. Danish innovators characterize this product ripening period as very critical because it is often longer than expected; government support programs are insufficient in this stage; external investors are more reluctant towards financing immaterial investments in marketing etc., compared to financing technical development (Nelleman, 1990, p.22), and the risk of the project is large compared to the documentation (DTI, 1990, p.14).

There is however evidence that innovators tend to start with a relatively small equity. Therefore financial slack is too small to cope with unexpected events (DTI, 1990, p.15) (Nelleman, 1990, p.72), (Industriministeriet, 1991, p.15). If innovators use all of their personal savings and possibilities for loans before they ask external investors like venture capital firms for equity financing of marketing etc., they are likely not to achieve a reasonable share in the firm if an investor agrees to finance further expansion. A consequence may be that innovators are demotivated because they feel excluded from running the firm and carrying their idea into effect.

In Denmark government funds are still an important source in this stage but also banks, and to some degree venture capital firms, also finance start-ups.

---

10 Mønsted (1985), T.Bak-Jensen (1982), Håndværksrådet (1983).

In addition, there are some less important funds for financing this stage including private funds, other firms, pension funds and Lønmodtagernes Dyrtidsfond.[11]

Informal investors make up an area which is very little used and until recently little examined. There may be an unused potential in these private placements because private investors often have management experience to give in addition to risk capital (DTI, 1990, p.19) (Nelleman, 1990, p.22,75). However, there seems to be a lack of channels of contacts between potential investors and projects looking for risk capital.[12]

The competence of management is perhaps the most important criteria for evaluating innovation projects. If the innovator, be it a single person or a firm, does not convince investors that the necessary competence to carry the project through is present, then the project is likely to be turned down.[13] Alternatively the competence can be supplied to the firm by education, new employees or the investor becoming actively engaged in working management.

In Denmark, as well as in other countries, it seems as if there are considerable differences between the way of thinking, or culture, of the financier and the innovator. Financiers tend to focus upon financial criteria whereas innovators are often obsessed by the idea of the project and may disregard economic realities and thorough budgetting. The degree of competence mis-match between innovator and financier may be reduced through a closer interaction and exchange of information.

---

11 LD (The Employees' Capital Funds) have had a large influence in the latter part of the 1980s and 1990s by purchasing a large amount of unlisted shares. However, this strategy has now turned to investments in later stage, established firms which demand less monitoring and advice.

12 Koppel (1992) reports a recent attemt to bring informal investors together with the purpose of registering potential "angels". Main (preliminary) results show that with an effort to arrange contacts, considerable amounts of risk capital may be available. Key barriers for matching an investor with a suitable project were found to be (exept for lack of channels of contrats) the personal character of the two parties and geographical distance.

13 OECD (1985) lists lack of confidence in the quality of management as the reason for 71% of rejections on hi-tech venture capital applications.

9.3.5. Expansion - financing growth and market entrance

If the project proves viable the firm may wish to expand, and then a whole range of problems arise concerning the basic principles for running a firm. Again competent management is important as is additional capital for exploitation of economics of scale. The firm often seeks equity at this stage or it looks for industrial cooperation or a financial partner. A wider range of different investors are relevant at this stage, including pension funds and venture companies.

For two reasons the limited home market in Denmark is insufficient as the only market for most product innovations. Shortened life cycles for most products and increased costs for developments necessitate a full-scale exploitation of the time the "market window" (the time when the product is sellable) is open. Many Danish product innovations are niche products, which makes it difficult to find a national industrial partner. Consequently, innovators are forced to be exporters as well and this demands additional capital for the usual extra costs connected to exporting.[14]

9.3.6. Summing up and relating to theory

In chapter 5 the process aspect of innovation was emphasized and it was pointed out that financial requirements differ during the life cycle of a project. Small firms were seen as having major disadvantages when raising funds compared with larger firms. In general the theoretical conclusions also seem to hold for the Danish case, if judged on the basis of the reports mentioned above. More specifically major barriers for financing innovations in Denmark may be grouped into two: information dependent barriers and competence dependent barriers. The former relates to the fact that borrowers do not have information on all possibilities and prices of funds. For example, firms - especially small firms - do not know about all government support programmes. Moreover firms rarely "shop around" to get the best offer for financing of its' project. Therefore, they have limited information on prices on funds. A "market price" does not exist for innovation projects. Lenders are also constrained by information. They are,

---

14 DUF (1991) lists the export share of manufacturing in their portfolio firms as on average over 90% within a couple of years of start-up.

of course, not aware of what potential projects are seeking seek finance, but even at the single project level lenders do not have access to information about all relevant aspects of a project.

Concerning competence dependent barriers borrowers - in particular entrepreneurs and small firms lack the ability to fill out applications for government programmes and to conduct a thorough business plan. Moreover they are often not competent in running a small, volatile business and managing an innovation project. Finally, they are unable to assess the way of thinking and the specific products in the financial sector. Lenders are, on the other hand, not able to judge innovation projects and knowledge based small firms. They tend to stick to judgments based on criteria they know about from financing routine investments whereas the idea, the technical possibilities, and the knowledge base of the firm is not valued highly.

These barriers are enhanced if it is a small firm or single entrepreneurs who applies for funds.

In the following I shall treat the most important financial sources in further detail, including considerations of the set-up of the Danish financial system in respect to support of firms in later stages financially.

9.4. Features of the financial system in Denmark of relevance to innovation financing

9.4.1. Public support - political, historical background, and specific institutions

Not only financial institutions select project to be undertaken. Firms themselves select which projects they find worth while carrying out. The criteria for this selection are primarily financial. Firms choose the project they believe will render a profit in the short or long term. These choices may however not necessarily coincide with what is socially desireable. The rationale for government is to adjust the direction of technological change in a way which not only fulfills the needs of private enterprises but also, when they are not the same, fulfil the needs of society. A classic argument

251

for government intervention is the one put forward by Arrow (1962). In his opinion public returns of R&D in a firm exceed private returns because of spillovers both between firms in the same industry and across industries. The fact that not all the returns of R&D are appropriated by the firm may discourage it from using resources on R&D. To uphold these incentives government must compensate.[15]

From our theoretical discussions arguments for the role of government in innovation financing can be derived. Given risk aversion to very uncertain projects and given the larger uncertainty the further "upstream" in the innovation process (as discussed in chapter 4 and 5) the large risk connected to R&D is likely to require extensive risk spreading to achieve external financing. Government agencies are able to provide such risk spreading. Furthermore, expenses on R&D amount to still larger sums and some projects are too large for a single financier.

Another argument for government subsidies could be to support infant industries. A deliberate government strategy to select certain key industries or key technologies to give favorable conditions (see chapter 7 for examples of this) may be a way to promote an internationally competitive industry in certain areas. A counter argument would be that government intervention may crowd out private financing of innovation (Fölster & Pelikan, 1991). However, private financial institutions are reluctant to finance the early stages of the innovation process and this is precisely where government usually step in.

Earlier the main way of conducting policy, was to give subsidies through tax deductions. Obviously, this is not very effective in terms of accumulation of knowledge and inducing closer interaction between borrower and lender which was discussed in the theoretical part as important to innovation projects. However two important initiatives were taken.

In 1970 "Udviklingsfonden" (The development fund) was established. Its purpose was to increase Danish industrial competitiveness and growth by

---

15   A survey of arguments for and against government subsidies can be found in Grossman (1990) and Fölster (1992).

financing development of new products and processes. The main part of the funds went to larger companies. The funds were administrated by the Ministry of Industry, who appointed a board with financial, industrial and technical expertise. As a supplement to this fund, a product development fund was established in 1977, which aimed more to aid smaller firms and provide seed capital. In 1990 the Development Fund was closed down. In 1992 a new fund was established but it is not working yet.

The other main initiative - and in our context the most important one - was the reorganizing of the technological service centre and the establishment of a technology council. Its purpose was to support technological development with financial aid, but not only that. An important part of its work was to give firms access to consultative support. Technological information centers were established on a regional basis for providing local firms with technical and market advisory aid and knowledge about further financial aid. These information centers have been successful in helping small and medium sized firms through their knowledge about these firm with a local basis. In addition, their knowledge about possibilities for advice and their relations to other, national institutions and programmes make them an important part of support to small and medium sized enterprises (T. Bak-Jensen, 1992). In the beginning of the 1980, a political climate for a more conscious and resource demanding technology policy grew. In this period the government increased funds for technological support substantially:

Table 9.5. Funds for technological support as a percentage of total industrial support.[16]

1981	1982	1983	1984	1985	1986	1987	1988
14,2	15,0	21,6	26,3	40,9	58,1	62,3	61,1

(Source: Sidenius,1989,p.54)

---

16 Even though there was this shift in support to technology the absolute figures show only a gradual increase, and actually fell substantially between 1985 and 1986 from 755.1 mio. D.kr. to 619.3 mio. D.kr. The total expenses for industrial support decreased since 1982.

As a consequence a third way of conducting technology policy was introduced. With a starting point in areas of special interest, identified by the Technology Council, technology programmes were indicated in the areas of information technology, biotechnology, technology of materials, a program for industrial design and a programme for new firms. This kind of programmes had considerable weight in the eighties as well as now.[17]

From the theoretical discussions in previous chapters it should be expected that government agencies would finance a large part of R&D. This expectation is confirmed by the tables below. 68% of external financing of R&D was government financed.

Table 9.6: External R&D financing in manufacturing - sources distributed.(in 1000 D.kr) 1989.

I & H support		Governme nt support	Danish firms	EEC	Other foreign sources	Other sources	Total[18]
a	b	c					
224167	55920	37804	44847	8387	32056	11544	52837	467562
47.9	12.0	8.1	9.6	1.8	6.9	2.5	11.3	100

Source: Ministry of Education, the Research department (1990, p.19).

As explained, the figures are far from being representative of innovation financing, because they cover R&D expenditures in established firms only. It is though interesting to see that government agencies - especially Udviklingsfondet (The Development Fund) supply firms with a very large part of their external finance for R&D.[19] As R&D is an increasingly important element of innovation (as discussed in chapter 4) government agencies financing R&D are likely to have an even larger impact in the future.

---

17 Recently the programmes have been cut substantially in order to reduce budget deficits.

18 The internal financing amounted to 4827 mio.kr in 1989.

19 In 1990 The Development Fund was closed down. This decision was critisized heavily by firms and corporate consultants.

In an international comparison industrial subsidies for R&D are high in Denmark.[20] In 1986-1988 industrial support in Denmark as a percentage of total industrial subsidies was 17.0% which is high compared to the EC average on 5.2% (Ford & Suyker, 1990, p.63). As indicated above there was a shift in policy during these years though focusing more on technology programmes and at the same time reducing total industrial support. it was also indicated that most of R&D support went to larger firms. This is reflected in the table below, which shows that the relatively increased focus upon technology might have been at the expense of small firms.

Table 9.7.:   Industrial support in the EC by type[a]. As percentage of total industrial subsidies.

	Small and medium-sized enterprises
Germany	2.8
France	2.2
Italy	5.1
UK	5.2
Belgium	7.0
Denmark	0.4
Greece	3.4
Ireland	4.5
Luxembourg	3.5
Netherlands	20.3
Portugal	1.9
Spain	0.6
EC-12	4.3

Source: Ford & Suyker, 1990, p.51.
a)   EC countries (1986-88 average): manufacturing plus mining, quarrying, gas and electricity sectors.

---

20 But the level of R&D expenditures is very low compared to other OECD countries.

Table 9.8.   Support to manufacturing in the EC countries by instrument [a] As percentage of total support.

	Grants	Tax concessions	Equity partic- ipation	Soft loans	Guaranties
Germany	30	63	0	6	1
France	33	16	18	15	19
Italy	54	36	7	3	0
UK	69	6	16	7	2
Belgium	81	11	6	12	10
Denmark	70	0	0	29	1
Greece	88	0	9	0	3
Ireland	52	37	6	1	4
Luxembourg	68	9	5	18	0
Netherlands	64	30	0	6	0
Portugal	26	60	12	2	0
Spain	78	0	19	2	1
EC-12	49	30	9	8	5

Source: Ford & Suyker, 1990, p.63.
a)   EC countries (1986-88 average): excluding supranational support, and support to energy and transport.

Table 9.8. shows how government support was given. It is notably that equity participation is absent in Danish support.[21] For small, innovative firms an equity gap is often a barrier to development.

In summary, the Danish level of R&D is very low but the government finance a relative large part of it. Industrial support as a whole is however well below the EC average (3.8% of GDP in Denmark, 7.5% in EC) (Ford & Suyker, 1990, p.46). It seems as if a government effort to increase the level and direct more technology support to small and medium sized firms - in particular as equity participation - would bring the policy more in line with other countries.[22]

---

21 In 1988 a government initiated venture company was established directed to financing innovations by equity participation. See section 9.5. for further information.

22 This is not to say that it is a goal in itself to harmonize policies to other countries. The national policy must be adapted to the specific needs of the national industry.

9.4.2. Mortgage institutions and the Danish market for bonds

When studying the Danish financial system two aspects appear to be distinct from the norm in most other countries: a very well developed market for bonds and three large mortgage institutions.

What is the reason for mentioning mortgage institutions in relation to the Danish system of innovation financing, when they almost exclusively finance buildings? The point is that many entrepreneurs start on the basis of personal loans with real estate as security. At a later stage it is much easier to borrow cheaply in banks, when there are buildings to put as security. Thus, this method of cheap financing of initial investments in buildings can ease borrowing for other purposes - e.g. technological investments. Recently mortgage institutions have tightened up lending procedures, and one can have a fear that high-technology investments at the start-up stage will have tougher conditions in the future.

The mortgage institutions are based on issuing bonds, and the Danish market for bonds is very well functioning and large. As distinct from to the case in the U.S., Danish firms do not issue bonds directly. Could it be possible to use the Danish bond market for financing investments directly? If firms issued bonds it might even be cheaper to obtain finance, because intermediaries would be avoided. Concerning technology and start-up financing, bonds could be issued with a larger nominal interest rate to cover the additional risk premium. In the U.S. these bonds are called "junk bonds".

There are however factors counteracting this possibility. One is that finance by debt in stead of equity makes the firm dependent on a rather steady cash-flow from sales of the products to redeem payments on the loans. Financial crises within the firm can easily occur before the project reaches break-even if sales do not show the expected performance, if development of the product is longer or other unexpected problems occur. If the firm was financed by equity, it could reduce or stop payments of dividends. It is, therefore an inappropriate way of financing early stages when the firm is very sensitive to deviations in expectations and thus often need financial slack. The experience with junk bonds are not unequivocally positive. In the

U.S. issuing has decreased substantially recently (The Economist, 5. May 1990, p.12).

This is a general argument. Another - related to the Danish system - is that many innovating firms are small. A small amount of bonds issued would not yield an incentive to judge the bonds. In other words, there is likely to be an information problem in that gathering information on a small firm is as costly as on a large firm. Furthermore, this method financing of is "arm-lengths". Investors need not have anything to do with the firm in question, except for the one-time buying and selling of the bonds.[23]

9.4.3. The pension funds and ownership/management of firms

Another important group of financial institutions in Denmark is the pension funds. In this connection they are interesting, because it has been discussed as to whether they would invest more in innovative firms provided legislation permits it. Legislation has put some limits on the investment of the pension funds, and financial institutions in general. This is to protect principal lenders, but in generally it is not considered appropriate, that preferred financial institutions own a too large proportion of stocks.[24]

Pension funds invest through equity and this makes them particularly interesting in relation to innovation financing because they provide "patient" capital. Other investors like insurance companies and banks have also invested in unlisted shares but banks generally avoid these shares if possible. In connection with bankruptcy, restructuring or credit arrangements with a firm a bank may take over shares but direct investments shares are not very common.

Pension funds, on the other hand, have actually provided firms with a considerable part of equity in the form of un-listed shares. They have both invested directly and indirectly through ownership of venture capital firms.

---

23 In addition, there is a tax legislative discrimination of direct issuing of bonds compared to ordinary debt financing.

24 In 1987 the 170 pension funds plus ATP and LD owned 45.7% of all stocks listed on the stock exchange (Industriministeriet, 1987, p.153). In the following LD and ATP are included in the term "pension funds".

The amount of direct investments exceed that of the total venture capital branch.

The experiences with these investments in the 1980s are, however, not exclusively positive. Monitoring and advising firms is a resource-demanding task and many investors realized that they did not have the necessary competence and other resources for monitoring. However, some of the pension funds continued and expanded investments in un-listed shares and they developed an actual investment department. In addition, they use professional boards for monitoring. Furthermore, an expansion of the total amount of investments made diversification possible (Venture News 7/91, p.4-5).

Quite recently the most active pension funds (LD and PKA) changed strategy because of too many failures in their portfolio of firms. Instead of unlisted shares they invest in firms in later stages which provides a better possibility for exit.

The story of pension fund investments in unlisted shares shows that providing capital only is not enough. Investments in high-risk firms like small, innovative firms, requires competence and resources. If the pension funds are not prepared to make "hands-on" investments they should perhaps rather concentrate on bonds and well-known, listed stocks. However, if they build up their competence and resources in this area, and legislation[25] permits them to be controlling owners, it may become an important source for financing innovations.

The above described investments by pension funds have similarities to those undertaken by traditional venture capital firms. In the next section the venture capital industry in Denmark is discussed. The purpose is to investigate if this industry has or can provide firms with risk capital for innovations.

---

25 In Denmark there are two kinds of stocks - A- and B-stocks, where A-stocks give more influence, but they are rarely traded. In a survey (Forum For Industriel Udvikling, 1988, p.32) it was found that A-stocks accounted for 30% of the total capital, but 74% of the votes in the firms.

9.5. Venture capital in Denmark and other non-regulated financial institutions

As previously mentioned the venture capital industry only provides firms with a fraction of the financing for their investments. In spite of its negligible importance, this market deserves special attention. The reason why venture capital firms are interesting in this context is that in their original idea they are supposed to finance high technology firms in the early stage.

> "..though small, venture capital can have a disproportionately large influence through its *catalytic* effect in inducing industrial structural shifts."
> (OECD,1985,"Venture capital for the development of new technology and the creation of companies",p.3)

Although there is some disagreement on how to define venture capital there are other common characteristics of venture capital financing, which relate to innovation financing. For example, in the original idea venture capital firms are generally considered to be over-average risk willing investors, financing is, to a large extent, with equity, time perspectives are long - often four to seven years, and above all they are active owners, that is to say, they add competence to the firm and take part in some decisions on the management of the firm.

The venture capital concept originated in the U.S. in the 1950's. At that time the U.S. venture capital firms were an important (often described as heroic) inducement in the creation of successful firms like Digital Equipment and Apple Computers. In many cases venture firms were spin-offs from universities or industrial firms. An essential feature of venture financing was a gradual build-up of competence through a mutual beneficial learning process between industrial firms and the venture capitalist.[26] However, the original idea of venture capital firms seems to have vanished somewhat not only in the U.S. but throughout the world. Rather than financing start-ups and risky, but promising, projects, the venture capital industry is now

---

26 Bullock (1983) describes this development.

oriented towards financing buy-outs and -ins, restructuring and LBO's in established firms[27].

The venture capital industry in Denmark is relatively young. Most venture capital companies were established in 1982, 1983 and 1984. There are several reasons why there was a boom in the number of venture capital firms shortly after the first were established. Firstly, there was an effect from the rapid development of the industry abroad. Secondly, even though the level of interest rates decreased, making debt financing attractive for the firms, the stock market was booming as were investments in industry. This boom in investments gave a great optimism with regard to introductions on the stock exchange and in the beginning most venture firms actually believed that introduction on the stock exchange was the exit. Investments in bonds became less attractive for pension funds and other institutional investors, also as an effect of tax on real rates of interest, and shares became more attractive due to legislative changes in the taxing of capital gains. Consequently, needs for capital in firms increased and institutional investors wished to channel some of their investments through affiliated companies with a venture capital profile. Legislation prevented them from putting too much capital in the corporate sector directly. Institutional investors are still the dominant investors in venture capital firms in the DK[28]

The venture capital industry has indeed been in flux in the past decade. Thus, in 1987 a magazine stated that

> "One thing is for certain: Venture capital is not a temporary phenomenon in Danish business. The industry is sustainable as an important partner and capital supply to especially young, fast growing firms, who, within a reasonably time span, have possibilities for being

---

27 Perhaps it is possible to trace precisely when this change began. 12/12-1980 Apple Computers was introduced on the stock exchange and the tremendous success this emission attracted both a lot of people and institutions to the venture capital industry and induced a boom in emissions of high-technology stocks. However, the newcomers to the industry was more directed towards fast, large profits than towards building up industrial firms (Finans/Invest, Nov.1984). The industry lost its original industrial base.

28 In 1987 the investors in the 21 Danish venture capital firms were banks (37.7%), pension funds (26.6%), private placements (16.8%), insurance companies (8.7%), others (10.2%).

introduced on the stock exchange III." (translated from
Danish)(Børsens Nyhedsmagasin, 26/6, 1987, p.32).

The state of affairs of the venture capital industry today would hardly
render statements as confident as this.[29] In 1990 a new deficit-record in
venture capital firms was set (78,5 mio. dkr) and both new corporate
investments and capital supply to the venture capital industry stagnated.
An accumulated loss of 362 mio dkr since the start of the industry adds
even more risk aversion to the cautious investment strategies in some of the
firms today. Out of the original 25 venture capital firms only 12 are left, and
4 out of these did not invest in 1990 or 1991 (Venture New 5/91, p.18).[30]
The remaining venture firms can be grouped into two. One group with a
relatively large amount of capital investing in well known, established firms,
and another group of venture firms with a smaller amount of resources
investing either passively, small amounts in larger firms, or concentrating
on a few small firms (ibid., p.24). A possible exception to these groupings
is "Dansk Udviklingsfinansiering A/S",(Danish Development Finance
Corporation LTD (DUF)).

Just like the development in the U.S., and also in the European venture
firms, the profile of the industry as such has changed towards risk avers
investment strategies, with the main part of investments in the later stage
of the firm. The table below show part of this development. Measured in
values instead of number of firms the trend would be even more significant.

Thus, buyouts and restructurings are important areas of business for some
of todays venture capital firms. Entrepreneurs and technological
development are not considered attractive investments[31] Actually it can be
questioned if there are any special characteristics of the venture capital

---

29 The magazine "Venture News" describes the development of the industry in Denmark.
Publications from EVCA - European Venture Capital Association - cover the European, and
partly the U.S., venture capital industry.

30 Not all of the disappeared venture firms went bankrupt. Some were merged, bought
out or restructured. But the trend is clear: still fewer venture firms.

31 A venture capital firm manager mentioned that in their opinion profitability is a
reverse function of the degree of technology in the projects.

industry in Denmark, which distinguish them from other investors in unlisted shares (like those dealt with above).

Table 9.9.: New investments - stages distributed.

[% number of firms]

	New firms	Expansion	Others	Number of firms
1983				3
1984	55	34	11	55
1985	39	42	19	52
1986	37	30	33	68
1987	29	35	36	52
1988	32	29	39	41
1989	47 (26)	29 (42)	24 (35)	38 (26)
1990	52 (29)	26 (35)	22 (36)	27 (17)

() DUF excluded.

Source: Venture News, 5/91, p.5.

The reasons for this change in the number of venture firms and in the investment strategies of the remaining part are presumably mainly three fold. Firstly, the losses during the 1980s was to a large extent on start-ups. The portfolio of applicants are likely to have an aspect of adverse selection. A relatively large share of applicants have presumably been rejected elsewhere due to bad reputation, inadequate documentation, disclosed information, etc. This adds to the already risky profile of start-ups.

Secondly, venture capital firms have presumably under estimated the amount of resources they had to devote to time consuming screening and monitoring of new, small firms. Especially when the new firm went from the development stage to the marketing of the product new problems arose, which took more resources, also with regard to additional capital. Compared to the size of the investment these resources were not in balance with the expected profits.

Thirdly, it can be questioned if the venture capital firms actually had adequate amounts and kinds of resources. Some of them started with a too small capital portfolio. The disadvantages of this are that they were unable to diversify their investments in order to minimize risk, and they were not always able to supply their portfolio firms with second and third round capital. Furthermore, they were not always competent to be active owners. Most venture firms were established "top-down", that is, established by one or several financial institutions, rather than as a spin-off from the industrial sector, as in the early, U.S. development of the venture capital industry. It is likely that some of the managers in the new venture firms came from the financial sector and brought with them investment policies from that sector. In other words the corporate sector did not always buy the "intelligent capital" that the venture capital concept was associated with.

Even though it has been heavily criticised for being much too cautious in its investment policy DUF is now about the only venture firm investing in start-ups of new, innovative firms.

DUF was established in 1988.[32] Compared to the other venture capital companies its initial capital pool was somewhat larger, and it was set up to finance R&D projects, both in existing firms and in start-ups. In addition it covers a wide range of consultancy functions in relation to its investments. From the start in 1988 to 1/3 1992 180 mio. dkr. has been invested in 35 projects. The staff in DUF is divided into areas of specialization and a thorough screening of applicants is done both by technicians and economists.

The main part of investments are in the early stage of projects. Large firms did not seem, until recently, to need venture capital for R&D projects (DUF, Newsletter, march 1991, p.4). This is in contrast to the development in venture capital firm activities abroad. Other differences are that DUF rarely

---

32 Initially it was meant to be a purely government firm, with a somewhat larger pool of funds, than it has now (1/2 bill.d.kr), but for various reasons, it ended up being a private company with capital from pension funds, insurance companies, the National Bank and others. On the one hand criticism was expressed against DUF for being in competition with the already established venture capital companies, but in fact it was intended to be so, because the existing companies apparently had to much risk aversion. On the other hand the existing venture firms had already changed investment strategies away from the areas of business DUF was set up for, and therefore there was no competition. Actually most venture firms were glad that they now had somewhere to send entrepreneurs and technology based projects.

cooperate with other Danish venture firms in financing projects, and investment activity is larger in DUF than the average venture firm abroad (ibid., and Newsletter oct. 1991, p.2).

Four factors provide the main criteria for screening projects: the technical, sales- and market perspectives, financial structure, experience and competence of management. Experience has showed that the latter is by far the most important. In the press heavy criticism has been made at the venture capital firms, and especially against DUF, because it was meant to be a risk willing investor, who not only invested in bonds, but also in development projects[33]. However, a cautious investment strategy may be the right thing to do in a new institution, which needs to build up competence in project screening and management. In addition, it is necessary to keep a reserve for follow-up investments in the portfolio firms. The development phase is usually not as expensive as later phases when the firm needs to set up an organization and hire people for production and marketing. Maybe there is some truth in the criticism, but, on the other hand, the lessons from the venture industry in the 1980s are that competence for managing development projects should be strongly emphasized, and it is equally important to recognize that investing capital only is inadequate.

Related to the possibilities for innovation financing the development of the industry is obviously inexpedient. Investment strategies have shifted in the same direction as have pension funds: investments in well-established, larger firms. Technology is not regarded as a sound investment project and losses on previous investments make venture firms reluctant to finance innovations.

---

33 In a survey of Danish venture capital firms (Industriministeriet, 1987,p.248a) it was found, that in the 10 most important Danish venture capital firms in 1985 only 37.4% of the total capital was invested in equity in companies not listed on the stock exchange or loans(1.4%). No less than 29.9% was deposits in banks and 20.1% was invested in bonds.

9.6. The financial system and possibilities for high-technology financing in Denmark

The features of the financial system is Denmark resemble some of the features from the theoretical discussion. In particular, barriers to innovation over the life time of a project in Denmark seen from the firms point of view, are almost similar to those presented in chapter 5. The characteristics of the system with heavy bank financing and little direct government influence would place the system in the category "credit based, institutional" further explained in chapter 7. In chapter 5 some requirements were derived for financial institutions if they were to support financing innovations efficiently. It would be reasonable to evaluate the Danish financial system on the basis of these criteria. However, before that evaluation is possible an important part of the analysis must be undertaken. We miss the point of view of the financing side and an analysis of the most important group of financial institutions in Denmark, i.e. the banks.

In the next chapter these are provided. I present an empirical analysis of the role of banks in innovation financing in Denmark.

Chapter 10. Bank financing, interplay with industry and criteria for judging innovation projects

10.1. Introduction

As mentioned in chapter 9 banks[1] dominate the Danish market, especially for loans. In chapter 5 and 6 some hypotheses were developed concerning how banks behave and how financial barriers may be made easier if they cooperate closely with industry. In this chapter I shall investigate in more detail the validity of the hypotheses by taking a closer look at the Danish banking sector and in particular the banks' attitudes toward financing innovation. I do not however, within this relatively small survey, claim to be able to verify or reject all aspects of the theories above, some of them referring to an international context. But some of the results presented in this chapter are unequivocal, strong indications on verification or rejection of the previous discussed theories.

More specifically some of the questions to be answered are the following:

- how do Danish banks behave under uncertainty, or more precisely, when faced with innovation projects?
- What degree of importance do they attach to a close relationship with industry, and how has this relationship developed in the 1980s?
- What induced the development of these relationships?
- What criteria are used for screening innovation projects?
- What are the specific advantages of close relationships?
- Are banks in Denmark willing and able to take and assess risks associated with innovation projects?

---

1 The term "bank" denotes both of the two kinds of banks in Denmark ("banker" and "sparekasser"). Today there is hardly any difference between them although legislation traditionally has been divided into two on the regulation of the two groups.

The material used for giving the answers is mainly contained in a survey on the Danish banking sector[2]. The survey of the banking sector in Denmark was conducted for three main purposes. They can be summarized as a) to provide information on the interplay between banks and industry; b) to see what criteria banks use for judging innovation projects; c) to acquire information on selected subjects dealt with in the theoretical chapters. This information may help to compare some of the theoretical statements in chapter 5 and 6 with the actual practice in Danish banks.

Below I shall report results from the survey under these three headings, divided into topical subgroups. I shall start each sub-section with a short statement of the problem. The questions asked are included in the presentation of data. Before all that I shall introduce the methods used in carrying out the survey.

10.2. Method and design of the survey of the Danish banking sector

The investigation of bank-industry relationships and criteria for judging innovation projects was intended to reveal information, which is usually considered confidential or at least issues not spoken of. As a consequence the design of the survey had to take into account that the respondents must be anonymous. Previously such investigations based on personal interviews rendered sparse results. The method employed for assuring anonymity was to make respondents send the enquiry to their branch organization, Finans-rådet, who took away the front page with the name and address of the respondent, and then returned the enquiries and front pages to me separately. The reason for asking for names and adresses was to be able to send a later reminder.

The procedure of contacting the banks was to write a letter to either the manager of industry credits or the information manager in the main offices,

---

2 The survey is useful for analyzing a range of other interesting topics, but I shall here concentrate on a few central questions related to the theoretical discussions especially in chapter 6 but also in other parts of this thesis. In a report to the Ministry of Industry (forthcoming, nov. 1992) I investigate several other aspects of the behavior of Danish banks and further, more detailed, statistical tests are used.

explaining the purpose and design of the investigation and asking if the manager would distribute questionnaires to relevant respondents in their branch offices. Then this person was phoned and asked if the bank would participate. Some banks responded that they did not have decisions on such loans decentralized, and therefore preferred answering centrally. A few others were not able to participate due to major restructuring or take-overs. Only 3 out of the 39 banks resisted taking part at all. The remaining 35 banks cover an estimated 90% of the Danish market measured by borrowing.

On the basis of the positive results from phone calls to the main offices of the banks, expectations to the answering rate were high. Previous investigations in the financial sector has shown that a rate of 25% would be reasonably good. However, the procedure used gave expectations that one out of three would answer. The actual rate showed to be far better than the norm for these kinds of investigations. 58 out of 128 (45.3%) answered the enquiry, which is satisfactory. The defections are considered to be randomly distributed and therefore not a problem for the interpretation of results.

The selection of participants was done on the basis of size criteria, a geographical distribution criteria, and the type of bank. 39 banks were selected as major Danish banks according to the above criteria and the likelihood of firms with borrowing needs for investments in new technology among its customers. A total of 128 questionnaires were sent to decision makers on industrial credits. Of the 58 answers 22 were main offices, 22 regional offices, and 7 local branch offices (7 are non-classified). One reminder was sent approximately a month after the first shipment. Another, including a new questionnaire a month after the first reminder. Because the questionnaire was sent to main offices for distribution it is uncertain how many of the questionnaires actually reached the respondents. The identification sheets indicate that a substantial part of the questionnaires were never distributed. Thus, the actual rate of responses is likely to be substantially higher.

There are, of course, pros and cons of the method used. One serious bias is that the results do not reflect if the bank is a major one, preferring to (insisting on) answering centrally. Thus, in principle, the largest bank in

Denmark, to take a fictive example, covering one third of the market, would have the same weight in the results as a relatively small, local branch office of a minor bank, if they participated by answering from the main office only. To compensate, it would be possible to weight the answers with the size, or number, of loans to industry in general, or even to innovations. However, such a disaggregation would hide important differences in the local interplay between the bank and firm. Attempts to persuade the banks to answer decentralized, when possible, were made, but in some cases in vain. In all cases the opinions of the main offices were respected, even if I asked for help, not permission to send the questionnaires.

Another bias is of a more general, fundamental character, namely the attitudes of the respondents and the influence from the debate about whether banks are risk willing or if there is a lack of well documented projects. Presumably, respondents are prone to respond in favour of the financial sector and the bank, when answering questions concerning the capacity and competence of the bank versus the skills of innovators. Likewise, a general weakness of postal enquetes is possible differences in how some of the concepts should be understood. A thorough definition of some of the terms is included in the questionnaire, as is a telephone number in case some did not understand the questions.

Two things indicate that the reliability of the results was high. First, the quality of the answers were controlled in the questionnaire. Subsequent tests of these control questions produced results indicating high levels of reliability. Thus, of five control questions three of them had significance levels above 99% and the other two above 95%. Cramer's V were high and Pearson chi-square were significant for all control questions. Second, the category "other.." in the questionnaire was rarely filled in. This is taken as an indication that the catagories listed are exhaustive. The questionnaire was tested on potential respondents and adjusted before the final version. Experts in judging a firm were consulted for comments on the section about criteria for credit. Unfortunately in one of the questionnaires only a small percentage of the questions asked were answered. Therefore, in the tables below you will usually find at least one (= 1.7%) missing case.[3]

---

3 Conclusions would be a bit stronger if this questionnaire was not included in the computations.

In the frequency tables a mean was calculated on a value for all the categories of answers. If the respondents agreed on the statement or attached great weight to the factor asked, the weight of the answer was valued as 1. Less importance was weighted 2 etc. Therefore, the smaller the mean the larger the importance of that statement/factor. If the mean is for example 2.0 it means that, on average, the respondents think the factor in question has a large impact. The specific value of the mean should however be interpreted with caution.[4] In this context it is only used for ranking the importance of the answers.

Criteria for rejecting or confirming the importance of a statement or hypothesis was that 60% or more of the respondents should answer either a large or a very large impact. It was however taken into account how the answers were distributed within these two groups. It could be argued that this is a very strict criteria, but the percentage was chosen that high because of the relatively small sample. For this reason I wanted only to draw unequivocal conclusions from the figures.

A Pearson chi-square test was used for correlation tests and Cramer's V was taken as an indication of the strength of the relationship. The level of significance rather than the value of Pearson chi-square is important in these tests. Due to the small number of respondents it was generally accepted at a low level (90% - marked by **. An above 80% level is marked by *). In some tables the number of observations in some of the cells is lower than three and this disturbs the meaning in using chi-square statistics. In these cases comments are only directed to the specific number of observations.

10.3. Bank - industry relationships

In chapter 6 the interplay between banks and firms was emphasized as an important determinant of the possibilities for financing innovations because

---

4 The reason why the mean is not a 100% precise measure of the importance is that the answers "no importance" are included in the calculation of the mean. Actually it should be excluded because a rejection of a statement is a stronger indication of a negative importance than if the respondent did not answer. To test the sensitivity of this argument a ranking scheme for most of the tables was calculated in which only "very large impact", "large impact", and "some impact" was included. As expected results were roughly the same as when using the mean as ranking measure.

learning processes in these relationships could reduce uncertainty and add to the competence in both firm and bank. In the long term aggregated transaction costs would then be reduced for the bank, although initial investments in creating the relationships with industry may be large. A close relation between the borrower and the lender is an advantage, because it reduces asymmetries in information and thus the reasons for credit rationing. Furthermore, it was argued that monitoring would be easier and that a mutual understanding of the way of thinking is both a result of the relationships and a pre-requisite for their maintenance.

In Denmark the relationships between banks and the industry has been said to have become weaker in recent years (e.g. Østrup, 1989, p.431). Several reasons have been put forward for this for instance increased competition in the financial sector, dispersion of the National Bank set limits to lending, expansion of financial departments and activities in firms, the development of information technology etc. I shall test how the relationships have actually developed and why banks enter such relationships. Furthermore, I shall see if the development is explained by the above mentioned events.

10.3.1. The development of the relationships.

Relationships change over time, but the above hypothesis, that strong relationships have grown weaker is clearly rejected. In fact, *all* respondents answered that the relationships have grown stronger in the 1980s.

Table 10.1. Development of bank-industry relationships in the 1980s.

Question: "Have relationships to firms grown a) stronger b) looser c) unchanged in the 1980s?"

Stronger	96.6
Looser	0
Unchanged	0
Not answered	3.4
Number of answers	56

Personal contacts through the use of the telephone have especially become more frequent[5]. The reason for answering that relationships have grown stronger was that the frequency of contacts has increased (93.1%). Furthermore, but not as significant, the number of industrial customers increased (65.5%) and the number of a firm's banking connections has increased (65.5%). Table 10.2 below shows what the most frequent reasons for the contacts were. It fits well with what was mentioned earlier about increased needs for advice in a increasingly more complex world.

Table 10.2   **The reason for contact between banks and firms**

Question: **"What is the reason for the contact?"**

	Advise	Monitoring the development of the firm	Keep customers
Often	62.1	55.2	39.7
Sometimes	34.5	39.7	39.7
Rarely	0	3.4	17.2
Never	0	0	0
Not answered	3.4	1.7	3.4
Number of answers	56	57	56
Mean	1.357	1.474	1.768
Standard deviation	0.483	0.570	0.738

10.3.3. The importance and actual effects of close relationships

The general importance of these relationships is considered high. Responding to

---

5 This, and some other passing remarks in the following further explain actions about various aspects of the relationships, cannot be read from the tables presented here. The background evidence is included in Christensen (1992b).

"Please estimate the importance of a close relationship to firms investing in new technology", 51.7% viewed the importance very large and 43.1% considered it to be large.

Figure 10.1. The general importance of close relationships

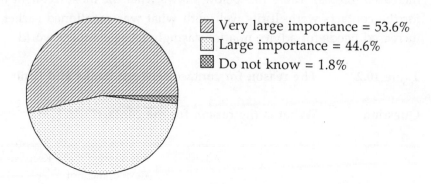

Why do the majority attach very great importance to a close relationship and the rest of the respondents see it as of great importance? Following the theory above a close relationship should reduce asymmetric information between borrower and lender through several mechanisms. First, access to information about the firm may improve, which is important both to initial screening and to monitoring. Secondly, in the longer term communication channels may develop quantitively and qualitatively, in particular as a result of a better mutual understanding of the way of thinking of the other party. Thirdly, trust is build-up which reduces the likelihood of opportunistic behaviour and thus reduces potential problems stemming from asymmetric information. Fourthly, a learning process may improve the banks' ability to assess projects and they also get to know the specific area of business of the firm.

Possible effects on the behaviour of banks would, again according to the theory, be that projects with high risk have better possibilities for obtaining financing, that monitoring costs in the bank decreases, and that banks put less emphasis on "objective" criteria like accounts and collateral.

Banks were both asked to judge the importance of a list of different possible advantages by a close relationship to firms, and they were asked to give their opinion on what the actual effects have been from a closer relationship to firms.

Banks saw the following advantages from having a close relationship to firms:

Table 10.3   **Advantages in a close relationship**

Question: **"What importance have the following advantages of a close relationship to firms?"**

	I	II	III	IV	V	VI
Very large importance	65.5	39.7	34.5	25.9	25.9	27.6
Large importance	32.8	53.4	50.0	63.8	58.6	55.2
Some importance	0	5.2	12.1	8.6	10.3	12.1
No importance	0	0	1.7	0	3.4	0
Do not know	0	0	0	0	0	3.4
Not answered	1.7	1.7	1.7	1.7	1.7	1.7
Number of answers	57	57	57	57	57	57
Mean	1.333	1.649	1.807	1.825	1.912	1.947
Standard deviation	0.476	0.582	0.718	0.571	0.714	0.854

I   - confidence between lender and borrower increases
II   - the bank gets to know the area of activity of the firm
III   - a close relationship keeps competitors out
IV   - a better understanding of the way of thinking with the other part develop
V   - better possibilities of monitoring the firm
VI   - build up of better, and maintenance of existing, communication channels

In table 10.4 below the banks were asked to evaluate a list of statements concerning the actual importance of closer relationships to firms. Ranked by importance the results were the following:

Table 10.4.   **Effects from closer relationships to firms**

Question: **"A closer relationship between bank and firm has meant:"**

	I	II	III	IV	V	VI	VII	VIII
Fully correct	56.9	37.9	25.9	13.8	13.8	5.2	10.3	3.4
Fairly correct	34.5	41.4	29.3	31.0	27.6	31.0	25.9	17.2
Partly correct	1.7	12.1	25.9	27.6	31.0	37.9	34.5	44.8
Wrong	0	1.7	8.6	15.5	17.2	12.1	17.2	20.7
Do not know	0	0	3.4	5.2	3.4	3.4	5.2	6.9
Not answered	6.9	6.9	6.9	6.9	6.9	10.3	6.9	6.9
Number of answers	54	54	54	54	54	52	54	54
Average	1.407	1.759	2.296	2.648	2.667	2.750	2.796	3.111
Std. deviation	0.533	0.751	1.093	1.102	1.064	0.905	1.053	0.925

I   -   better information about the borrowers
II   -   better possibilities for building up competence for credit judgement in the bank
III   -   new, unknown costumers are rejected more often
IV   -   projects with high risk have easier access to financing
V   -   the bank saves resources
VI   -   lower risk premia
VII   -   previous accounts and alike, gets relatively less importance when judging projects
VIII   -   requirements for collateral decreases

The following conclusions are from these two tables: Banks see the potential advantages of a closer relationship to firms as, primarily, improved trust between borrower and lender. This is by far the most important advantage of having a close relation to industry customers. The second most important advantage is that the competence of the bank improves because it gets to know about the area of business of the firms. In fact, all the possible advantages are viewed as generally of large importance, which reflects the large importance a close relationship has in general (see figure 10.1). The category "other advantages" was not filled in by any of the respondents and is taken as an indication of that the catagories listed are exhaustive.

The actual effects from the closer interaction in the 1980s are that banks have better information about borrowers and they have improved their ability to judge applicants. To a lesser extent the close relationship with customers tends to disclose other, new applicants from credit. Most banks think that high risk projects have better access to credit but almost equally many do not think that this has been an effect of closer relationships.[6] In spite of the closer relationships, banks did not put less weight on "objective" criteria. Thus, most banks answered that they do not take lower risk premia and it was not thought that accounts, budgets, and collateral are less important now compared to when the relationships were not as close.

Thus, the expectations derived from theoretical considerations are both confirmed and rejected. From the results it is true that a closer relationship between borrower and lender improves the information level and the competence of banks. In particular, improved mutual trust is considered an important advantage and better information and credit judgement competence have been the most important effects of closer relationships. However, the hypothesis is rejected that banks have used "objective" criteria to a lesser extent because of the closer relationships.

---

6 The questionnaire was made in a way that allowed those who thought relationships have grown stronger and those who had the opposite opinion to answer different questions on the same topic. For example, a question on this topic was formulated for those who thought relationships to be still less tight in the 1980s. The question was thus if dismantling of relationships has had the consequence that applications for credit to high risk projects were more often rejected. By mistake 1/5 of the respondents answered these questions. On this specific topic 84.6% answered that it has in fact been the case that high risk projects are rejected more often.

10.3.4. Explanations of the actual development of relationships

In chapter 6, 7 and 8 likely impacts on bank behaviour of recent trends in financial systems were discussed. From this discussion we would expect to find explanations as to why banks and firms have become closer in the past decade in increased needs for advice as a result of a more uncertain environment and more complex financial options, in the past performance of the bank, and in changes in competition. The latter was considered both nationally between banks, between banks and other financial institutions, and internationally. In theory, increased competition may induce banks to tie customers closer to the bank in order to keep other competitor banks away. Increased competition from other kinds of financial institutions was seen as unfortunate for borrower-lender relationships because diversification often is accompanied by despecialization. Finally, increased international competition and internationalization were also considered to be inexpedient for these relationships. To see why relationships between bank and firm have grown stronger I asked

Table 10.5. Explanations to the development of relationships

Question: "What are the reasons for the development of closer relationships between firm and bank?"

	I	II	III	IV	V	VI
Very large importance	20.3	24.1	27.6	10.3	8.6	1.7
Large importance	62.1	53.4	32.8	51.7	37.9	8.6
Some importance	10.3	13.8	22.4	22.4	32.8	48.3
No importance	0	1.7	6.9	6.9	10.3	31.0
Do not know	0	0	1.7	0	1.7	1.7
Not answered	6.9	6.9	8.6	8.6	8.6	8.6
Number of answers	54	54	53	53	53	53
Mean	1.889	1.926	2.151	2.283	2.547	3.245
Standard deviation	0.572	0.696	1.008	0.769	0.889	0.731

I   - firms need more advisement
II - increased competition between banks
II - losses on new unknown customers
IV   -   firms need more hedging against interest rate and exchange rate fluctuations
V - increased competition from other financial institutions
VI   -   expectations of increased competition in the European single market

How do the results fit with theory/expectations? Increased needs for advice were seen as the most important development causing borrower-lender relationships to have grown stronger. Hedging against interest rate and exchange rate fluctuations could in fact be considered to be part of the increased needs for advice. This development fits with theory. Past performance of the bank is also important. 60.4% answered that losses on new, unknown customers have had an impact on the closer relationships to established customers. Competition was seen as an even more important factor. 77.5% thought competition from other banks was a reason for a closer relationship. On the other hand, competition from other kinds of financial institutions was not considered important and expectations of the development to the European single market had no impact at all. All these observations fit with theory. Competition from other financial institutions and internationalization were in chapter eight seen as dismantling links between borrower and lender, and here they are not considered to induce such relationships. To reverse the argument, that is to say, to take these results as an indication of dismantling of the relationships would, however, be to interpretate the figures without respect for possible alternative possibilities.[7]

Recently heavily debate has been made on what impact large losses on corporate customers has for risk willingness and credit policy in banks. Are those banks who experienced these losses reluctant to give credit to innovation projects or do they perhaps rely on established, known customers to a larger extent. The latter hypothesis may be tested by using cross-tables of the question on how important banks think a close relationship to innovative firms is and the question on the effect of corporate losses. In other words, have corporate losses meant that banks emphasize close relationships to firms with innovation projects.

Table 10.6   The importance of corporate looses on relationships to firms

Question: The importance of close relationships by - Question: Rejecting new firms

Q	4	3	2	1	0	Row	Total
4	10	7	8	2		27	50.9
3	5	10	7	2	1	25	47.2
0					1	1	1.9
Colum	15	17	15	4	2	53	
Total	28.3	32.1	28.3	7.5	3.8		100

---

7 Checking with the reverse questions (see footnote 3) does, however, indicate that such an interpretation is reasonable.

0   Do not know
1   No importance
2   Some importance
3   Large importance
4   Very large importance

	value	DF	significance
Pearson Chi-square	28.69190	8	.00036
Cramer's V	.52027		.00036 *1

According to this additional test the connection between a close relationship and past performance is strong (**). Cramer's V is also at a high level, in comparison with computations on other factors in table 10.5.

10.3.5. The impact of firm size on the relationships between borrower and lender

In the theoretical chapters, in particular chapter 5, the importance of firm size was considered with regard to the opportunities for small firms to obtain credit. A consideration was also made whether there are differences in how a small and a large firm interact with a financier. More specifically, the following hypotheses were developed: i) In general there is a difference in logic between financiers and innovators, but this mis-match is particularly severe when financiers deal with small firms. ii) small firms lack the competence in presentation and preparing of business plans. iii) small firms are organized differently from banks; larger firms have an organizational structure which is more like that in a bank and this enables them to communicate better. iv) for these reasons banks have better contact with larger firms. v) financial innovations are developed as a response to larger firms' demand.

Table 10.7 shows the results from questions related to firm size.

Table 10.7   Firm size and relationships between banks and firms.

Question: "In this question statements relating to small and large*
             firms are presented. Please estimate to what degree the
             following statements are correct."

	I	II	III	IV	V	VI
Fully correct	39.7	34.5	32.8	22.4	12.1	15.5
Fairly correct	44.8	43.1	39.7	53.4	36.2	36.2
Partly correct	12.1	17.2	19.0	17.2	37.9	25.9
Wrong	0	1.7	3.4	1.7	6.9	10.3
Do not know	0	0	1.7	1.7	3.4	8.6
Not answered	3.4	3.4	3.4	3.4	3.4	3.4
Number of answers	56	56	56	56	56	56
Mean	1.714	1.857	1.982	2.036	2.518	2.589
Standard deviation	0.680	0.773	0.924	0.808	0.934	1.156

I   -   large firms are easier to communicate with and have a better understanding of the
        banks
II -   the organizational structure of the firm is important to the interaction with the banks
III -   the bank has better contact with firms in which they have a big engagement
IV -   small firms lack competence in presentation and preparing of business plans.
V   -   financial innovations are developed as a response to larger firms demand.
VI -   banks has better contact with larger firms

Small and big firms: The firm size is defined by number of employees, in the following
                          categories: small = 1 - 49 employees, larger = 50 - 199, large= 200 -

The first three of these hypotheses are confirmed by the figures whereas the
latter two are rejected. From table 10.3 and 10.10 we learnt that in general
there is a difference in the way of thinking between borrower and lender.
The results in the table above demonstrate that the difference is even more
pronounced between banks and small firms. 79.3% of respondents (table
10.10) think that there is a difference in culture and 84.5% think that this is
the case with small firms. Most banks (75.8%) agree with the statement that
small firms lack the competence to prepare and present business plans

(hypothesis ii)). Even more of the banks (77.6%) confirm hypothesis iii). The organization of the firm is important for the interaction with the bank. Only some of the banks found that financial innovations are developed in the interactions with larger firms. Finally, the quality or intensity of the contact generally seems to be more related to the amount of investment in the firm than to the size of that firm. Firm size is however still important to the interaction.

10.4. Criteria and competence for credit to innovations

In chapter 6 some determinants of bank behaviour with regard to judging innovation projects were developed. I wanted to test whether banks were capable of judging innovation projects, and what criteria they used for this judgement. The hypotheses developed are that banks are in general not sufficiently capable of judging innovation projects. Consequently their credit judgement criteria will tend to be biased towards emphasizing what their competence actually is, i.e. what have previously been named "objective" criteria. It was also proposed that banks choose not only by analyzing the applicant. Their choices are also determined by a number of factors internal to the bank as well as the environment in which the bank operates.

10.4.1. Resources and competencies for credit judgement

A prerequisite for a good credit judgement is an adequate amount and quality of resources for this task in the bank. It was suggested in chapters 6 and 9 that banks generally do not have the expertise to judge innovation projects and in particular they lack competence in judging the technical risk in innovation projects. Two strategies could alleviate potential problems from this lack of competence. One is to build up competence internally perhaps by organizational changes aimed at establishing a special department or even affiliates for handling innovation projects. Such affiliates are often more prone to invest equity capital rather than loans. Another strategy is to buy specialized advice form outside the bank.

It is, of course, always problematic to ask anyone to evaluate his/her own competence. Answers can be expected to be biased towards over-estimating the competencies of the banks.

Figure 10.2. Competencies for credit judgement

The banks were asked:
i) "Do you find that competence in the bank for judging innovation projects is sufficient?"
ii) "Do you have any technical expertise within the organization?"
iii) "Is external technical expertise used for judging innovation projects?"

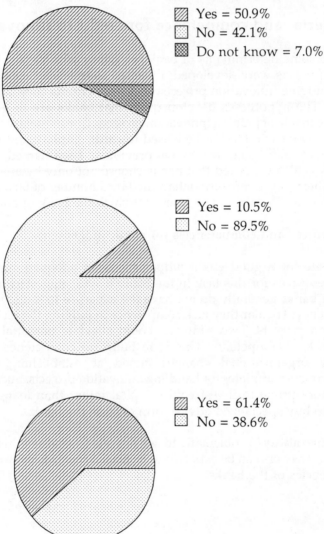

Yes = 50.9%
No = 42.1%
Do not know = 7.0%

Yes = 10.5%
No = 89.5%

Yes = 61.4%
No = 38.6%

Despite the potential bias quit many of the banks think that their competence for judging innovation projects is insufficient. Only half of the

284

banks are satisfied with their internal competence. Only a few of the banks had technical expertise employed. If those banks who answered 'no' in question i) are the same as those who answered 'yes' in question iii) it would be an indication of a deliberate strategy to primarily use external advice when faced with innovation projects with great technical risks. If this is the case it is not possible to conclude from question i) that the competence of banks is insufficient. Checking to what degree there is overlap between no-answers in i) and yes-answers in iii) does not support the hypothesis that those who evaluate their own credit judgement ability as insufficient are those who use external advice. The banks who answered no in i) are randomly distributed on the yes category in iii) with half of the "no-banks" on each category in iii).

One could think that a conclusion derived from the figures on competence in these questions would be that there is a correlation between whether there is technical expertise employed and sufficient credit judgement ability. The table below shows cross-tables for the questions i) and ii)

Table 10.8   Credit judgement competence to technical expertise

Question: Sufficient credit judgement competence by Question: technical expertise employed

Q81/Q82	Yes	No	Row	Total
Yes	6	23	29	50.9
No		24	24	42.1
Do not know		4	4	7.0
Colum	6	51	57	
Total	10.5	89.5		100

Apparently the hypothesis holds. In fact, all those who found their credit judgement capacity insufficient had no technical expertise employed. Of those who found their competence to be sufficient only 6 had technical staff. However, checking frequencies reveals that this is actually all the banks who had such expertise internally. In conclusion, credit judgement competence in banks is generally insufficient, but internal technical expertise is a major determinant of ability to judge the technical risk in innovation projects.

It is, of course, not important to have technical expertise internally or externally in the organization if technical risk is not important in the banks' credit judgement. Checking for correlation between "yes-answers" in i) and low priority in the question about technical uncertainty in credit judgement criteria shows no correlation. Of the 12 respondents who thought technical uncertainty is of minor importance only, 5 thought their credit judgement competence to be sufficient. On the contrary there seems to be a correlation between those who value the technical uncertainty high in their credit criteria and those who actually have the competence to access these risks. This is confirmed by cross-checking those who had technical expertise internally with credit criteria. All of the banks who had this expertise employed gave a high priority to technical risk in their criteria.

Table 10.9   Correlation between competence and the criteria technical uncertainty

Question: sufficient credit judgement competence by Question: technical uncertainty

Q81/Q93	4	3	2	1	Row	Total
Yes	11	13	5		29	51.8
No	8	9	6	1	24	42.9
Do not know		1	1	1	3	5.4
Colum	19	23	12	2	56	
Total	33.9	41.1	21.4	3.6		100

0   Do not know
1   No importance
2   Some importance
3   Large importance
4   Very large importance

The development of the modes of production towards increasing complexity and still more emphasis on human capital (as discussed in chapter 5) makes credit judgement increasingly difficult for the banks. Thus, the statement

"It has become increasingly difficult to judge borrowers, because immaterial factors (education, organization, marketing, research and development) has become more important relative to machines and buildings"

was evaluated as true by most (81.1%) respondents (in the table below is included some other issues are included which I shall comment upon later):

Table 10.10. Statements on various issues.

Question: "Please estimate to what degree the following statements are correct"

	I	II	III	IV	V
Fully correct	50.0	25.9	32.8	15.5	8.6
Fairly correct	36.2	53.4	48.3	62.1	29.3
Partly correct	5.2	10.3	8.6	19.0	44.8
Wrong	1.7	5.2	3.4	0	12.1
Do not know	1.7	0	3.4	0	0
Not answered	5.2	5.2	3.4	3.4	5.2
Number of answers	55	55	56	56	55
Mean	1.618	1.945	1.929	2.036	2.636
Standard deviation	0.828	0.780	0.951	0.602	0.825

I   -   it is particular critical for the firm if it does not receive additional capital when faced with the need for immaterial investments
II   -   usually there is a difference in culture between the firm and the bank. The firm is very focused upon technical features of the project and the industry and less on economic management
III -   it has become increasingly difficult to assess borrowers because immaterial factors (education, organization, marketing, R & D) has become more important relative to fixed capital
IV -   when financing new technology or new ideas collateral is more important due to the extra uncertainty in the project
V   -   firms often change their strategy when they get to know possibilities and conditions for debt financing

10.4.2. Criteria for credit to innovation projects

In chapter 6 a theory of behaviour of banks under uncertainty was developed. It was suggested that banks are likely to consider not only the specific applicant firm but also other criteria. The development of both the environment of the bank and internal factors have an impact as well. These former factors can be considered first. The theoretical discussions provided

287

us with a lot of different firm specific factors likely to be of importance in granting credit for innovation projects. For example, it is important for the bank to assess the technical and market uncertainty of the project. Furthermore, banks judge the organization of the firm and its management and the applicant himself is an important part of this. Budgets, collateral, accounts, and thorough business plans are also likely to be major determinants in granting credit. It was also hypothesized in the theoretical discussion that the fund raising ingenuity and personal karisma of the applicant is important. In chapter 9 it was also pointed out that the Danish home market is relatively small. As innovation projects are often niche products the Danish market is often too small to render a sufficient turn-over. Consequently, it could be that banks would be more willing to accept firms who are export oriented. Ranked against importance the following factors were central to banks:

Table 10.11. Criteria for credit judgement.

Question: Please estimate the importance for granting credit to innovation-projects of the factors below.

	Very large impact	Large impact	Small impact	No impact	Dont know	Not answered	numbe r of answers	Mean	Standard dev.
Firm specific factors									
Various budgets 1-2 years ahead	65.5	29.3	1.7	0	0	3.4	56	1.339	0.514
Organizations and management of the firm	60.3	36.2	1.7	0	0	1.7	57	1.404	0.530
Market prospects	55.2	43.1	0	0	0	1.7	57	1.439	0.501
The business plan	53.4	43.1	1.7	0	0	1.7	57	1.474	0.538
Past accounts	37.9	48.3	10.3	0	0	3.4	56	1.714	0.653
The knowledge base of the firm	36.2	50.0	10.3	0	0	3.4	56	1.732	0.646
The reputation of the firm	39.7	41.4	12.1	3.4	0	3.4	56	1.786	0.803
The technical uncertain	32.8	39.7	20.7	3.4	0	3.4	56	1.946	0.840
The project is within a fast growing technology	25.9	51.7	13.8	0	3.4	5.2	55	1.982	0.871
Dependency on subcontractors	27.6	43.1	25.9	1.7	0	1.7	57	2.018	0.790
Production and technology	19.0	51.7	25.9	1.7	0	1.7	57	2.105	0.724

	Very large impact	Large impact	Small impact	No impact	Dont know	Not answered	Number of answers	Mean	Standard dev.
The presentation of the project	17.2	50.0	27.6	1.7	0	3.4	56	2.143	0.724
Collateral	19.0	43.1	32.8	1.7	0	3.4	56	2.179	0.765
The firm is home market oriented	8.6	15.5	51.7	13.8	5.2	5.2	55	2.909	0.948

	Very large impact	Large impact	Small impact	No impact	Dont know	Not answered	Number of answers	Mean	Standard dev.
Bank specific factors									
The development of outstanding loans	25.9	41.4	24.1	3.4	0	5.2	55	2.055	0.826
Business cycles	15.5	58.6	19.0	1.7	0	5.2	55	2.073	0.663
Time profile on outstanding loans	8.6	34.5	41.4	6.9	3.4	5.2	55	2.600	0.894
Legislation on the financial sector	8.6	25.9	37.9	15.5	5.2	6.9	54	2.815	1.011
Structural changes in the financial sector	3.4	24.1	41.4	19.0	6.9	5.2	55	3.018	0.952

The table includes criteria related to internal conditions within the bank and to the surrounding institutional set-up of legislation and the financial sector in general. For the banks it was suggested in chapter 6, that they typically learn from the past and adjust their credit judgement criteria in accordance with how successful they were in the near past. Furthermore it was suggested that the time profile of previous loans may have an impact. In general, banks tend to borrow long-term and lend short-term. If the portfolio of outstanding loans are relatively long-termed it may reduce flexibility of the bank - especially if loan limits are imposed. The latter consideration indicates that legislation was another potential factor as pointed out in that chapter. Other external developments may be important to loan policies. Business cycles and the general business climate may influence both the aggregate risk of the portfolio of firms and the market prospects for potential new projects. Finally, it was suggested that structural changes in the financial sector may influence competition between banks and criteria for credit.

Results for the firm specific factors actually confirm that all of the factors mentioned are to some extent important in credit judgement. The question of export orientation was formulated in a somewhat reverse manner and therefore rejected. All the other factors were seen as having a very large impact or large impact on credit judgement by at least 60% of the respondents. This indicates that a wide range of things are taken into account when judging projects. It is for example, not enough that an entrepreneur is good at presenting his project to a financier. This is an important criteria but a lot of other criteria are used and some of those are more important.

Four criteria are a bit more important than others: i) budgets, ii) organization and management in the firm, iii) market uncertainty and - prospects, iv) the business plan

It was suggested in the theoretical part of the present book that production in general and innovations in particular are increasingly knowledge based. This fact, it was argued, is likely to influence negatively possibilities for obtaining credit because the knowledge base of a firm is worthless as collateral. Banks are likely to be unable to assess immaterial investments and this knowledge base. Investigations into this important topic demonstrate that banks actually do rank the knowledge base of the firm high in their credit judgement (86.2%, table 10.11). Collateral, on the other hand, although important it is not as important compared to other criteria (62.1%, table 10.11). Less emphasis on collateral may be a consequence of the development described above. The assets of the innovative firm are to a large extent intangible and firm specific. Therefore they are worthless as collateral and difficult to assess. As mentioned earlier this interpretation is confirmed by table 10.10 in which Statement III, described the just mentioned development.

The bank specific factors are in general not as important as the firm specific factors. A rejection was made of the hypotheses that time profile of the loan portfolio, legislation, and structural changes in the financial sector have a large impact on the judgement of innovation projects. The development of previous loans is the most important of these criteria. The answers largely follow the answers in table 10.5 no. III, the category "losses on new, unknown customers".

10.5. Various subjects

In the questionnaire questions were included not directly related to the two overall subjects of the survey. Their purpose was to use the opportunity for confronting some of the general, theoretical statements relating to the practice of Danish banks.

10.5.1. Credit rationing in Danish banks?

In chapter 3 credit rationing and asymmetric information was discussed. It was argued that banks are likely to abstain from using the interest rate as an instrument for getting rid of bad borrowers. Instead rationing credit is used. How do Danish banks behave in this sense?

Table 10.12 confirms that credit rationing is more frequently used than taking a risk premium when projects are risky. 81.1% agree with the statement in the table.

Table 10.12 Credit rationing

Question: "The bank more often reject applications rather than raise interest rates when faced with high-risk projects."

Fully correct	48.3
Fairly correct	32.8
Partly correct	6.9
Wrong	10.3
Do not know	0
Not answered	1.7
Number of answers	57

In chapter 3 it was argued that credit rationing is induced by asymmetric information and that the scope for asymmetric information and opportunistic behaviour is reduced by trust, and a close relationship between borrower and lender produces this reduction. It could, therefore, be expected that there is a correlation between those who emphasize credit rationing and those who emphasize the importance of increased trust, monitoring, and information as a result of close relationship to corporate customers.

Below results are presented from cross-tables for the question above and three questions that cover trust, monitoring, and information.

Table 10.13 Credit rationing and trust

Q	4	3	Row	Total
4	18	10	28	49.1
3	12	7	19	33.3
2	4		4	7.0
1	4	2	6	10.5
Column	38	19	57	
Total	66.7	33.3		100

Table 10.14 Credit rationing and monitoring

Q115/Q31	4	3	2	1	Row	Total
4	9	16	2	1	28	49.1
3	6	10	3		19	33.3
2		4			4	7.0
1		4	1	1	6	10.5
Column	15	34	6	2	57	
Total	26.3	59.6	10.5	3.5		100

Table 10.15 Credit rationing and better information

Q115/Q65	4	3	2	Row	Total
4	16	10	1	27	50.0
3	12	6		18	33.3
2	2	2		4	7.4
1	3	2		5	9.3
Column	33	20	1	54	
Total	61.1	37.0	1.9		100

0 Do not know
1 No importance
2 Some importance
3 Large importance
4 Very large importance

Of those who think that the statement on credit rationing is fully correct 2/3 (66.7%) think that trust is very important and the other third think that trust is important. Out of those of the opinion that banks sometimes do use interest rates 12/19 attach very large importance to trust. The relationship between the importance of monitoring and credit rationing shows that the results are not quit as unambiguous. Nevertheless, the majority (41/47) of those who agreed fully or almost with the statement on credit rationing attached either very large or large importance to monitoring firms in a close relationship. Finally, the importance of information about the borrower was valued high by all except one respondent. Chi-square statistics is not included because of the small number of observations in each cell.

Together these figures demonstrate that Danish banks prefer to ration credit rather than take a risk premium. These banks emphasize trust, possibilities for monitoring, and information about the borrower, which in theory are important factors in reducing credit rationing. Formulated in the reverse manner; if information, trust, and possibilities for monitoring the firm are insufficient, credit rationing is imposed.

10.5.2. Financing different phases of development

In chapter 5 it was emphasized that problems with financing innovations differ according to which stage of development the project is in. Uncertainty decreases the more the project is developed and this will ease financial constraints it was argued. At a certain point of time when the firm is in a transition from start-up to expansion firms may for reasons discussed in chapter 5 meet severe financial constraints. In chapter 6 it was argued that likely sources of external finance differ with the development of the project as well. Banks are likely to avoid financing the early stage. When do Danish banks actually finance innovation projects, and is the hypothesis about a certain "death-valley" point of time in the development of the firm confirmed?

The latter question can be answered by looking at table 10.10 above. In that table the statement on a critical phase in a firm's life cycle with regard to external finance was agreed with by 86.2% and it was found to be the most correct statement of the five presented. In other words the statement deduced from theory was confirmed.

The former question is answered by table 10.16 below.

293

Table 10.16 Stage of development and bank financing

Question: "When do the bank usually finance innovation projects by entrepreneurs and existing firms respectively?"

	New firms/ entrepreneurs	Existing firms
Early stage	17.2	19.0
Start-up	65.5	55.2
Expansion	13.8	22.4
Not answered	3.4	3.4
Number of answers	56	56
Mean	1.964	2.036
Standard deviation	0.571	0.660

Two subjects in this table should be commented upon. First, banks primarily finance innovation projects when the project is in its start-up. But banks do in fact also finance early stage, although less than 1/5 of the banks take part in that stage. Second, there is a small difference between new firms/entrepreneurs and existing firms in how early banks enter the project. Banks tend to enter later when innovations are carried out by existing firms. The difference is, however, too small to render valid conclusions.

10.6. Risk aversion in Danish banks towards innovation projects ?

According to the surveys of the firm point of view presented in chapter 9, Danish banks were characterized as risk avers by industrial firms in Denmark. What information on this issue does this survey from the financier's side provide?[8]

---

8 Some would, perhaps, question if this information is reliable because it comes from the banks, who may not be objective on this matter. However, banks were both directly asked and tests were undertaken which yield an indirect answer. A more fundamental problem

The general impression by Danish observers of risk willingness in Danish banks is that risk willingness was large in the middle of the 1980s but has since then decreased substantially. Lately, risk willingness is said to be at a very low level due to large losses on corporate customers, and to financial scandals in well-established firms. In the near future banks are expected to continue a very cautious credit policy.

This general impression is shared by most banks in the survey. A majority think that risk willingness has decreased since the mid-1980s and most of the banks think that it will remain the same in the near future.

Table 10.17. Past and future risk willingness

Question: "Has the risk willingness of the banks to innovation projects decreased, increased, been unchanged in the last half of the 1980s and is it going to decrease, increase, remain the same in the next few years?"

	1980s in general	In the near future
Stronger	51.7	17.2
Looser	10.3	6.9
Unchanged	34.5	70.7
Not answered	3.4	5.2
Number of answers	56	55

The statement above - that it is the same banks who think that risk willingness has decreased as those who think it will remain the same - can be documented by a cross table for the two questions.

---

is that risk willingness is not something objectively, easily measured. borrower.

Table 10.18. Assessment of riskwillingness in the 1980s compared to future risk willingness

Q112/Q113	Looser	Stronger	Unchanged	Row	Total
Looser	5	1	23	29	52.7
Stronger	2	2	2	6	10.9
Unchanged	3	1	16	20	36.4
Column	10	4	41	55	
Total	18.2	7.3	74.4		100

The table shows that a large proportion (23/29) of those who answered that risk willingness has decreased think that it will remain the same in the future. The chi-square test has no meaning in this case because of the small number of observations in most of the cells.

In the questionnaire respondents were asked to give some data on their actual loans. From these figures it is in principle possible to calculate various measures for risk willingness. However, this section of the questionnaire asks for sensitive information, and consequently the number of missing cases were about half of total respondents. A reliable interpretation of data is invalidated by these defects. I shall only give one piece of information from these figures. On the average the proportion of loans without full security in the banks who answered amounted to 50%.

10.7. Conclusions

In Denmark as well as in several other countries a standing issue, as previously discussed, is whether there is enough finance and a lack of good projects or if there is a lack of finance but plenty of good projects. As mentioned the financial sector maintains the former statement whereas the entrepreneurs maintain that lack of finance is the problem. The analysis above has, hopefully, introduced some light and shade into the debate. It is however interesting to see that the banks do not reject the statement "a financial barrier to innovations exist" completely in spite of their anticipated reluctancy to admit that this should be a fact. In table figure 10.4 the distribution of answers is presented.

Figure 10.3. The existence of a financial barrier to innovation

Question: A financial barrier to innovations exist

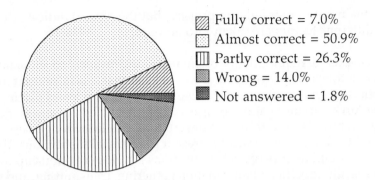

Fully correct = 7.0%
Almost correct = 50.9%
Partly correct = 26.3%
Wrong = 14.0%
Not answered = 1.8%

Results from this survey have demonstrated that Danish banks have closer relationships with firms than they had in the 1980s. This is in contrast with previously maintained perceptions of the development. Banks value a close relationship with firms with innovation projects very high. The primary reasons for this view are that the interaction with the borrower increases trust and understanding between the parties, and it enables banks to judge applications more competently in the future. This has meant that the information level on borrowers has increased. Explanations of why these relationships have become closer could be found in an increased need for advice in firms, in increased competition between banks, and in the poor, past performance of many banks recently. Banks pointed to a difference in the interaction with small and large firms. Culture, logic, and understanding in a large firm is closer to the banks' than that of a small firm.

The competencies for judging credit were generally regarded as insufficient, and a relationship was found between internal technical expertise and sufficient credit judgement capability. Technical expertise was rarely found inside the organization. Firm specific factors were estimated as having high priority in a credit judgement. Budgets, organization and management, market uncertainty and prospects, and the business plan were found to be the most important firm specific criteria. Past performance of the bank and (related) business cycles were the most important bank specific factors. Credit rationing is commonly used in Danish banks according to the survey. The figures also indicate that risk willingness in Danish banks has decreased since the mid-1980s and is likely to remain at same level in the near future.

As discussed in the various sub-sections most of the observations fit to the theory above. Some hypotheses and established opinions have, though, been questioned. For example, it was rejected that internationalization in the form of the European single market would have an impact on the interaction between borrowers and lenders. It is to some extent also rejected that banks emphasize collateral when judging a project and they do in fact take the knowledge base of the firm into account. On the other hand, budgets are the main criteria for judging projects, but the figures indicate that a number of different factors are taken into account.

In chapter 5 requirements of financial institutions to efficiently support innovations were developed. It was argued that it is important that financial institutions have a time perspective long enough to avoid placing short-term pressures on innovation projects. Competencies to assess not only the figures but also the technical uncertainty, the knowledge base of the firm, and the management must be present in financial institutions. Furthermore, an important feature of such institutions is a close relationship to borrowers. This facilitates efficient information gathering, transmitting, and storing. The advising capacity of financial institutions must be high and it is an advantage if financial institutions are flexible.

With respect to the time perspective there is no evidence that Danish financial institutions will be particular short-sighted. Pension funds have increased corporate lending and investing and these investments may on average be long-termed. On the other hand they have lately concentrated on later stage financing and low-risk investments. Traditional early stage financing sources, in particular government agencies, are providing a substantial part of early stage financing and R & D financing as well, and these agencies may have long time horizons. From the survey on the banking sector and from chapter 9 it seems as if competencies for judging industrial firms in Denmark are generally inadequate. At least it was indicated that competencies are directed toward evaluation of projects mainly on the basis of figures.[9]

Even though venture capital firms in Denmark apparently have dismantled their ties with corporate customers investing in new technology, banks have closer relationships with firms now compared to the late 1980s. There is however, still scope for an even stronger relationship to the typical Danish firm. The dominance of institutions in the Danish financial system can facilitate a potential for further development in that direction, and the variety of institutions may potentially induce flexibility in the system. Thus, if the Danish system is to change to more market orientation it must do so with the advantages of the present system in mind. In particular, changes must be made in a way that facilitates further information storing, gathering, and transmitting. In the present system the information provided to the other party by lenders and borrowers respectively is generally inadequate, oriented in different directions, and transmitted in a way which does not fit with the logic, organization, or competence of the other party.

---

9 A Swedish report (NUTEK, 1991, p.66) pointed out that in Swedish banks personnel dealing with credit judgement were mainly trained in assessing figures rather than technology, even though the person and the idea were claimed to be more important.

Chapter 11. Conclusions

11.1. Introduction

This chapter closes my discussion on innovation financing. It restates some of the most important conclusions made from the discussions above and it discusses, in an explorative way, some possible ideas for innovation financing arrangements primarily derived from the theoretical discussion.

11.2. Needs for theoretical development

Despite its great importance this part of economic theory has suffered from inadequate, fragmented attempts to theorize on financing innovation, as was discussed in chapter two. More specifically, innovation theory has primarily focused upon real phenomena and has generally disregarded financial aspects. Financial theory, on the other hand, has focused upon price relations and arbitrage under conditions of risk rather than uncertainty, and it has generally disregarded the purpose of the investment that needs finance. One part of financial theory however is focused upon the interaction between a borrower and a lender under imperfect information conditions. However, as explained in more detail in chapter three, that part of financial theory is insufficient for the present purpose although it does focus upon the borrower-lender interaction and points out informational constraints in this interaction.

Even though increased information may reduce uncertainty and thus ease possibilities for obtaining finance, another constraint is equally important. It was discovered in the theoretical discussion above, and also in the empirical investigation, that a competence constraint may hamper innovation financing. It is not because financiers and innovators are not skillful in financing and innovating respectively, but their competencies are oriented differently, and this poses problems in the interface between borrowers and lenders. Moreover, they are often different in culture and logic, which further enhances financing problems.

In chapter 9 and 10 it was found that similar problems do in fact exist in the Danish financial system. Thus, in chapter 9 it was found that Danish firms claimed that competencies in banks are oriented towards assessing their budgets and past performance only, and the banks do not have the right understanding of what was going on in the corporate sector. In chapter 10 the survey showed that increased trust, understanding between the parties, better information, and improved competencies were seen by Danish banks as major effects from a closer relationship to firms in recent years.

With this problem identification and the working hypotheses in chapter 1 in mind, important elements of my suggestion of a theory of innovation financing can be restated. The present approach has attempted to integrate aspects of innovation theory, considerations of the behaviour and needs of the firm and the financier over time, and the systemic perspective.

This integration has resulted in an understanding of financing innovations as a *process* which is characterized by uncertainty in three dimensions. Thus, an innovation project is uncertain with respect to the time and costs of the development and adjustment process, or in other words, there is a technical uncertainty. Second, an innovation project is uncertain with respect to the market prospects of the project. Finally, there is an uncertainty on the honesty and ability of the person or the firm undertaking the project.

An uncertain project in a volatile environment may cause potential lenders to be reluctant to finance this process. A natural reaction when faced with a great uncertainty would be to rely on conventional behaviour which has proven successful in the past. The innovation process is, however, not totally random and chaotic. At least four coordinating factors of importance to the financing of that process has been identified. First, the innovation process was characterized as an incremental, social process, drawing upon, and combining knowledge accumulated in an interplay with a wide range of other people and institutions. Thus, innovations are rooted in a specific institutional surrounding, and an innovation system - often based in the nation - is one such environment, which may reduce uncertainty in innovations. Second, the innovation process was characterized as path-dependent. The past pattern of production, the means of production, and consumption patterns determine to a large extent in which direction technological development is going and this reduces uncertainty. Third, the structural linkages between suppliers, firms, users, financiers and the environment in which they operate are other coordinating factors referred to as development blocks. Finally, and most important, it is a coordinating, and uncertainty reducing factor that a lender and a borrower form a long-term relationship. This enables them to learn about the other partys' logic and culture. This proximity in culture and way of thinking is important in reducing the third dimension of uncertainty mentioned above, i.e. the build up of trust and mutual understanding reduces the scope for opportunistic behaviour, increases the level of information, and increases both parties competence.

Uncertainty and coordination has implications for financing innovations in several respects. Uncertainty is not fixed in magnitude or character over time and the above dimensions of uncertainty have varying importance according to how developed the firm or the project is. Small firms may experience severe problems with financing innovations due to a greater uncertainty on their financial and managerial abilities but in addition to the mere size of the firm an obstacle to financing innovations may be that particular financial institutions are not equally well suited to access the specific problems in different stages in a life cycle of an innovation project. Consequently, financiers behave differently according to when they are asked to finance an innovation project, and there are, in fact, most often different sources of financing over time. Therefore, one could perhaps talk about a financial life cycle for a firm. As a consequence the different financial requirements over time produces some requirements to financial institutions if they are to support the process of financing innovations efficiently. Features of such institutions were found to be a sufficiently long time perspective to avoid short-term pressures on innovation projects, an ability to assess the market prospects for the particular innovation and to give advise in managing the project in order to exploit these prospects, a close relationship with its' corporate customers, and a flexibility allowing them to adapt to changing needs in industry and the economy as a whole.

How would financiers behaviour typically be compared to these requirements? External finance may come from either markets or institutions, and I found that institutions are generally likely to better suited

301

for financing innovations their main advantage being the ability to learn from experience and to accumulate this knowledge for later use. Past experience is one of the determinants of risk willingness in the theory of bank behaviour above. Other important determinants were found to be the institutional and regulatory framework, the financial and strategic position of the bank, business cycles, and considerations by the bank which is not directly profit maximising in the short term. Together these determinants have a major influence on the credit policy of the bank as was further explained in chapter 6 illustrated by a model of linkages in the process of financing innovations.

That model was illustrating how the growth, selection, and contraction of financial institutions influence the structure of the financial system. Institutions are not the only way to finance innovations though. A financial system is a mix of different institutions and markets and this mix is important to innovation financing because different financial systems employ different time perspectives, they are more or less flexible, and in particular they support and generate borrower-lender interaction differently and with different intensity.

The closer relationships between Danish banks and firms had come about due to increased needs for advice in firms, increased competition between banks and in the past performance of banks recently. Communication was generally more smooth between large firms and banks than between small firms and banks. It was found that sufficient internal competencies for credit judgement was lacking. Emphasis in credit policies were found to be on budgets, organization and management, market uncertainty and market prospects, and the business plan, but a wide range of different factors were considered important.

Confronted with actual figures for how major financial systems look like today the theoretical conclusions were found in chapter 7 to be in relatively nice coherence with the empirical evidence. Grouping financial systems in three provided us with an analytical framework useful for analysis of actual financial systems. With the approach taken in this analysis in mind it was found that credit based financial systems are likely to generate and maintain relationships between borrowers and lenders better than do capital market based financial systems. In spite of this it was found in chapter 8 that recent changes in financial systems is going in the direction of coherence, and in particular the credit based financial systems are moving towards more capital market based corporate financing and other features of these financial systems.

I shall comment further on the systemic aspects of this theory as an intermediate step to discuss specific policy issues.[1]

The discussion of financial systems and technological development in this book has, hopefully, clarified some of the features of the workings of different types of financial systems, in particular with regard to how borrower-lender interactions are in these systems. But a number of questions in relation to innovation financing naturally follow those in the discussion above: Which system is better in supporting technical change? Are there differences in when and what they are good at supporting? Which system promotes risk willingness as discussed in chapter 6? A fundamental question is: If credit based financial systems are superior to capital market based systems in terms of supporting innovations financially, is there any correlation between type of financial system and the innovative capability of the country?

Some of the answers have been given in the discussion above. But what has been said so far may sound a bit biased towards the advantages of credit based financial systems. However, disadvantages of these systems as well as merits of the capital market based systems must be added to the arguments posed in chapter 6,7 and 8. In a credit oriented financial system, it is easier to accumulate knowledge and develop competence to judge projects. But in times of rapidly changing technologies it is difficult to take advantage of this. The competence built up during the previous technological regime quickly becomes irrelevant. Time between technical changes may be too short to build up lending routines and exploit economies of scale in lending. In a capital market oriented system routines are not built up to the same extent. The lack of routines may sometimes be an advantage in a volatile environment because routinized behaviour may

---

1 Actually the OECD has at the time of writing started a more intense focus upon systemic aspects of financing corporate investments.

be hostile to innovation. Thus, the centralized market may have some advantages concerning flexibility. But flexibility is also dependent on a variety of financial institutions, and their capability to adapt to new states of the environment.

In conclusion, one may argue, that these systems have their respective advantages in two different ways of supporting technological change. One (the credit based) could be termed the learning mode, where development of, and development within, financial institutions are essential. The other (capital market based) has its strengths in one-time selection, and here the market mechanism is the main way of selecting between projects.[2]

11.3. Future developments in the financial system and specific policies improving possibilities for high-technology financing in Denmark

The Danish financial system was characterized as credit based with dominance of institutions, mainly banks, in the credit allocation. It was also pointed out that the industry structure is characterized by a relatively large number of small firms. In recent years production and technological development has changed. Competition has become increasingly international, product life cycles has shortened, barriers to entry are higher, R & D is increasingly important to innovations but is simultaneously more costly than earlier, and the knowledge base of the firm is a crucial competition parameter when evolutionary viability of the firm is to be maintained. These changes are not to the advantage of small firms. This highlights the importance of that changes in financial systems must be in line with changes in national industry.

---

2 Thus, a counter argument against the present approach would be that the U.S. economy has been one of the most innovative but simultaneously it has a capital market based financial system. However, it could equally well be argued that *in spite of* the financial system the economy is highly innovative. The innovative viability of the economy may in this system to a larger extent depend on other factors than financial. The precise answer to such questions must thus be given after careful examination of the specific national financial systems and in particular of the way the innovation process is taking place in the nation.

The financial system in Denmark (and the world) is today undergoing fast changes. This makes it even more important to recognize, that how the financial system supports technological development does make a difference. It is also necessary to supervise how financial barriers to innovation change and to analyze what they actually consist of, in order to carry an effective policy through.

In the process of changing the financial system, the Danish system has changed towards more market orientation, but is still a bank oriented financial system. Probably the small size of the Danish capital market will limit a further change, in spite of internationalization and integration. To prevent inexpedient effects from rapid changes in the present institutional set-up, and to avoid being "stuck in the middle" between two types of financial systems with different merits and incentive structures, adequate institutional development must proceed, but in the right speed and aimed at reducing specific problems in industry. In the Danish case the challenge is to adapt to the changes in production compared with the specific industry structure. As was emphasized in the discussion on the origin of financial systems institutional changes do not happen overnight. Whether this is possible in a process of harmonization and integration is an open question for the 1990s.

A fundamental question to clarify before policy actions are taken is to consider if new institutions must be build or if the present institutions can be changed to support innovation financing better[3]. This clarification must rest on close examination of a) whether the present institutions are working satisfactory under the conditions they have and b) what the requirements are for new ideas to work properly.

I shall not embark on different proposals and experience from other countries. It is important to consider different measures in other countries in order to learn from experience abroad. Many of these measures are

---

3 It is important to consider different measures used in other countries in order to learn what might be efficient policies towards overcoming financial barriers to innovation. I shall not embark on different proposals and experience from other countries though. Many of these measures are evaluated thoroughly elsewhere. Consequently I shall only present a few provisional ideas which I think follows from the approach taken above.

evaluated thoroughly elsewhere. Consequently I shall only present a few provisional ideas which I think follows from the approach taken above.

i)

One possible innovation within the banking sector, and perhaps other sectors as well such as the venture capital sector, could be to introduce a kind of "out of job-training" of the staff dealing with credit judgement. Bank employees could be placed in customer firms for a period of time and learn about practice in the firm, the way to handle financial control, the way to steer innovation projects, and above all to learn about corporate culture.

Several advantages of this method could be mentioned. One would be increased intensity of learning processes between the specific firm and the bank. The bank is better able to monitor that particular firm during the stay of its' employee, and the firm will benefit from on-the-spot advise and direct access to the skills of the financier. In the long run credit judgement competence is improved. Differences in logic either diminish or becomes a minor problem because the two parties have a better understanding of why this difference exist and how it should be handled. Finally, trust and personal relationships between borrower and lender will improve.

Disadvantages for the bank may be in dispensing with resources in this training. This is, of course, a trade-off between short-term needs and long-term benefits for the bank. A complicating factor could be that the firm may have more than one bank connection. The idea is to a large extent beyond the scope of government policy. Rather it is perhaps relevant to consider internally in the banking sector. However, it might be possible to design government instruments for inducing incentives for such measures.

ii)

Training should though not be restricted to the financiers. Entrepreneurs and firms may alleviate competence problems through appropriate training in management and start-up of a business. One way of training could be local courses in entrepreneurship, for example arranged in joint cooperation between regional technological information centres (TIC) and a local bank. Such courses should include teaching in what the financial possibilities are, how a business plan is prepared, etc. In Denmark such courses have started appearing. Some are arranged by The Technology Institute (DTI) and others are more local arranged by a municipality. It would perhaps induce a further knowledge on the financial sector, and mutual understanding and personal acquaintance if financial institutions, in particular local banks, were involved in running these courses also.

iii)

To reduce problems outlined above concerning adapting the financial system to changes in production, then at least government agencies could perhaps help by changes in the way support programmes are run. In section 5.2.3. it was pointed out that linking financing of each stage and the transition from one stage to another is important for such programmes to be efficient. If the programmes were not only focused upon early stage and start-up, firms might have better possibilities for managing transition and they could, perhaps, be better advised if they are able to handle problems stemming from new trends in production and competition in later stage. This proposition may meet resistance with the argument that government funding of later stage will crowd out private financiers.

iv)

Another means of improving borrower-lender interactions and thus innovation financing ability of financial systems in general and the Danish system in particular should be considered. Further integration of the financial and the corporate sector through increased equity holdings in financial institutions might pave the way for financing more innovations. Several ways of designing such legislative changes are possible. A consideration can be made of which institutions should be allowed to participate in innovation projects with equity, to what extent it should be allowed, if the option should only be open for investing in innovation projects, if equity should be in a form that limit the access to control the firm, etc.

Advantages would be that profit sharing would improve incentives to participate financially in innovation projects and maybe fill the equity gap many firms face in their development phase. It may also intensify the interaction between borrower and lender (rightly "firm" and "investor" in this instance) because financiers have more incentives to emphasize "non-

307

objective" criteria like market prospects, possible further developments and uses of the technique in question, the knowledge base of the firm, and possibly several other criteria which require another kind of interaction than exchange of a sheet of paper. In addition, cultural proximity is likely to improve. Financiers will become more involved in the corporate culture.

Disadvantages could perhaps be alleviated through appropriate design of how this measure should be taken. It would, though be difficult to avoid increased administration and more bank supervisors. It should also be considered if banks are actually competent and willing to assess the long-term prospective of a firm, which is necessary when financing with equity. With this step there is a danger that power may be concentrated in some financial institutions. The coordinating power of Swedish banks referred to earlier is in some cases an advantage of such a concentration, but it may not be socially, politically desireable to have such a power if it is likely that the interests and the time horizons of decisions of the financial institution and society do not coincide. In relation to the history of Swedish industrialization it should be emphasized that Swedish financial institutions were prohibited from owning large proportions of shares in industrial firms because of the bankruptcy of the industrial concern Krüger in 1933, which also caused crisis in the financial sector. Whether the stability of the financial system will improve or will be more fragile is an open question. Neither theory nor experience from actual financial systems give us unequivocal answers.

For the Danish financial system and in particular the banking sector the timing of measures in this direction should be considered carefully. At the moment prices on bank shares are relatively low and most banks have experienced large and increased losses on corporate customers. It is likely that increased equity holdings in banks will make the financial system more fragile because the portfolio of banks gets more risky.[4] Bank failures could be the unfortunate result. Measures for compensating that effect are that

---

4 This is a standard argument, which may be reversed. In times of crisis in the financial sector - even a rumour may make depositors question the solidity of their bank - it may be an advantage and a stabilizing factor to have a number of well-established, solid industrial firms in their port folio (provided, of course, that there isn't a similar crisis in the industrial sector). In this way risk is actually diversified on several sectors of the economy, not only the financial sector.

capital requirements to banks could be increased. Another is to allow the universal bank model to a greater extent. That would help banks diversify and spread risk, provided they enter areas of business they are well-equipped to deal in.

v)

The stability of the financial system is indirectly relevant to the next point. This possible innovation relates to one of the central problems in innovation financing. The recent problems in the Danish as well as in other countries' banking sector with large losses on corporate customers are not simply an over-banking problem. In fact, the problems resembles those of the American banking system in the early 1930s. An incorrect estimation of the risks may have deterrent macro economic consequences. On this point Keynes wrote an article probably inspired by a visit to Chicago in july-august 1931. During that stay he was observing the fragile structure of the American banking system, a fragility which stemmed from an extensive financing of dubious projects and businesses without security in real assets or in (reasonable) expected profits. In his paper he wrote that

> It is for this reason that a decline in money values so severe as that which we are now experiencing threatens the solidarity of the whole financial structure. Banks and bankers are by nature blind. They have not seen what was coming...." (Keynes, 1931, "The Consequences to the Banks of the Collapse of Money Values.")

What was coming was a break down of the banking system, which occurred eighteen months after Keynes predicted it, in february 1933.

It seems as if credit judgement of corporate customers in Danish banks was not careful enough in the past decade, probably as a result of intense competition between banks in the 1980s, which urged banks to increase lending substantially. This is not necessarily a problem in itself. However, the collateral for these loans was often real estate or shares valued at an unrealistic high price. When the stock market did not develop at the speed expected in the mid-eighties, and when prices suddenly went down on for example real estate after many years of increase - it was actually taken for granted that prices would keep rising - the value of collateral decreased also

309

and banks were faced with large losses when firms went bankrupt. It is only natural that this effects the credit policy at banks to being more cautious, but this may harm innovation financing.

If an insurance against large falls in the value of accepted collateral could be established, e.g. in the form of an option market for collateral, then this inexpedient effect on the risk willingness of banks may be avoided. It may not be practically feasible as a central market but at a local level between a limited number of financial institutions it may work. The system resembles that of the insurance companies who reinsure their portfolio of contracts with other insurance companies. The important difference in the idea above is that options make the value of collateral fixed at the time of contracting. For some innovation financing there might, however, be negative, or at best neutral effects. Innovations are increasingly knowledge based and investments immaterial, and this leaves firms with little possibilities for offering any second-hand valuable collateral.

vi)
In chapter 4 different kinds of distance were discussed and for example cultural proximity in the borrower-lender interplay was emphasized. Geographical distance might have an impact too. In spite of the small size of the country, recent Danish surveys (Maskell, 1992, Koppel, 1992) have pointed out the importance of geographical distance. In Sweden the government has established venture capital companies on a regional basis. Another dimension may equally be important. In chapter 8 it was argued that financial institutions specialized on a particular industry are likely to be superior in assessing investment proposals of firms. Merging these two elements would create a regional, industry specific way of organizing innovation financing. It could perhaps be argued that this is only relevant in countries where large differences in industrial structure between regions exist. However, in the surveys mentioned above even very small geographical distances could prevent financiers from being interested in innovation projects.

The specific design of an industry specific, geographical bounded innovation financing arrangement could follow several models. One is a government run model, and another is a industry run - perhaps initiated and subsidized by government or municipalities. Would it, for instance work if textile producers in Herning-Ikast formed a venture capital company for the local textile industry only? In fact, a somewhat similar way of organizing innovation financing existed in Denmark at the turn of the century. The cooperative movement in Denmark was made up of networks of local, industry specific firms who also cooperated economically and eventually formed their own bank. In principle, organizing financing in this way would be extended self-financing in the sense that the capital for the venture company comes from the very same firms who benefit from access to finance for investments in innovations. The point in the arrangement is that a mutual benefit would arise from a degree of risk spreading, and that the venture company is likely to develop competence to assess investment proposals, to advise firms in the industry, and to have a coordinating function because it will have access to information on all similar firms in the area.

A problem for a specialized venture company - at least in Denmark - would probably be to diversify risk sufficiently. If the industry is in a crisis the venture company will also be seriously affected. A problem for a local venture company would probably be to have enough viable ventures to invest in - depending on how "local" it is and depending on what area the company is located in and consequently how much industry is in the area. A venture capital company like the one described above would face both problems. Therefore, it is only suitable for regions with a high density of a specific type of firms with great innovative potentials.[5]

Several other policy measures to improve innovation financing could be thought of. The ideas above are derived from the approach and the problem identification in the book and are only a few out of many possibilities. The precise instrument and the precise design of that instrument should be considered carefully. It should be recognized that the institutional set-up of financial systems affects how the interaction between agents in the system takes place. An understanding of this interaction is crucial when designing technology policy.

---

5 In the U.S. venture capital companies were established in "Sillicon Valley" and between them they specialized on specific areas of business but were still located in the same, geographical limited area.

List of references

Abernathy, W.J. and J.M. Utterback (1975): "A Dynamic Model of Product and Process Innovation", Omega, Vol.3, No.6, pp 639-56.

Akerlof, George A. (1970): "The market for lemons: Quality Uncertainty and the market mechanism", Quarterly Journal of Economics, 84, 488-500.

Alchian, A.A. (1950): "Uncertainty, evolution, and economic theory", Journal of Political Economy, vol.58, pp. 211-221.

Amendola, M. & J.-L. Gaffard (1988): "The Innovative Choise", Padstow, Basil Blackwell.

Amendola, M. & J.-L. Gaffard (1989): "Liquidity and the Process of Creation of Technology", Paper prepared for "International Seminar on Science, Technologh and Economic Growth.

Andersen, E.S. (1991), "Techno-economic paradigms as typical interfaces between producers and users", Journal of Evolutionary Economics, 1991:1, pp 119-144.

Arrow,K.J. (1973): "Information and Economic Behaviour", Stockholm.

Arrow,K.J. (1974): "The Limits of Organization", New York.

Arrow, K.J. (1962): "Economic Welfare and the Allocation of Resources for Invention", NBER, Princeton.

Arthur, W.B. (1983): "Competing Techniques and Lock-in by Historical Events. The Dynamics of Allocation Under Increasing Returns", IIASA, Laxenburg.

Arthur, W.B. (1988): "Competing technologies: an overview", in G. Dosi et.al. (eds.): Technical Change and Economic Theory, Pinter Publ., London.

Artus, P. and de Boissieu, C. (1988): "The Process of Financial Innovation: Causes, Forms, and Consequences", in Hertje (1988).

Ayres, C.E. (1944): "The Theory of Economic Progress", Chapel Hill, the University of North Carolona Press.

Ayres, C.E. (1961): "Towards a Reasonable Society", Austin.

Bak-Jensen, T. (1982): "Midler til fremme af udviklingen i mindre virksomheder".

Bak-Jensen, T., Venture News, No.5 og 7, 1991.

Bank of England, Quarterly Bulletin, Vol. 30, 1990, No.4, pp. 511-513.

Berglöf, E. (1988): "Ägande och inflytande i svenskt näringsliv -Ägarna och kontrollen över företaget - en jämförende studie av sex länders finansiella system", SOU,38.

Berglöf, E. (1990): "Capital structure as a mechanism of control: a comparison of financial systems", in Aoki, Gustafsson and Williamson (eds.) "The firm as a nexus of treaties", Sage publications, London.

Berglöf, E. (1991): "Corporate Control and Capital Stucture", Stockholm.

Bieber, R. (ed.) (1988): "1992: One European Market?", Baden-Baden.

Bingham, R.D., E.W. Hill & S.B. White (1990): "Financing Economic Development", SAGE Publications, Newbury Park.

Bingham , T.R.G. (1989): "Recent Changes in financial Markets: The Implications for Systemic Liquidity", ETLA Discussion Paper no. 308.

Birch, A. & E. Büchert/Nelleman A/S (1990): "En lys ide", Søborg.

Blundell-Wignall, A. (1991): "Macroeconomic Consequences of Financial Liberalisation: A Summary Report", OECD.

Bolton Committee (1971): "Report of the Committee of Enquiry on Small Firms", HMSO, London Cmnd 4811.

Boulding, K.E. (1985): The World as a Total System, Beverly Hills, Sage Publications.

Bresolin, F. (1986): "Corporate Finance and Financial Structure", Paper from Conference on Innovation Diffusion, Venice 17/22 March 1986.

Bullock, M. (1983): "Academic Enterprise, Industrial Innovation and the development of high technology financind in the United States", London, Brand Brothers and Co.

Bullock, M. (1987): "Funding of Technological Change: R&D for the 21st. Century. An Analysis of Trends affecting Strategies for Industrial Innovation", The Research and Development Society, London.

Cable,John (1985): "Capital Market Information and Industrial Performance: The Role of West German Banks", The Economic Journal (March).

Cainarca, G.C. (1992): "Agreements between firms and the technological life cycle model: Evidence from information technologies", Research Policy, vol.21, no. 1,Feb., pp 45-62.

Carlsson, Bo and Stankiewiez, Rikard (1990): "On the Nature, Function and Composition of Technological System", Case Western Reserve University and University of Lund.

Carrington and Edwards (1979): "Financing Industrial Investment", Macmillan Press.

Chan, Yuk-Shee (1983): "On the Positive Role of financial Intermediation in Allocation of Venture Capital in a market with Imperfect Information", The Journal of Finance, vol. XXXVIII, No. 5.

Christensen, Jesper L. (1992): "Pengeinstitutternes samspil med virksomhederne i industrien og kriterier for lån til innovationsprojekter", Rapport til Industriministeriet om spørgeskema-undersøgelse, dec.

Christensen, Jesper L. (1992): "The Role of Finance in National Systems of Innovation", in Lundvall (ed).: National Systems of Innovation, Pinter Publ., London, pp 146-168.

Christensen, Jesper L. (1990): "Information and financial constraints on innovation projects", paper presented at the workshop "Process of knowledge accumulation and the formulation of technology strategy", Røsnæs 20.-23./5.

Christensen, Jesper L. (1991): "The Danish national system of innovation financing", in "Approaching the danish system of innovation", FAST Occational Papers.

Clements, Alan W. (1985): "Company-bank relationships", in Journal of International Banking Management and Strategies.

Clower, R. (1965): "The Keynesian Counterrevolution: A Theoretical Approisal".

Coase, R.H. (1937): "The nature of the Firm", Economica, Vol.4, No. 16, pp 386-405.

Cohen, Stephen S. and Zysman, John (1988): "Manufacturing innovation and American industrial competitiveness", Science, Vol. 239, pp.1110-1115,

Coombs, R., P. Saviotti, V. Walsh (1987): "Economics and Technological change", London, MacMillan.

Cox, A. (1986): "The state, finance and industry", St.Martins, New York.

Courchene, Thomas J. (1989), "Crumbling Pillars: Creative Destruction or Cavalier Demolition?". Paper prepared for conference on Deregulation and Reregulation, Alberta, September.

Crawford, Vincent P. (1987): "International Lending, Long-Term Credit Relationships, and Dynamic Contract Theory", Princeton Studies in International Fiance, No.59.

Cyert, R.M. and J.G. March (1963): "A behavioral Theory of the Firm", Englewood Cliffs, Prentice-Hall.

Dahmén, Erik (1950/70): "Entrepreneurial Activity and the Development of Swedish Industry 1919-1939", Homewood, American Economic Association translation Series.

Dahmén, Erik (1961): "Innovationer i kreditväsendet under den svenska industrialiseringen", i Hegeland, Hugo (ed.), Money, Growth and Methodology.

Dahmén, Erik (1988c): "Dynamics of Entrepreneurship, Technology and Institutions", Paper presented at a conference on "Evolution of Technology and Market Structure in an International Context", Siena.

Dahmén, Erik (1988a): "Development Blocks'in Industrial Economics", Scandinavian Economic History Review, No.1.

Dahmén, Erik (1988b): "Entrepreneurial activity, banking and finance, historical aspects and theoretical suggestions", Industriens Utredningsinstitut, Working Paper No. 209.

Dalum, Bent et.al. (1991): "Internationalisering og erhvervsudvikling", Notat, Industri- og Handelsstyrelsen.

Dansk Teknologisk Institut (1992): "Højteknologiske iværksættere", København og Århus.

Danmarks Nationalbank: "Beretning og regnskab" div. årgange og "kvartalsoversigt", div. numre.

Dansk Teknologisk Institut (1990): "Højteknologiske iværksættere - erfaringer fra stipendie-ordningen", januar.

Dansk Teknologisk Institut (1990): "Paradoksproblemet", December.

Dansk Udviklingsfinansiering A/S, nyhedsbreve, marts og oktober 1990.

Dansk Udviklingsfinansiering A/S (1991): Årsberetning.

Dasgupta, Partha & Stiglitz, Joseph (1980b): "Industrial Structure and the nature of Innovative Acitivity", Economic Journal, Vol.90, no.358, pp 266-93.

Dasgupta, Partha & Stiglitz, Joseph (1980): "Uncertainty, industrial structure, and the speed of R&D.

David, P.A. (1975): "Technical Choice, innovation and Economic Growth", Cambridge, Cambridge University Press.

Davidson, Paul (1978): "Why money matters: Lessons from a half-century of monetary theory", Journal of Post Keynesian Economics, Vol.1,no.1.

Dean, Robert, Jr.(1974): "The temporal mismatch - innovation's pace vs management's time horizon", Research management, may, pp.12-15.

Derian, Jean-Claude (1990): "Financing the needs of small technology oriented companies: The case of France", Paper for the conference Technology and Investment, 21-24 january, Stockholm.

Diamond,D.W. (1984): "Financial Intermediation and Delegated Monitoring", Review of Economic Studies LI.

Diamond, Douglas W. (1989): "Monitoring and reputation: the choice between bank loans and directly placed debt", CRSP Working paper series no. 254, University of Chicago.

Dosi, G. (1982): "Technological paradigm and technological trajectories", Research Policy, Vol.11, no.3.

Dosi, G. (1988c): "Finance, Innovation and Industrial Change", stencilat.

Dosi, G. (1988a): "Source, Procedures, and Microeconomic Effect of Innovation", Journal of Economic Literature, Vol.26, No., pp 1120-1171.

Dosi, G. (1988b): "The Nature of the innovative process", in G. Dosi m.fl. (eds.): Technical Change and Economic Theory, Pinter Publ., London.

Dosi, G. and L. Orsenigo (1988): "Industrial structure and technical change", in Heertje (ed.): Innovation, Technology, and Finance, Basil Blackwell, Oxford and New York, pp 14-37.

Dosi, G. and L. Orsenigo (1988): "Coordination and transformation: an overview of structures, behaviours and change in evolutionary environments", in G. Dosi m.fl. (eds.): Technical Change and Economic Theory, Pinter Publ., London.

Dosi, G., Freeman, C., Nelson, R., Silverberg, G., Soete, L.(eds) (1988): "Technical change and economic theory", London, Francis Pinter and New York, Columbia University Press.

Driscoll, Michael (1991): "Deregulation, credit rationing, financial fragility and economic performance", Working Paper, Middlesex Polytechnic school of Economics.

Edenius and Bäckstrand (1989): "Marknadens agerende ved vissa förandringar av det statliga företagsstöd", SOU.

Edwards, J.S.S. and Fischer, Klaus (1991): "Banks, finance and investment in West Germany since 1970", Cepr.

Edquist, Charles & Lundvall, Bengt-Åke (1992), "Comparing the Danish and Swedish Systems of Innovation", Forthcoming in Richard R. Nelson (ed). "National Systems of Innovation".

Eliasson, Gunnar (1981): "The financing of new Technological Investment", i Grandstrand and Sigurdson, "Technological and Industrial Policy in China and Europe", Proceedings from the First Joint TIPCE Conference, pp 227-247.

Eliasson, Gunnar (1990): "The Firm as a competent team", Journal of Economic Behavior & Organization", Vol.13, No.3, pp. 275-299.

Eliasson, Gunnar m.fl. (1990): "The Knowledge based information economy", Stockholm, Almqvist & Wiksell International.

Elliott, J.E. (1983): "Schumpeter and the Theory of Capitalist Economic Development", Journal of Economic Behavior and Organization, 4.

Ellsworth, Richard R, (1985): "Capital markets and competitive decline", Harvard Business Review, No.5.

Engwall, Lars & Jan Johanson (1990): "Banks in Industrial Networks", Scandinavian Journal of Managment, Vol. 6, No.3, pp 231-244.

Falciglia, A. (1986): "Some reflections from the theory of investment financing", paper for Conference on Innovation Diffusion, Venice 17/22 march 1986.

Fazzari, Hubbard and Peterson (1987): "Financial constraints and corporate investments", NBER Working Paper 2387.

Finans/Invest, November 1984.

Ford, R. & W. Suyker (1990): "Industrial Subsidies in the oecd Economies", OECD Economic Studies, No. 15.

Forum for Industriel Udvikling (1988): "Har Danmark en fremtid som industrination?", København.

FoU-Trender, (1990:2).

Frankel, Jeffrey A. (1989): "Japanese Finance: A Survey", NBER Working Paper no. 3156.

Frankel, Allan B. & Montgomery, John D. (1991): "Financial Structure: An International

Perspective", Bookings papers on Economic Acitivity, Vol.1.

Franks & Mayer (1990): "Take overs", Economic Policy 10, april.

Freeman, C. (1982): "The Economics of Industrial Innovation", Cambridge, Mass.

Freeman, C. (1987): "Technology Policy and Economic Performance: Lessons from Japan", London, Frances Pinter.

Freeman, C. (1988): "Preface to part II", in Dosi et.al (1988).

Freeman, C. & Perez, C. (1986): "Business cycles, long waves, investment behaviour and technological changes", SPRU.

Fölster, S. (1992): "The Art of Encouraging Invention", IUI.

Garlato,G. (1986): "The Role of Government in Innovation Financing", paper for conference on innovation diffusion, Venice, march.

Gasslander, O. (1962): "History of SEB to 1941".

Gertler, Mark (1988): "Financial Structure and Aggregate Economic Activity: An Overview", Journal of Money, Credit, and Banking, vol.20, No.3.

Gjerding, Allan Næs m.fl. (1990): "Den forsvundne produktivitet (The lost Productivity), Charlottenlund, Jurist- og Økonomforbundets Forlag (forthcoming in English).

Glete, Jan (1989): "Long-Term Firm Growth and Ownership Organization", Journal of Economic Behavior and Organization, Vol.12.

Gnes,P. (1983): "The financial structure and financing of firms: developments and prospects", Review of economic conditions in Italy, no.2.

Goldsmith, R. (1985): National balance sheets for 20 countries", NBER, New Haven.

Goodhart, C.A.E. (1989): Money, Information and Uncertainty, Macmillan Press, Hong Kong.

Godballe, Karsten m.fl. (1987): Finansielle barrierer for teknologisk udvikling?", Speciale forvaltning, RUC.

Grandstrand, O. & Jon Sigurdson (1981): "Technological and Industrial Policy in China and Europe", Proceedings from the First Joint TIPCE Conference, pp 31-70.

Greenwald, B.C. & Stiglitz, J.E. (1988): "Money Imperfect Indformation, and Economic Flucturations", in Kohn & Tsiang (eds.): Finance Constraings, Expectations, and Macroeconomics, Clarendon Press, Oxford.

Greenwald, B.C. & Stiglitz, J.E. (1990): "Asymmetric information and the new theory of the firm: Financial constraints and risk behavior", NBER Working paper 3359.

Greenwald, B.C. & Stiglitz, J.E. (1990): "Information, Finance, and markets: The Architecture of Allocative Mechanisms", paper prepared for the Conference on the History Enterprise:

Finance and the Enterprise in a Historical Perspective, Italy, September 1989.

Grilli, V. (1989): "Financial markets and 1992", Brookings papers on Economic Activity, No.2, pp. 301-324.

Grossman, G.M. (1990): "Promoting new Industrial Activities: A Survey of Recent Arguments and Evidence", OECD Economic Studies, No.14.

Gurley,J.G. and Shaw,E.S. (1955): "Financial Aspects of Economic Development", The American Economic Review, Vol. XLV, sept.

Hallwirth, Volker (1990): "Financing problems of small and medium-sized enterprises", OECD, Paris.

Hall, B. (1991): "Corporate Restructuring and Investment Horizons", NBER Working Paper 3794.

Hall, G. (1990): "Lack of Finance as a Constraint on the Expansion of Innovatory Small Firms", in Barber, J. J.S.Metcalfe and M. Porteous: "Barriers to Growth in Small Firms", Routledge, London.

Hansen, P.H. (1991). "From Grwoth to Crisis", Scandinavian Economic History Review, Vol. 39, No.3, pp 20-40.

Harrison, R.T. & C.M. Mason (1991): "Informal Investment and the Venture Capital market in the United Kingdom: A Strategy for closing the equity gap", RENT V, Vaxjo University.

Haubrich, J.G. (1989): "Financial Intermediation", Journal of Banking and Finance, Vol.13, No.1, pp 9-20.

Heertje, A.(ed.)(1988): "Innovation, Technology and Finance", Oxford.

Heiner, R. (1983): "The origin of Predictable Behavior", American Economic Review, vol.73, No.4, pp 560-95.

Hicks, J. (1979): "Causality in economics", Basil Blackwell, Oxford.

Hicks, J.R. (1935): "A Suggestion for Simplifying the Theory of Money", Economica, Vol.22, No.5-8.

Hilferding, R. (1910): "Finanzkapital", Frankfurt A.M., 1968.

Hirschman, A. (1970): "Exit, voice and loyalty", Cambridge, Mass., Harvard University Press.

Hollingsworth, B.M. (1988): "Økonomisk rådgivning af små virksomheder", Samfunds-litteratur, København.

Holmstrom, Bengt (1989): "Agency costs and innovation", Journal of Economic Behavior and Organization", Vol. 12.

Hoshi, T. Kashyap, A. and Scharfstein,D. (1989): "Bank Monitoring and Investment: Evidence from the changing structure of japanese corporate banking relationships", NBER Working Paper 3079.

Hoshi, T. Kashyap, A. and Scarfstein, D. (1990): "The role of banks in reducing the costs of financial distress in Japan", NBER Working paper 3435.

Hoshi, T., Kashyap, A. and Scarfstein, D. (1991): "Corporate structure, liquidity and investment: Evidence from Japanese industrial groups", Quarterly journal of economics, Vol. CVI, feb., pp.33-60.

Hu, Yao.Su (1984): "Industrial banking and special credit institutions: A comparative study", Policy studies institute, London, Oct.

Hubbard, R. Glenn (1990): "Asymmetric information, corporate finance, and investment, The University of Chicago Press, Chicago.

Hutchinson, T.W. (1979): "On Revolutions and Progress in Economic Knowledge", CFambridge Univ. Press.

Högberg, Leif (1981): "Industriel innovation", JTI,Århus.

Håndværksrådet (1983): "Ungskoven i dansk erhvervsliv", København.

Håndværksrådet (1991): "Konjunkturanalyse for den mindre industri".

Industriministeriet (1987): "Brancheglidning i den finansielle sektor", Betænkning nr. 1108.

Industriministeriet (1990): "10 erhvervspolitiske temaer", København.

Industriministeriet (1990): "Vækst gennem nye virksomheder", København.

Industriministeriet (1992): "En styrket indsats over for iværksætterne og de mindre virksomheder - en rapport fra tværministeriel aktionsgruppe", København.

Industri- og Handelsstyrelsen (1992): "Nye virksomheder og iværksættere i tal 1985-89", København.

Jaffee, D.M. & Russell,T. (1976): "Imperfect information, Uncertainty and credit rationing, Quarterly Journal of Economics, Vol. 90, 651-666.

Jaffee, D.M. & Stiglitz, J. (1990), "Credit Rationing", Handbook of Monetary Economics, Vol. 2.

Jain, A.K. & Gupta,S. (1987): "Some evidence on "Herding" behavior of U.S. banks", Journal of Money, Credit and Banking, Vol.19, 78-89.

Jensen, Holger (1986): "Lønmodtagerfondes rolle som formidlere af risikovillig kapital", Nationaløkonomisk Tidsskrift, nr. 2.

Jespersen, C. (1991): "Den mindre industris vækstmuligheder i 90'erne", København.

Johnson, Björn (1992): "Institutional Learning", in Lundvall (ed.): National Systems of Innovation, Pinter Publ., London, pp 23-44.

Katona, G. (1975): "Psychological Economics", Amsterdam.

Kay, N. (1988): "The R and D function: corporate strategy and structure", in Dosi et.al.(1988).

Keynes, J.M. (1921): "Treatise on Probability", JMK, Vol.3, MacMillan.

Keynes, J.M. (1930): "Treatise on Money", JMK, Vol.6, MacMillan.

Keynes, J.M. (1936): "The General Theory of Employment, Interest and Money", JMK, Vol.7, MacMillan.

Kiemer, Bent (1986): "Billige og risikovillige penge til finansiering af teknologi", Økonomisk Perspektiv, oktober.

Kiemer, Bent (1988): "Finansiering af teknologiudvikling - en udfordring for virksomhed og bank", Overblik, No 1, pp 24-26

Knight, Frank (1921): "Risk, Uncertainty and Profit", Boston, Houghton Millfin.

Koppel, Peter (1992): "Pilotforsøg vedr. formidling af privat kapital til særlige projekter", DTI/Innovation, København.

Kristensen, Arne (1990): "Innovationsaktivitet i Dansk Industri 1984-1988", Notat Industri- og Handelsstyrelsen.

Kristensen, Arne (1992): "Industriel innovation i Danmark", Serie om Industriel Udvikling no.37, Aalborg University.

Kristensen, Peer Hull (1984): "Økonomisk Evolution - et spørgsmål om information?", Skriftserie nr. 11, Inst. f. Samfundsfag, RUC.

Landau, R. & N. Rosenberg (1986): "The Positive Sum Strategy", National Academy Press, Washington.

Landström, Hans (1988): "Småföretagens försörjning med riskkapital", Stockholm.

Landström, Hans (1991): "Private Investors in Sweden: An Agency Theory Approach", paper for the RENT V research in Entrepreneur-ship - 5th Workshop, Växjö 28-29 1991.

Laudy, J. (1991): "Financial Strategies", in Bowen et.al.: "The European Challenge: Industry's response to the 1992 programme", Harvester, pp. 422-433.

Lawson, T. (1985): "Uncertainty and economic analysis", The Economic Journal, No.95.

Lawson, T. (1985): "The Relative/Absolute Nature of Knowledge and Economic Analysis", The Economic Journal, No.97.

Leijonhufvud, A. (1968): "Keynesian Economics and the Economics of Keynes", London.

Leland, H.E. and Pyle, D.H. (1977): "Informational Asymmetries, Financial Structure, and Financial Intermediation", The Journal of Finance, Vol.XXXII, no.2.

Lindgren, Håkan (1987): "Bank, investmentbolag, bankirfirma. Stockholms Enskilda Bank 1924-1945", Norstedts.

321

Lindgren, Håkan (1991): "Tradition och förnyelse i 1980-talets bankhistoriska forskning",

Lindgren, Håkan (1990): "Long-term Contracts in Financial Markets: Bank-Industry Connections in Sweden, Illustrated by the operations of Stockholms Enskilda Bank, 1900-70", i Aoki, Gustafsen 6 Williamson (eds.), "The Firms as a nexus of treaties".

List, F. (1841/1959): "Das Nationale System der Politischen Oekonomie", Basel, Kyklos-Verlag.

Llewellyn, David T. (1990): "Competition and regulation: Trends in financial systems", Pennings- & Valutapolitik, Nr. 4.

Lundvall, Bengt-Åke (1985): "Product Innovation and User-producer Interaction", Aalborg University Press.

Lundvall, Bengt-Åke (1988): "Innovation as an interactive process: from user-producer interaction to the national system of innovation", In Dosi et.al. (1988).

Lundvall, Bengt-Åke (1991): "Explaining Inter-firm cooperation and innovation-limits to the transaction cost approach", paper for workshop in Berlin, june.

Lundvall, Bengt-Åke (1992): "User-Producer Relationships, National Systems of Innovation and Internationalisation", in Lundvall (ed.): National Systems of Innovation, Pinter Publ., London, pp 45-67.

Mackie-Mason, J. (1989): "Do firms care who provides their finance", NBER Working Paper 3039.

Macmillan Committee (1931): "Report of the Committee on Finaance and Industry", London MHSO, Cmnd 3897.

Masera, R.S. (1989): "Monetary and Financial Markets in Europe: Regulation and Market Forces", Review of Economic Conditions in Italy, No.1, pp. 13-41.

Mayer, Colin (1988): "New issues in corporate finance", European Economic Reveiew 32, 1167-1189, North-Holland.

Mayer, Colin (1990): "Financial systems, Corporate finance and Economic Development", in Hubbard (1990).

Mayer, C. and Alexander, I. (1990): "Banks and securities markets: corporate financing in Germany and the UK.", CEPR discussion paper No.433.

Mayer, H. and Kneeshaw, J. (1988): "Financial Market Structure and Regulatory Change", in Hertje (1988).

Maxwell, Maurice (1990): "The financing of small and medium sized business in the European community", Paper for OECD-seminar in Paris 2.-3/7.

McKelvey, M. (1991): "How do national Systems of Innovation Differ?", Working Paper No.79.

Minsky, Hyman P. (1975): "John Maynard Keynes", Columbia University Press, New york.

Minsky,H.P. (1982): "An Exposition of a Keynesian Theory of Investment", in "Can "it" Happen again?", New York.

Minsky,H.P. (1989): "Financial Structures: Indebtness and Credit", in Barrère, A. (ed.): "Money, Credit and Prices in Keynesian Perspective", Macmillan.

Minsky, H.P. (1990). "Schumpeter: Finance and Evolution", in Heertje & Perlman (eds.), Evolving Technology and Market Structure: Studies in Schumpeterian Economics, University of Michigan Press.

Mishkin, Frederic S. (1990): "Financial Innovation and Current Trends in U.S. Financial Market", NBER Working Paper Series, No. 3323.

Modigliani,F. and Miller,M.H. (1958): "The Cost of Capital, Corporation Finance, and the Theory of Investment", American Economic Review, 48.

Moore, Robert R. (1987), "Financial Constracting and Asymmetric Information", University of Wisconsin-Madison.

Mowery, D.C. (1992): "Finance and Coprporate Evolution in five Industrial Economies, 1900-1950", Industrial and Corporate Change, Vol.1, No.1, pp 1-36.

Mullineux, A. (1987): "International banking and financial systems: A comparison", Graham & Trotman, London.

Myers, Stewart C. and Majluf, Nicholas S. (1984): "Corporate financing and investment decisions when firms have information that investors do not have", Journal of financial economics, 13(2)

Mønsted, Mette (1985): "Små virksomheder i rådgivningssystemet", Nyt fra Samfundsvidenskaberne, København.

Neave, E.H. (1991). "The Economic Organisation of a Financial Systems", Guildford, Routledge.

Nelson, Richard R. (1990): "Incentives for Entrepreneurship and Supporting Institutions.

Nelson, R. (1988): "Institutions supporting technical change in the United States", in G. Dosi m.fl. (eds.): Technical Change and Economic Theory, Pinter Publ., London.

Nelson, R.R. (1992): "National Innovaton Systems: A Retrospective on a Study", Industrial and Corporate Change, Vol.1, No.2, pp 347-374.

Nelson, R.R. and S.G. Winter (1977): "In Search of a Useful theory of Innovations", Research Policy, Vol.6, No.1.

Nelson, R.R. and S.G. Winther (1982): "An Evolutionary theory of Economic Change", Cambridge, Mass.

Nielsen, Klaus (1986): "En teori om samspillet mellem institutionel og teknologisk udvikling", TPØ Vol.9 nr.3, Roskilde.

Nordic Industrial Fund (1991): "Innovation Activities in the Nordic Countries" (tabelsamling), Oslo.

Närings- och teknikutvecklingsverket (1991): "Att Skapa livskraft", No.4, Stockholm.

Nordic Industrial Fund, Newsletter, No.4. 1991.

OECD (1985): "Venture Capital in Information Technology", Paris.

OECD (1986): "Financial ressources for industry's changing needs".

OECD (1988): "Reviews of R&D policies - DENMARK", Paris.

OECD (1989): "Financial Market Trends", no.44, oct.

OECD (1982): "Innovation in Small and medium-sized Firms".

Oxelheim, Lars (1990): "International financial integration", Springer-Verlag, Heidelberg.

PA Consulting Group (1992): "TIC-systemets nuværende indsats og udviklingsretning". Rapport udarbejdet for Industri- og Handelsstyrelsen, København.

Pasinetti, Luigi (1981). "Structural change and economic growth", Cambridge University Press.

Pavitt, K. (1984), "Sectoral Patterns of Technical Change: Towards a Taxonomy and a Theory", Research Policy, Vol. 13.

Pelikan, P. (1991): "Efficient institutions for ownership and allocation of capital", IUI, Stockholm.

Penrose, E. (1980): "The theory of the Growth of the Firm", Oxford, Blackwell.

Perez, C. (1983): "Structural Change and the Assimilation of New Technologies in the Economic and Social System", Futures, Vol.15, No.4.

Polanyi, K. (1962): "Personal Knowledge: Towards a Post-Critical Philosophy, Chigago University Press, Chigago.

Porter, M.E. (1990): "The Competitive Advantage of Nations", The Free Press, New York.

Prakke, Frits (1988): "The Financing of Technological Innovation" in Heertje (ed.)(1988).

Ray, G.H. and P.J. Hutchinson: "The Financing and Financial Control of Small Enterprise Development", Gower Publ., Chippenham.

Reed, J.S. & G.R. Moreno (1986): "The role of Large Banks in Financing Innovation", in Landau and Rosenberg (eds.): The Positive Sum Strategy, National Academy Press, Washington, pp. 453-466.

Rosen, B.N., S.P. Schnaards and D. Shani (1988): "A comparison of approaches for setting standards for technological products", J. Prod. Innov. Manag., 5, pp 129-139.

Rosenberg, N. (1976): "Pespectives on technology", Cambridge, Cambridge University Press.

Rosenberg, N. (1982): "Inside the black box", Cambridge, Cambridge University Press.

Rothwell, R. & Zegveld. W. (1985): "Reindustrialization and technology", Essex.

Rothwell, R. & W. Zegveld (1982): "Innovation and the Small and Medium Sized Firms", Frances Pinter, Exeter.

Rybzinsky, T. (1984): "Industrial Financial Systems in Europe, U.S. and Japan", Journal of Economic Behaviour and Organization 5.

Rybzinsky, T. (1988): "Financial Systems and Industrial Re-Structuring", National Westminster Bank, Quarterly Review.

Rybzinsky, T. (1989): "Innovative Activity and Venture Financing. Japan, the US and the Europe", Working Paper no. 216, Industriens Utredningsinstitut, Stockholm.

Sahal, D. (1981): "Patterns of technological innovation", New York, Addison-Wesley.

Sahal, D. (1985). "Technology, Guide-Posts and Innovation Avenues", Research Policy, Vol.14, No.2, pp 61-82.

Sako, Mari (1989): "Competitive Cooperation: How the Japanese Manage Inter-firm Relations", paper prepared for the Copenhagen Workshop on Inter-firm Relations, Copenhagen 9-11 October.

Sampson, A. (1981): "The Money Lenders, Coronet Books, London.

Santarelli, Enrico (1987a): "The financial determinants of technological change. An Expository Survey", Economic Notes, Vol.16, no.3.

Santarelli, Enrico (1987b): "Financial and technological innovations during the phases of capitalist development", in Matteo, Goodwin, Vercelli (eds.): "Technological and social factors in long term fluctuations", Springer Verlag.

Schackle, G.L.S. (1967): "The Years of High Theory", Cambridge Univ. Press.

Schackle, G.L.S. (1974): "Keynesian Kaledics", Edinburgh Univ. Press.

Schotter, A. and G. Schwödiauer (1980): "Economics and the theory of Games: A Survey", Journal of Economic Literature, Vol.18, pp. 479-527.

Schuette, H.L. (1980): "The Role of Firm Financial Rules and a Simple Capital market in an Evolutionary Model of Industry Growth", UMI publ., University of Michigan.

Schumpeter, J.A. (1912/31): "Theory of Economic Development", Harvard University Press.

Schumpeter, J.A. (1939): "Business cycles", Abridged, Porcupine Press.

Schumpeter, J.A. (1942): "Capitalism, Socialism and democracy, New York.

Sejersted, Francis (1986): "Routine or Choise", Mimeo.

Sejersted, Francis (1988): "Bank og samfunn", Bergen Bank Kvartalsskrift no 4.

Sharpe, Steven A. (1990): "Asymmetric Information, bank Lending, and Implicit Contracts: A Stylized Model of Customer Relationships", The Journal of Finance, Vol. XLV, No.4, pp. 1087.

Sidenius, Niels Chr. (1989): "Dansk Industripolitik", Skive.

Simon, H. (1982): "From Substantive to procedural Rationality", Models of bounded Rationality, Vol.2.

Simon, H. (1982): "On How to Decide - on what to do", Models of bounded Rationality", vol.2.

Simon, H. (1986): "Rationality in Psychology and Economics", The Journal of Business, Vol.59, No.4, part 2.

Simon, Herbert A. (1991): "Organizations and Markets", Journal of Economic Perspectives, Vol.5, No.2.

Sjögren, Hans (1991): "Long Term Contracts in the Swedish Bank-Orientated Financial System During the Inter-War Period", Business History, Vol.33, No. 3.

Smith, Eric Owen (1990): "The West German Economy", Croom Helm.

Statens Industriverk (1988): "Riskkapitalet och de mindre företagen", SIND, No.3.

Statens Industriverk (1989): "Venture Capital-marknaderna i de Nordiska Länderna", SIND:1.

Stiglitz, J. and Weiss, A. (1981): "Credit Rationing in Markets with Imperfect Information", American Economic Review, 71, 393-410

Stiglitz (1984): "Information and economic analysis. A perspective", Economic Journal.

Stiglitz, J.E. (1987): "Learning to learn, localized learning and technological progress", in Dasgupta and Stoneman (eds): "Economic Policy and Technological Performance", pp 125-153.

Stiglitz, J. and Weiss,A. (1988): "Banks as social Accountants and screening devices for the allocation of credit", NBER Working Paper 2710.

Stiglitz, J.E. (1988): "Why Financial Structure Matters", Journal of Economic Perspectives, Vol.2, No.4.

Storper, Michael (1991): "Telchnology Districts and International Trade: The Limits to Globalization in an Age of Flexible Production", University of California.

Strange, S. (1986): "Casino Capitalism", Oxford.

Storey, D.J. (1990): "Is there a gap in the financing of small firms?: A review of evidence from the United Kingdom". Paper from OECD-seminar on small and medium-sized industrial enterprises, Paris.

Suzuki, Yoshio (1990): "The Japanese Financial System", Clarendon Press, Oxford.

Svensson, Per (1988): "Ekonomisk styrning av produkt-utvecklingsprojekt", Uppsala, Mekanförbundets Förlag.

Svenska Bankföreningen (1991): "Bankerna och EG 6", Februari.

Teichova, A. (1988): "Rivals and Partners", Uppsala Papers in Economic History, Working Papers no.1, Uppsala.

Thurow, L. (1992). "Head to head", William Morrow & Co., New York.

Torell, H.S. & Dohner, R.S.(1987): "A simple simulation model of international bank lending", International finance discussion papers no.307.

Townsend, R.M. (1979): "Optimal contracts and competitive markets with costly state verification", Journal of economic theory 21, 265-93.

Tylecote, A. and Demirag, I. (1991): "Short-termism: Culture and structures as factors in technological innovation", mimeo from research project on "Performance pressures and technological progress in British industry".

Utterback, James M. m.fl. (1988): "Technology and industrial innovation in Sweden: A study of technology-based firms formed between 1965 and 1980", Research Policy, Vol.17, No.1.

Vasan, P.C.S. (1986): "Credit Rationing and Corporate Investment", UMI, Hardvard University.

Veblen, T. (1904): "The Theory of Business Enterprise", New Brunswich, New Jersey.

Veblen, T. (1919): "Captains of Finance and the engineers", Dial, June, pp 599-606.

Vercelli, A. (1985): "Money and production in Schumpeter and Keynes: Two Dichotomies", in Arena & Graqiani (eds.), Production, Circulation et monnaie, Paris.

Vinals, José & Berges, Angel (1988): "Financial innovation and capital formation", in Hertje 1988.

von Hippel, E. (1988): "Sources of Innovation", Oxford University Press, Oxford.

Walker, D.A. (1989): "Financing the small firms", Small Business Economics, Vol.1, pp 285-296.

Wellhöner, V. & H. Wixforth (1989): "Bank-industry Relations in Theory and Practice", Uppsala papers in Economic History, Working Paper No.4, Uppsala.

Williamson, Oliver E. (1988): "Corporate finance and corporate governance", The Journal of Finance, Vol.43,no.3,july.

Williamson, Oliver E. (1986): "The Economic Institutions of Capitalism", London.

Williamson, Oliver E. (1975): "Markets and Hierakies", Cambridge, Mass.

Wilson Committee (1979): "The financing of small Firms", Interim Report of the Committee to review the functioning of Financial Institutions, HMSO, London, Cmnd 7503.

Winter, Sidney G. (1984): "Schumpeterian competition in Alternative Technological Regimes", Journal of Economic behaviour and Organizations, 5, pp 287-320.

Winther, Sidney G. (1987): "Knowledge and Competence as Strategic Assets", in teece, D. (ed.): "The Competitive Challenge - Strategies for Industrial Innovation and Renewal, Cambridge, Mass., Ballinger.

Wärneryd, Karl-Erik (1988): "The Psychology of Innovative Entrepreneurship", i Raaij van, Veldhoven & Wärneryd (eds.) Handbook of Economic Psychology, Kluwer Academic Publ., Dordrecht.

Zander, Udo (1991): "Exploiting A Technological Edge - Voluntary and Involuntazry Disseminaiton of Technology", Stockholm.

Zysman, John (1983): "Governments, Markets and growth - financial systems and the politics of industrial change", Cornell University.

Zysman, John (1986): Financial systems and technological change", paper for Conference on Innovation Diffusion, Venice 17/22 march.

Zysman, John (1990): "Trade, Technology and National Competition", Paper for OECD conference in Paris 24.-27/6.

Østrup, F. (1989/1992): "Det Finansielle System i Danmark", København.